DOES GOD HELP?

NB: When
Rizzuto an
all me h
to dis
representatin, me
can discuss is God
as a mental
thing...

an aspect of the self

"That aspect of the self I call 'God'."
                    MYSELF

wished for

And if, as in the T, the Asd wants to
be "right" or "acceptable" to God, then it
is about being right or "acceptable" to this
designated "unassimilated" aspect of the self...

Projectn   } Seems to be about
Projective Ident.   resolving (intra projectn-
Projective Counter-Ident   introject
                                    processes
                                intra subjectively)

                        how one
                        feels/thinks
                        about one's TOTAL
                            self experience.

                aspecting the
∴ God are one's self
            made cs for
        transitional phenomena purpose

    but also to
resolve/evolve aspects of one's DESIRE
                    into BROADENED csne.

DOES GOD HELP?

Developmental and Clinical Aspects of Religious Belief

edited by
SALMAN AKHTAR, M.D.,
and HENRI PARENS, M.D.

JASON ARONSON INC.
Northvale, New Jersey
London

This book was set in 12 pt. Bembo by Alabama Book Composition of Deatsville, AL, and printed and bound by Book-mart Press, Inc. of North Bergen, NJ.

Library of Congress Cataloging-in-Publication Data

Does God help? : developmental and clinical aspects of religious belief /
edited by Salman Akhtar and Henri Parens.
        p.   cm.
    Includes bibliographical references and index.
    ISBN 0-7657-0319-X
    1. Psychotherapy patients — Religious life — Congresses.   2. Psychotherapy — Religious aspects — Congresses.   3. Psychoanalysis and religion — Congresses.   I. Akhtar, Salman, 1946 July 31–   II. Parens, Henri, 1928–

    RC489.R46 D63   2001
    616.89'14 — dc21

                                                                        00–067595

Printed in the United States of America on acid-free paper. For information and catalog write to Jason Aronson Inc., 230 Livingston Street, Northvale, NJ 07647-1726, or visit our website: www.aronson.com

To the memory

of

Margaret S. Mahler

teacher, friend, source of inspiration

Contents

Acknowledgments

The chapters in this book, with the exception of 1 and 8, were originally presented as papers at the 31st annual Margaret S. Mahler Symposium on Child Development held on May 6, 2000, in Philadelphia. First and foremost, therefore, we wish to express our gratitude to the Margaret S. Mahler Psychiatric Research Foundation. We are also grateful to Michael Vergare, M.D., chairman of the Department of Psychiatry and Human Behavior at Jefferson Medical College, as well as to the Philadelphia Psychoanalytic Institute and Society for their shared sponsorship of the symposium. Many colleagues from the Institute and Society helped during the symposium, and we remain grateful to them. Finally, we wish to acknowledge our sincere appreciation of Maryann Nevin for her efficient organization of and assistance during the symposium. Her outstanding skills in the preparation of this book's manuscript came to our aid, as did the assistance of Melissa Nevin during the later stages of this book's production.

Contributors

Yasser Ad-Dab'bagh, M.D., D.P.M.
Resident in Psychiatry, McGill University Hospital; Candidate,
Montreal Psychoanalytic Institute

Salman Akhtar, M.D.
Professor of Psychiatry, Jefferson Medical College; Training and
Supervising Analyst, Philadelphia Psychoanalytic Institute

Philip J. Escoll, M.D.
Clinical Professor of Psychiatry, University of Pennsylvania School
of Medicine; Training and Supervising Analyst, Philadelphia Psychoanalytic Institute

M. Hossein Etezady, M.D.
Clinical Director of Psychiatric Services, Paoli Memorial Hospital;
Faculty, Philadelphia Psychoanalytic Institute

Ruth M. S. Fischer, M.D.

Clinical Professor of Psychiatry, University of Pennsylvania School of Medicine; Training and Supervising Analyst, Philadelphia Psychoanalytic Institute

James S. Grotstein, M.D.

Clinical Professor of Psychiatry, UCLA School of Medicine; Training and Supervising Analyst, Los Angeles Psychoanalytic Society/Institute and the Psychoanalytic Center of California; a North American Vice-President of the International Psycho-Analytic Association

William W. Meissner, S.J., M.D.

University Professor of Psychoanalysis, Boston College; Training and Supervising Analyst, Boston Psychoanalytic Society and Institute

Mortimer Ostow, M.D.

President, Psychoanalytic Research and Development Fund; Sandrow Visiting Professor Emeritus of Pastoral Psychiatry at the Jewish Theological Seminary of America

Henri Parens, M.D.

Professor of Psychiatry, Jefferson Medical College; Training and Supervising Analyst, Philadelphia Psychoanalytic Institute

Dwarkanath G. Rao, M.D.

Clinical Faculty, Department of Psychiatry, University of Michigan Medical School; Faculty, Michigan Psychoanalytic Institute

Satish Reddy, M.D.

Clinical Assistant Professor of Medicine and Psychiatry, Mt. Sinai School of Medicine; Faculty, Columbia University Center for Psychoanalytic Training and Research

Ana-Maria Rizzuto, M.D.
Training and Supervising Analyst, The Psychoanalytic Institute of New England, East

J. Anderson Thomson, Jr., M.D.
Assistant Director, Center for the Study of Mind and Human Interaction, University of Virginia School of Medicine

1

IS GOD A SUBJECT FOR PSYCHOANALYSIS?

Henri Parens, M.D.,
and Salman Akhtar, M.D.

M any thoughts are evoked by the question "Does God help?" It may lead some to think that there are psychoanalysts who are assuming that God exists or out to prove that he does not exist. Therefore we wish to state at the very outset that proving or disproving the existence of God is not our concern. Psychoanalysis can no more prove or disprove God's existence than it can prove or disprove that there is or is not a death instinct or, for that matter, even an id or ego. These are abstractions. And there is no shame in the fact that to date, given our methods of investigation and so far as we know, proof (incontrovertible documentation) of any psychoanalytic hypothesis just cannot be achieved. The closest we can come to it is to pile up multicentered accumulations of inferential data—subjective data from which plausible hypotheses derive strong support.[1]

---

[1]Even the data of direct behavioral observation collected by clinical researchers such as Anna Freud (with Burlingham 1944), Spitz (1965), Mahler (Mahler and Furer

It is clear to analysts that many people believe that God exists, while others more or less firmly do not. Some just don't know. Usually individuals of any one of these persuasions cannot be swayed from their belief, nor is it the prerogative of, or appropriate for, an analyst to try to dissuade any patient from such belief. But with this understanding it would seem quite reasonable, though somewhat hazardous, for psychoanalysts to address the question "Does God help?" Given that an undetermined percentage of our patients believe in God, that believing in God no doubt influences their intrapsychic life, it seems to us that psychoanalysis can and ought to fruitfully consider and address the question. For those among our patients who believe there is a God, it may prove useful to consider whether believing in God helps them and if so, how. And, in all fairness, similar curiosity needs to be directed at those who vehemently deny and even mock God's existence.

The situation, however, is complicated by the nature of the subject itself for if God does exist, then we psychoanalysts can talk only of "God representation" (Rizzuto, this volume) in the human psyche and not God itself. After all, the purview of psychoanalytic theorizing is not external objects (e.g., chairs, trees, trains) themselves but their intrapsychic representations and meanings. On the other hand, if God does not exist, then paradoxically we can talk of God representation as well as of God, since the latter would be regarded as a projection of mental products anyway.

It might therefore be best to begin with the question "Can psychoanalysis bring some explanation toward understanding the roots and nature of religious belief?" This is not a new question for psychoanalysis. Much has already been written about it. On this

---

1968, Mahler et al. 1975), Parens (1979, Parens et al. 1976), McDevitt (1983), and Roiphe and Galenson (1981) as well as that collected by empirical researchers such as Sander (1964), Emde and colleagues (1976), Ainsworth and colleagues (1978), Stern (1985), and others are at best inferential and subjective. This is because, even while relying on manifest behavior, inference and subjectivity are brought to bear on cataloging these observational data.

point as on many others, we start with what Freud had to say about it.

A CRITIQUE OF FREUD'S VIEWS ON RELIGIOUS BELIEF

Freud's first substantial exploration of the origins of religious belief are to be found in his 1913 "Totem and Taboo." In readings of Freud's 1913 work and his 1927 and 1930 excursions away from "the natural sciences, medicine and psychotherapy [into] cultural problems" (Freud 1927, p. 3), we found that Freud came to some rather firm views on the psychic nature and origins of religious belief. Our attention was especially riveted on two points Freud (1927) made:

1. Religious beliefs derived from the child's earliest experiences of helplessness, which is continued in the adult.

2. "Religion is comparable to a childhood neurosis" and Freud wondered if "mankind [can] surmount this . . . neurosis" (1927, p. 53).

But we hasten to add that Freud also asked for forbearance saying that his views "are not . . . incapable of correction. [That] If experience should show . . . to others after me . . . that we are mistaken, we will give up our [assumptions]" (p. 53).

Speaking to the first point, it is not altogether surprising that, challenged by his Nobel Prize-winning interlocutor Romain Rolland to explain the nature of the "oceanic feeling," in 1930 Freud was both tempted and victimized by this alluring question. Freud proposed that this "oceanic feeling"—which the literary-musicologist luminary Rolland assumed to be a nuclear "religious" experience—derives from and is a continuation in the psyche of the child's helplessness. In their study on human dependence, Parens and Saul (1971), reviewing some of Freud's writings on the subject, took this significant connection between human helplessness and the origins of religious feelings some steps closer to addressing Rolland's question. Given the advances made in psychoanalysis since 1930, Parens and Saul were able to propose that "Rolland's description of feelings and the phase of development to which Freud assigns the origin of religious ideas are compatible within the framework of the normal symbiosis formulated by Mahler" (p. 26). That is to say, first, that the helplessness of the infant would make him/her turn to what the child perceives to be an omnipotent object. But in addition, the child's earliest experiences of feeling one with mother, that is, the infant's symbiotic experience, would be a reasonable antecedent explanation for the oceanic feeling, feeling one with the universe. Erikson (1959) and Mahler (1965, Mahler et al. 1975) especially detailed for us the powerful and indelible nature of the infantile symbiotic experience. Mahler, along with Lichtenstein (1961) and Jacobson (1964), held that this symbiotic yearning for such experience continues throughout life.[2] In this they were affirming Freud's observations not only of 1927 and 1930 but also those written in "An Outline of Psychoanalysis" that the earliest cathexes are indelible (1940).

Parens and Saul furthered the thrust of the proposition:

> In considering the mystical implication in Rolland's argument we point to Winnicott's . . . conceptualization that mystery and mysticism tend to be characteristic of transitional phenomena. The normal symbiosis would meet exactly the required conditions for a period characterized by such transitional phenomena, such mysticism and mystery. It is the developmental period when cognitive and affective structures [are such that] affects are experienced grossly and objects are [still quite unrealistically] perceived. It is a period when beginning secondary process functioning is substantially [in-

---

[2]Akhtar (1996) has traced the echoes of such longing in the human vulnerability to unrealistic optimism and inordinate nostalgia, labeling the two corresponding structures as "someday . . ." and "if only . . ." fantasies.

fluenced] by primary process functioning. This determines the mysticism and omnipotence of the symbiotic mother–child relationship . . . [which the child experiences as his/her] "symbiotic self-representation." [Parens and Saul 1971, p. 26]

This model, Parens and Saul added, would accommodate well Rolland's descriptions of the oceanic feeling as "a feeling of something limitless," an "indissoluble bond," "being one with the external world" (p. 27).

Winnicott (1953) made a distinction between transitional objects and transitional phenomena. *Transitional space*, Winnicott suggests, is where the feeling of oneness and vagueness experienced while being nurtured by mother resides. It is experienced as a confluence of reality and unreality but such matters do not form its content. It is the psychic area where imagination is born and paradox reigns supreme. *Transitional object* is a concrete representative of the experience of being nurtured by mother, whereas the *transitional phenomenon* is an affective-perceptual psychic state that is transportable into selective experiences. The transitional object can be held, cuddled, sucked on, thrown into a corner, subjected to abuse. The transitional phenomenon is not contained in a concrete structure; it cannot be held or discarded. It is subjectively experienced, enjoyed, and neither questioned nor not questioned for its verity. Religious feelings and belief seem to lie in this realm.

This reasoning, with a caveat, also lends itself well to what Freud proposed were the mechanisms at play in the image formation of deity. Parens and Saul (1971) said, "The mental representation of the archaic parent, overvalued as [she/he] appeared to the helpless child, at the behest of helplessness in the adult is displaced onto the image of a deity-object in the representational world which has attributes of the overvalued parent" (p. 29). Here's the caveat: Freud is known to have given preponderant emphasis to the importance of the father to the child. He first questioned this emphasis in a footnote in "The Ego and the Id" (1923) and seemed to decentralize it—at least for a time—in 1926 (in Addendum C to

"Inhibitions, Symptoms and Anxiety"). There, much more than before, he spoke of the importance of the mother to the child.[3] Nonetheless, given the cultural determination by monotheistic religions to make the representation of God a male figure, Freud seemed to have easily slipped into this assumption as well.

But Freud's specification that the representation of God as a male figure derives from the child's earliest experience of dependence on his/her father runs into difficulty with the generally accepted recognition in psychoanalysis that the child's earliest experiences lie in what we may now speak of as the parent–child symbiosis. It creates a significant conceptual dilemma. We assume that usually the primary object of the child's attachment is the mother. Where the father is significantly and factually involved in the care of the infant, such a symbiotic emotional investment in the father is also likely to occur. This is certainly inferred in the findings reported by Pruitt (1997). Thinking along this line leads to the view that if the earliest, most indelible emotional investments are in general predominantly attached to the mother and more selectively so to the father, the assumption of a monotheistic God in the image of a male does not flow with unquestionable credibility. Indeed, only fifteen years after Freud's death, Moloney (1954) published a detailed and well-reasoned essay on the maternal origins of religious belief.

Then, why is God generally assumed to be male? Is it by virtue of societal influence? Would it suffice to assume that this is due to the parents' teaching the child that the God representation is a male figure? Is it that the child who first turns to the mother for protection, as the years pass perceives the father as more physically powerful than the mother and is increasingly the one sought for protection against physical hazards? It is well known that represen-

---

[3]Freud (1926) referred to the distress caused by the rupture of the mother–infant bond as "*seelenschmerz*" (p. 171), literally "soul-pain." His choice of the word *soul* here gives an inkling of the potential confluence between the early feelings toward the mother and the religious-spiritual dimension of life.

tations of a monotheistic God, be it in paintings or in literature, tend to be male in character. But the doubt is this: Doesn't this male assignment to the representation of God create a disharmony with internal representations of those earliest childhood-derived godly functions that are ascribed by the child to the mother? Children assign functions to their parents. Each child selects—a process that is substantially unconscious—which functions each mother and each father will get assigned. There is overlapping and more or less transient substitution, but there is also specificity of function that tends to hold over time, over years, and indeed over a lifetime. So, from where does it come that God, for those who so conceptualize it, is perceived in a male form? One possible answer is that the view of God as man is a defense against the more alluring and terrifying view of God as woman.

But there is another more hidden problem with Freud's (1927) proposition that religious beliefs derived from the continuation of infantile experiences of helplessness in adult life. It reasons well that the fear of death, to which Freud pointed among humans' major fears, may play a large role in the adult's experience of helplessness. We infer, by the way, that Freud was probably burdened with the fear of death when he wrote these lines. He had feared death from early on in life, according to his physician Max Schur, had mouth cancer for several years by 1927, and was 71—old-age in 1927—when he made this statement. Death was no stranger to his thoughts.

We also want to argue against Freud's designation of religious belief as a "childhood neurosis." In a detailed exploration of the nature of dependence and its lifelong line of development, Parens and Saul (1971) assert that dependence is not a condition of childhood alone but a human condition, and that dependence is continued into adulthood. Such dependence is not a neurotic condition in either the child or the adult except where it results from a state of regression due to intense conflict-generated anxiety. Normal, healthy humans are dependent on a variety of others for a variety of functions from birth to the end of life. Freud (1914) was the first to infer its normalcy in suggesting that the more desirable and normal was the anaclitic type (anaclitic meaning "to lean upon another") of relationship as opposed to the narcissistic type, which merely propogated self-affirmation. Mahler (personal communication) agreed with Lichtenstein (1961) and Jacobson (1964) that however well resolved the symbiotic phase of development, the human life condition is essentially a symbiotic one, that is, reciprocally dependent on a beneficent other. Our needs for others and for things and functions change over time depending on the state of our adaptive abilities and the type of need at a given time. At best, as adults we become relatively self-reliant but never fully independent. As adults we are dependent as adults, not as children except in states of regression. With this reasoning, Freud's inference that dependence is a neurosis and therewith of religious belief as a neurosis cannot be supported. Indeed, religious belief can be a fulfillment of some people's adult dependency needs.

DOES FAITH IN GOD HELP?

For those among our patients who believe that there is a God, it may prove useful to consider whether believing in God helps them and how. This we can address independently of whether we ourselves believe in God or not.[4] As analysts we are accustomed to helping patients even while we do not share some of their experiences, interpretations of life, and beliefs. And we know that in these matters it is not helpful and indeed it is unacceptable for us to try to sway our patients to not believe as they do or to believe as we believe.

---

[4]For those among us who simply do not know, it is possible that they not only puzzle over such matters but that they are in awe of experiences that defy scientific explanation—at least to the extent we know today. Some have said that the uncertain feeling that some of life's questions are unanswerable is itself religious in character. They hold this to be the essence of "religious feeling" though without belief in a God.

We think that for those who do believe in God and who have faith in God, such faith and religious belief may help and may not help. But it is not a simple matter. We can start by saying that faith probably helps when it is linked to "basic trust" (Erikson 1959) and it may not help when it is not. We say this with the understanding that basic trust emanates from the "confident expectation" (Benedek 1949) that the primary object will appropriately and benevolently gratify the infant's basic needs in due course. Basic trust, like much of human development, of course, evolves and is age-appropriately continued in the adult. As Erikson emphasized, basic trust develops as a feeling not only attached to the object but equally attached to the self. It is trust in the object and in the self. And it is nuclear to a good symbiotic experience—the matrix for the origin of religious belief. Basic mistrust, on the other hand, yields a hurtful and hostile symbiotic experience that may become the matrix from which negatively valenced religious feelings arise. Thus, when our patient believes in God, whereas basic trust leads the patient to feel benevolently protected, basic mistrust is likely to lead the patient to feel malevolently held and threatened—by God. The belief in God helps the first, and probably pains the second. This need not always follow. For instance, it will not when the patient's basic mistrust is not generalized and is countered by an internal representation of an idealized mother. We have seen such inner support carried by an internal representation of an idealized mother in children and adults whose relationships with their mothers were highly negatively burdened with hate.

The question "Does God help?" comes into clinical context around an often-encountered clinical problem. In some patients, superego-triggered reactions of shame and guilt often derive from the breach of strictly enforced religious dictates internalized in childhood. Sex before marriage, an unwanted pregnancy, abortion, and so forth may trigger an unyielding harsh conscience reaction assumed by the patient to arise from the breach of a religious dictate.

One young woman came into psychotherapeutic treatment following a recent abortion. She was plagued with shame and guilt. She was convinced that her painful reaction was because she had breached her church's dictates against abortion. For several reasons, but especially because she seemed unable to tolerate the idea that her harsh conscience reaction might have other derivations, she could not accept the recommendation for more intensive therapy. As we worked twice a week we found that she seemed to have been rather selective in which of her church's dictates she had internalized. She had accepted and in fact exaggerated the component of teachings that enunciate sinfulness. There was this sin and that sin, and still another sin. She was on the lookout for her own sinfulness. But we never heard a word about the solutions recommended by her church for having sinned.

This was not the only clinical case where we found that such a patient fails to recognize that her church also provides the comforting measures of confession, penitence, and forgiveness. She seemed to derive a large degree of gratification from accusing herself of having sinned. It was clear to this therapist (Parens), and he did not fare so well in getting her to see that her harsh conscience reaction might have some other derivation she could not access by blaming the church's harsh indictments. Clearly, because of the way she assimilated her church's dictates, her religious beliefs did not help her. But if we are permitted to coalesce religious belief and God, and we can say that these were one to her, according to the well-known basic dictates of her church she had only internalized one part of her God, the critical, harsh, unyielding part. Hoping that we do not offend our Catholic readers, we (non-Catholics) would say that she left Jesus' principal message to his followers—forgiveness—out of her belief system. This selective internalization helped her shift accountability for her pain: her painful reaction was due to the harshness of the church's dictate, to "God's will," not to her own unanalyzed intrapsychic conflict(s).

This case shows that aspects of belief in God can be utilized by a harsh superego against the ego to cause suffering and loss of self-observation. A more benevolent belief, in contrast, can be self-sustaining and even joyous. For the latter type of individuals, God is indeed helpful.[5] To round out the picture, we must look in the same vein at lack of belief in God. On the healthy pole of the spectrum, disbelief in God can represent a firm grounding in reality and acceptance of lack of omnipotence without relegating it elsewhere. On the unhealthy end, disbelief in God can represent basic lack of trust, incapacity for any sort of faith, and a shifting and unanchored sense of self. Worse, it can be accompanied by the malignant narcissism and paranoid grandiosity (Kernberg 1984) whereby one can declare oneself to be God!

But there is another direction to which the question "Does God help?" leads us. Prior to the Mahler symposium that gave rise to this volume, we received a letter from a highly respected colleague who asked, "Would [anyone] give a categorical 'NO' . . . to the question 'Does God help?'?" Our colleague questions "the role of religion—at least in its organized form—in the world." We think this statement pertained especially to his questioning "the value of religious dependence, [especially in] its way of deferring or displacing responsibility, its shifting accountability from the socio-political world to the fantastic world of 'spirituality'" (Aaron Esman, personal communication, March 2000). Another colleague asked, "What of the crimes committed, over the centuries into the present, in the name of religion?" Crimes and wars of all kinds, stretching over the centuries, have been committed in the name of religious belief. This too is not simple.

For all of us, those who believe in God, those who do not, and those who do not know whether a God exists or not, what is it that has led so many for so long to commit crimes against others? This

---

[5]For instance, one study of 525 adolescents found that religious commitment significantly reduced the risk of suicide (Stein et al. quoted in Larson et al. 2000).

has occurred in the name of "my religion," in the name of "my God." For believers, even monotheistic religion believers who agree that there is only one God, have committed crimes against "their God's children" who believe in him differently. Might it not be that this knotty question takes us into the domain of "malignant prejudice" (Parens 1998) more than religion? It takes us into the domain of what makes human beings torture and kill other human beings who differ from them in one way or another. Has religion been a servant of malignant prejudice?

But religion cannot escape needing to address the question "Has believing in God wrought crimes against human beings?" To a point, some religious authorities have addressed this question, but certainly some have not. It is not the role of psychoanalysis to pose the question to religion. It is humanity, civilization, that has to ask the question. But it is in the domain of psychoanalysis to consider some effects wrought by religious dictates that condone or even advocate such crimes. It is within our realm of psychoanalytic concern, however complex the issue, to ask, Has belief in God helped humanity? Where and when has it, and where and when has it not?

However naive, it was not the intent of this symposium to have the question "Does God help" take us into this dark aspect of the history of civilization. But it was asked. And we want to touch on it here. The question "Has believing in God brought about crimes that afflict our patients?" can be asked within psychoanalysis. It is applicable to religion in that specific tracts of religious dictates and liturgy have long asserted that believers are better than nonbelievers, that believers will go to heaven while nonbelievers will go to hell. Dictates such as these can and have become the nucleus around which malignant prejudice has organized. And it is so that representatives of religious authority—like representatives of governmental authority in all continents—have over the centuries condoned, in fact even commanded, that the earth be ridden of the heathen. Has this psychologically or emotionally harmed humans? Unequivocally, yes. This aspect of the issue has been studied and

[handwritten top margin: Parents/children are glib/reductionistic; no interest in what is "normal"—vs "path..." How are the authorities?]

continues to be studied by psychoanalysts in the present. In this regard, we could say that believing in God—in what would seem to be a distorted way—has not helped.

CONCLUSION

[handwritten: i.e., their Mahlerian dev. theory]

We have briefly reviewed Freud's ideas about religious belief and examined them in the light of contemporary developmental theory. We have found his two main assertions—namely, that the idea of God emanates from childhood feelings regarding the father, and that religious belief betrays a neurotic form of dependent longing—to be questionable.

Continuing further along these lines, we have suggested that both the belief in God and the disbelief in God have normal and pathological variants. Belief in God seems healthy and normal if it emanates from identification with loving parents who were God believing *and* if such belief provides personal soothing and intrapsychic coherence. Belief in God seems pathological if harshness assigned to him is used by a punitive superego to torment the ego or if the specificity and intensity of a particular religion leads to prejudice and loathing of those belonging to a different faith. Disbelief in God seems healthy if it emanates from identification with loving but atheistic parents and is accompanied by the capacity for faith in the secular institutions of nation, love, work, parenting, and so on. Disbelief in God seems pathological if it represents cynicism, inner faithlessness, and psychic unbelonging on a wider basis *or* if it becomes an excuse for declaring oneself to be a God!

[handwritten right margin: I am not very interested in arguing for what is normal/normative vs path. ? ego alien vs ego syntonic]

Through all this we have attempted to change the question "Does God help?" to "Does belief in God help?" The latter, we believe, facts more squarely in the purview of our field, psychoanalysis. Our answer to the question—to the extent we have been able to come up with one—is that sometimes and for some people it does and sometimes and for some people it does not. We regret not being able to be more certain, but this uncertainty is actually

[handwritten right margin: How connected are they & what guides...]

[handwritten bottom margin: The question for me is how does this fit into their overarching object-relations matrix, inner + outer...; their narcissistic/developmental struggles (and attendant wants)! a sense of self, relational desires! successes]

not very different from the uncertainty that prevails in the understanding of many, many other realms of human life!

REFERENCES

Ainsworth, M. D. S., Blehar, M. C., Waters, E., and Wall, S. (1978). *Patterns of Attachment: A Psychological Study of the Strange Situation*. Hillsdale, NJ: Lawrence Erlbaum.

Akhtar, S. (1996). "Someday . . ." and "if only . . ." fantasies: pathological optimism and inordinate nostalgia as related forms of idealization. *Journal of the American Psychoanalytic Association* 44:723–753.

Benedek, T. (1949). The psychosomatic implications of the primary unit: mother–child. *American Journal of Orthopsychiatry* 19:642–654.

Emde, R. N., Baensbauer, T., and Harmon, R. (1976). Emotional expression in infancy: a biobehavioral study. *Psychological Issues*, Monograph 37. New York: International Universities Press.

Erikson, E. H. (1959). Identity and the life cycle. *Psychological Issues*, Monograph 1. New York: International Universities Press.

Fenichel, O. (1945). *The Psychoanalytic Theory of Neurosis*. New York: Norton.

Freud, A., and Burlingham, D. (1944). *Infants Without Families*. New York: International Universities Press.

Freud, S. (1913). Totem and taboo. *Standard Edition* 13:1–161.

——— (1914). On narcissism: an introduction. *Standard Edition* 14:69–102.

——— (1920). Beyond the pleasure principle. *Standard Edition* 18:1–64.

——— (1923). The ego and the id. *Standard Edition* 19:3–66.

——— (1926). Inhibitions, symptoms and anxiety. *Standard Edition* 20:77–174.

——— (1927). The future of an illusion. *Standard Edition* 21:3–66.

——— (1930). Civilization and its discontents. *Standard Edition* 21:59–145.

——— (1940). An outline of psychoanalysis. *Standard Edition* 23·141–207.

Jacobson, E. (1964). *The Self and the Object World*. New York: International Universities Press.

Kernberg, O. F. (1984). *Severe Personality Disorders: Psychotherapeutic Strategies*. New Haven, CT: Yale University Press.

Larson, D. B., Larson, S. S., and Koenig, H. G. (2000). The once forgotten factor in psychiatry: research findings on religious commitment and mental health. *Psychiatric Times* 17(10):78.

Lichtenstein, H. (1961). Identity and sexuality. *Journal of the American Psychoanalytic Association* 9:179–260.

Mahler, M. S. (1965). On the significance of the normal separation-individuation phase. In *Drives, Affects, and Behavior*, vol. 2, ed. M. Schur, pp. 161–169. New York: International Universities Press.

Mahler, M. S., and Furer, M. (1968). *On Human Symbiosis and the Vicissitudes of Individuation*. New York: International Universities Press.

Mahler, M. S., Pine, F., and Bergman, A. (1975). *The Psychological Birth of the Human Infant*. New York: Basic Books.

McDevitt, J. B. (1983). The emergence of hostile aggression and its defensive and adaptive modifications during the separation-individuation process. *Journal of the American Psychoanalytic Association* 31(5):273–300.

Moloney, J. C. (1954). Mother, God, and superego. *Journal of the American Psychoanalytic Association* 2:120–151.

Parens, H. (1971). A contribution of separation-individuation to the development of psychic structure. In *Separation-Individuation: Essays in Honor of Margaret S. Mahler*, ed. J. B. McDevitt and C. F. Settlage, pp. 100–112. New York: International Univsersities Press.

——— (1979). *The Development of Aggression in Early Childhood*. New York: Jason Aronson.

——— (1998). *Prejudice: Does paranoia explain it? A discussion of J. M. Post's* The Psychopolitics of Hatred. Meeting of the American Psychoanalytic Association, New York, December.

Parens, H., Pollock, L., Stern, J., and Kramer, S. (1976). On the girl's entry into the Oedipus complex. *Journal of the American Psychoanalytic Association* 24(5):79–107.

Parens, H., and Saul, L. J. (1971). *Dependence in Man: A Psychoanalytic Study*. New York: International Universities Press.

Pruitt, K. (1997). *Clinical reflections from a longitudinal study of fathered children: ten years and counting*. Presented to Discussion Group #10: *Issues in Paternity*, chair, S. H. Cath. Meeting of the American Psychoanalytic Association, New York, December.

Roiphe, H., and Galenson, E. (1981). *Infantile Origins of Sexual Identity*. New York: International Universities Press.

Sander, L. W. (1964). Adaptive relationships in early mother–child interaction. *Journal of the American Academy of Child and Adolescent Psychiatry* 3:231–346.

Spitz, R. (1965). *The First Year of Life*. New York: International Universities Press.

Stern, D. N. (1985). *The Interpersonal World of the Infant*. New York: Basic Books.

Waelder, R. (1956). Critical discussion of the concept of an instinct of destruction. *Bulletin of the Philadelphia Association of Psychoanalysis* 6:97–109.

Winnicott, D. W. (1953). Transitional objects and transitional phenomena. *International Journal of Psycho-Analysis* 34:89–97.

2

DOES GOD HELP? WHAT GOD? HELPING WHOM? THE CONVOLUTIONS OF DIVINE HELP

Ana-Maria Rizzuto, M.D.

to make the meaning explicit / touching; ? explic. to join in understanding...

When psychoanalysts ask whether God helps people or not, the question requires clarification of the terms involved: *God* and *help*. Who is the God analysts may talk about? Psychoanalysis is an empirical discipline and has no competence in philosophical or theological questions. As analysts we can neither affirm nor deny that any God exists. The affirmation or negation of God's existence exceeds the level of our competence as experiential and empirical experts in understanding intrapsychic processes. We are, however, competent in comprehending the patient's subjective experience of God. We have the expertise to give meaning to the analysand's developmental and dynamic processes of formation of a private conception of God during the growing-up years and its transformations in the course of life. We can also understand the psychic use of God as an object in everyday life and in pathological situations. We have the ability to help patients articulate and make sense of their conflicts and predicaments with a God that has not escaped the analysand's struggles for attachment and satisfaction with primary objects, resulting in contradictory wishes and a

a central player / "family"

disappointing life. Each person's manner of believing or not believing in God and of striving with a divine being reveals dynamic
processes deeply connected with the patient's life history, object
relations, narcissistic balance, and defensive structure—the areas of
our specific competence as psychoanalysts.

To develop my answer we need to define the terms of
the question. The first term—*God*—requires that we describe the
types of Gods encountered in people's lives and the psychic
functions different conceptions of God may provide to the believer.
My research suggests that at least in our culture, where the word
God and religious expressions are everpresent, all children form an
unconscious, and frequently conscious, representation of God in
the course of development. The help or lack of it coming from such
a God depends on the relational dynamics between a particular
personal God and the conception of oneself in relation to God.
This includes conflicts of desires, beliefs about personal worth,
shame and guilt about past crimes and misdemeanors, as well as
complex fantasies about fate, acceptance of rejection, love and hate,
reward and punishment. The combination of such a multitude of
factors makes the God of each individual a very original version of
the God presented by any official religion and the culture at large.

The second term of the question—*help*—is almost as broad as
the first. The dictionary defines help as to give assistance or support,
to make something more pleasant or bearable, to be of use to, to
benefit, to futher advancement, to change for the better, to keep
from occurring, to avoid or prevent (*Merriam Webster's Collegiate
Dictionary*, tenth edition, 1995). Thus, from the point of view of
type of action, help is a type of intervention that may occur at many
levels of interaction. *Interaction* is a critical term because by definition help requires at least two participants relating to each other.
We could call this the cross section of help, the help offered at a
given moment in time. For us psychoanalysts, help has a longitudinal meaning. We know that no one can come to existence,
thrive, and become an adult without the specific and timely help of
others. The long-lasting discussion about nature and nurture has

brought to light that each moment of natural emergence of capabilities and functions must be met by the nurturing and adequate
offerings of at least a caring adult for the normal integration of
functions in the overall development of the child. We know that
the child's babbling must be met by adult speech if the child is to
talk. We also know that the child's smiles and gestures must be met
by the adult's echoing face for the child to come to his or her own
inner experience of being a self. To say it briefly: from the point of
view of human develoment there are as many types of help as there
are emerging functions and experiences that cannot reach their
psychic fruition without interaction with a complementary human
being. The need to be complemented by the responsive gestures *mirrored*
and actions of others obtains throughout life, from the infant's first
smile, through adult social and sexual intercourse, to the elderly
person asking to be touched and to be talked to. No one is exempt
from it. Even those who may have chosen to retreat to isolated
places live in interactional company with their inner loved, hated, *= the help of*
or idealized objects. To say it in Edith Jacobson's (1964) terms, the *an inner community*
self is born, grows, and achieves maturity in interaction with the
help of its object world. There is a specific type of help that is
optimal for each moment of development and each type of function. Such help is not optional. At no point in life can we live
without the help of others, even if it is others as sustaining and
loving internal objects. Human beings cannot be islands.

The question about God's help must take into consideration
the myriad types of help that are indispensable to become and
remain a rounded enough human being. God's help, whatever
form it might take, must submit to the development and dynamic
needs of the one helped if it is to be of any use at all. God's help *NICE*
cannot bypass the psychodynamic laws that govern the functioning
of the psyche.

The question of whether God helps or not is not too different
from asking whether we, psychoanalysts and therapists, help or not.
Patients come to us for help as paying supplicants. God is free,
moneywise, but the divine being seems to ask for other returns. We

transactional

claim to help our petitioner patients by listening to them, helping them articulate and voice their most feared thoughts and feelings, clarifying their life's predicaments, and allowing them to love or hate us as they need to in order to experience themselves as they are in their involvement with us. Their struggles in the treatment reveal their personal histories and stories, the formation of their character structure, the resolved and unresolved conflicts in their lives, as well as the eternal hopes that spring up freshly in intimate encounters. These are hopes for acceptance, love, respect, understanding, admiration, and the resulting feeling that it is meaningful and good to be oneself with a reliable therapist. Our patients want to feel that they can trust and respect us and find some comfort in our knowledge of their inner world.

When adult patients relate to a God they believe in, their petitions to such a God may converge to a remarkable extent with what we know could help them. In their prayers people want God to hear and see them, to understand their problems, and to intervene on their behalf in order to straighten out those life circumstances that cause them pain. People want to feel loved and accepted by a trustable God and try to love God and behave as they believe their God wants them to. Similarly to the therapist, they want to feel that God is pleased that they exist, that their lives are meaningful. Believers are very much afraid that their "bad" thoughts, feelings, and actions make them unacceptable to God, and try their best to change, control, or suppress them. So, too, with their analyst. As analysts we should not be surprised that what analysands want from us they also want from God.

To illustrate the help people want from God we may listen to the 2500-year-old Psalms of the Hebrew *Bible* and then to today's patients' prayers.

Psalm 70 (King James version) petitions:

> Be pleased, O God to deliver me!
> O Lord, make haste to help me!

> Let them be put to shame and confusion
> who seek my life!
> . . . .
> who desire my hurt!
> . . . .
> I am poor and needy;
> hasten to me, O God!
> Thou art my help and my deliverer;
> O Lord, do not tarry!

Psalm 9 expresses gratitude to a good object:

> I will give thanks to the Lord
> with my whole heart;

Psalm 19 proclaims admiration for God's great works:

> The heavens are telling the glory of God
> and the firmament proclaims His handiwork.
> Day to day pours forth speech,
> and night to night declares knowledge

Psalm 22 cries out the pain of abandonment:

> My God, my god, why hast Thou forsaken me?
> Why art Thou so far from helping me,
> from the words of my groaning?

Psalm 13 describes abandonment as having lost the face of God:

> How long, O Lord? Wilt Thou forget me forever?
> How long wilt Thou hide Thy face from me?

And Psalm 23 expresses deep trust in a caring and healing God:

The Lord is my shepherd,
I shall not want
He makes me lie down in green pastures.
He leads me beside still waters;
He restores my soul.

Psalm 84 is exultant with the joy of closeness:

How lovely is Thy dwelling place
O Lord of hosts!
My soul longs, yea, faints
for the courts of the Lord;
My heart and flesh sing for joy
to the living God

God's love is proclaimed in Psalm 89:

I will sing of Thy steadfast love,
O Lord, for ever;
with my mouth I will proclaim
Thy faithfulness to all generations.

When the patients who were involved in my research were asked what prompted them to pray they responded by saying that they felt God would "be close to me," "answer my prayers," "listen to me," "hear me," "understand me," "understand my prayer," "guide me," "help me solve problems," "help me be a better person," "give me the strength to be a better father." For some, God offered a special company "when I am alone," a sort of conversation "because God and I are talking together," and "gives me companionship and strength I cannot get in the world," a companion who can "recognize when I am in trouble."

Those who did not pray said that they did not because "God would not answer," implying that God exists. "I never felt it [God] had any significance," "God does not exist," "there is no one to pray to." The history of these patients who felt there was no God who would respond to them revealed that they had suffered either early parental loss or felt terribly alone as children or at the time of their responding to the question. They had lost hope that a God they were able to represent unconsciously could or would have any interest in them when they were in need of help.

If we compare the need for help in the patients in my research, our patients in analysis, and the authors of the Psalms, we can say that they converge in representing humankind's basic relational needs, involving others and themselves as internal objects. These essential needs are for connection to a worthwhile, lovable, and loving object who hears us, understands us, and responds to our need not to be alone in the world in helpless pain or empty opulence, an object who is capable of participating in exciting exchanges and of creating excitement for us (such as the beauty of creation or the feeling of God's love in Psalms 19 and 89). The essential human need for deep attachment and relationship to a reliable object resonates with us when we hear a patient lament for the inevitable vacation's separation or abandonment at a time when the analytic relationship has brought about deep involvement. The thoughts of Psalm 22 are frequently addressed to us:

> . . . why has Thou forsaken me?
> Why art Thou so far from helping me,
> from the words of my groaning?

We should not be surprised that what people want from God is what we all want from significant objects. As analysts we know the power of relationships, be they actual or internal. We are convinced that the exploration of the patient's predicaments and conflicts in the context of a solid and respectful relationship has the power to help the patient. We cannot separate the depth of the necessary interpretation of experience from the relational analytic experience itself. The help and the helper are of one piece. And so it is with God. I mean that when people come to treatment they come with whatever God they have conceived in their life's experience, and consciously or unconsciously they have a certain type of relationship with God. Some of them are very aware of their God, others try as best they can not to be aware of a God that disturbs them, while others have private ego-syntonic dealings with their God and do not feel a need to bring God overtly into their analysis or even their own conscious awareness, while yet others may use their God as a secret protection against a painful transference. Finally, there are those who claim to have no God at all. Among them, there are some who may be surprised by the discovery of a private and *ad hoc* God and an unconscious religion. There are as many Gods for an analyst to attend to as there are patients. I am talking here about God as a psychic conception of the patient, as a manifestation of the analysand's psychic reality that may or may not be integrated with participation in private or public religious practices. The analyst must keep in mind that God's psychic origins and attributes do not change the patient's belief in the actual existence or nonexistence of a God they are capable of representing. For the patient, God has a psychic reality that must be respected, not so much because it is divine—a matter that should not concern the analyst—but because it is the personal creation of the patient as the result of his or her overall process of making sense of inner life, relational objects, and the world at large, including the cultural and religious background. As Winnicott might say, the patient's God is a paradox that must be explored but not challenged.

Religious beliefs are dynamic processes deeply connected with the patient's life history, object relations, narcissistic balance, and defensive structure. Each person's private God is the result of a very complex developmental and dynamic process integrating in private ways intricate experiences with early objects, narcissistic and libidinal investments of the body and the self, and interpretive and wishful fantasies in the context of a particular family constellation and a sociocultural and religious environment presenting official descriptions of what God is like. Few private Gods, however, conform to the official religious story, marked as they are by the idiosyncratic traits they have collected in the dynamic efforts the individual has made during the development years and later in order to make sense of the God the culture offered (Rizzuto 1979).

I am attempting to establish the fact that the word *help* in the title of the symposium *Does God Help?* can and must be understood in the broad sense in which we humans always need help from others, actual others early in life, and at least internal others in later life. Freud (1927) made a specific connection between childhood and adult helplessness and "the formation of religion" (p. 22) and of the representation of God based on the desire for the protection the father could offer against the helplessness of childhood. For Freud (1910, 1913) God is nothing but an "exalted" father based on the infantile wish for protection. Freud uses intense words: "The terrifying impression of helplessness in childhood aroused a need for protection—for protection through love—which was provided by the father; and the recognition that this helplessness lasts throughout life made it necessary to cling to the existence of the father, but this time a more powerful one" (1927, p. 30).

For Freud, God is the simultaneous result of the religious indoctrination of the child and the young person's need for psychic and external protection. The outcome is the formation of an internal object made out of the father's actual traits, and the "exalted" characteristics the child adds to it, in the context of its relationship to him, in order to feel protected. Today we call this "exaltation" an idealized parental representation or imago. My research has convinced me that there are few "pure" Gods resulting from the exclusive exaltation of a parent. When that happens the patient's psychic situation is frequently gravely pathological. Most God representations are collages of significant aspects of primary object, significant adults (grandparents, aunts and uncles, and at times siblings and religious figures) who have created meaningful, real or imagined libidinal ties with the child.

Freud's great contribution to the psychodynamic study of reli-

gion consisted precisely in establishing the now well-demonstrated
connection between early objects and the psychic representation of
God. In spite of such a momentous discovery, or perhaps because of
it, Freud wanted to do away with all religion and the infantile
clinging to a transformed paternal imago. He believed that "Men
cannot remain children for ever; they must in the end go out into
'hostile life'" (1927, p. 49), give up their God, and stop needing
help and protection from a divine being. Much has happened since
Freud enjoined his fellow humans to do away with religion and
their "exalted" fathers. Psychoanalysis has progressively understood
that, "in psychic reality the object is immortal" (Schafer 1968, p.
220) and we cannot make disappear a God representation we have
formed out of the psychic tissue of primary objects and our own
wishes and experiences with them. We have also learned that God's
psychic substance has earlier and more complex antecedents than
just the paternal imago (Rizzuto 1979). God obtains first some of its
traits from prolonged interactions with the mother and other
primary objects, including the father, and also from the sense of self
and from narcissistic self-valuations in the context of the child's
interpretation of life's events and also wishful fantasies. The God
representation is just that, a representation in progressive dynamic
elaboration as the result of the continued reconstruction and
transformation of the relation with the primary objects, exposure to
alleged manifestations of God such as religious services, as well as
the changes occurring in the developing child. This process of
internal transformation of self and object was described by Freud
(1887–1904) in relation to the reorganization of memory in his
December 6, 1896 letter to Fliess: "As you know, I am working on
the assumption that our psychic mechanism has come into being by
a process of stratification: the material present in the form of
memory traces being subjected from time to time to a *rearrangement*
in accordance with fresh circumstances—to a *retranscription*" (p.
207).

In the course of a child's development, God, as an internally
represented object, undergoes modifications as the result of the

child's and adult's encounters with significant objects and experiences. The new object may awaken feelings, desires, and wishes for reinvolvement with early objects or with God as an experienced relational object. Their emotional and relational impact may contribute to modify some aspect of the God representation. God also undergoes changes, as Freud (1913) suggested, when the relationship with the primary objects changes: "His [the individual's] personal relation to God depends on his relationship to his father in the flesh and oscillates and changes along with that relation" (p. 147). We know today that it is not only "the father in the flesh" but also the mother and other primary objects or their present-day representatives such as spouses and lovers, bosses, teachers, religious figures, and others that may, through relational facilitations or disruptions, contribute to the modification of the relationship with God. Among these figures, the analyst must also be considered as a significant modifier of the relationship to God and his representation, as the result of the transformation that the parental imagos undergo during a treatment made possible by the affectionate transferential tie to the analyst. We have no studies in this area, except isolated anecdotes. In my own clinical experience, I have seen several people at the end of analysis revisit their religious beliefs as part of the process of termination and separation from the analyst as an intimate object.

Freud was too narrow in his conception of what help people needed and wanted from God. A God who finds psychic sustenance in prolonged primary object-related experiences as well as in cultural encounters with religion and its human representatives has a breadth of relational, emotional, and intellectual meaning that by far exceeds Freud's narrow clinging to the father. The help God may be asked to offer and the needs God may be requested to satisfy are as simple and immature or as complex and mature as the subject who appeals to God. Such needs encompass the entire spectrum of human need from birth to death. The limits to the help such a God might be asked to offer are set by two aspects of the phenomenon. On the one hand, there are the restrictions that its origins in early

and later relational objects place upon the representation of God as
a helper. On the other, there are the constrictions imposed by
character structure and narcissistic self-appraisal at the time of
searching for help in God and in other external or internal objects.

Another point is essential. Claiming that one has received help
from God is always a matter of interpretation of external events,
interpersonal dealings, and internal states. God's help cannot be
demonstrated or proven to someone who is not willing to accept
the version of the person who believes in it. The impossibility to
demonstrate to an unbeliever what one considers God's help does
not shake the conviction of the believer. Emotionally this makes
sense, because the interpretation of the type of help obtained from
God is based on the deep conviction that certain events do result
from God's help. The experience evokes the relational emotion of
having been responded to by God. The conviction has equal
emotional force when the nonbeliever in God's help affirms, as one
of my patients insisted, "God won't listen to me." No rational
demonstration can change such a belief. In either case it behooves
the analyst to delicately explore such convictions, tracing their
sources to the patient's emotional and relational history in the
context of his family and cultural system of belief. The analyst must
be careful not to reduce the experience to its genetic source but to
understand it in the patient's present-day relational situation, the
transference in the first place.

These last remarks bring to focus a technical point. Religious
beliefs and feelings are a very sensitive matter in the patient's
experience. They carry in them deep-rooted feelings, wishes,
hopes, and fears that connect to old and new layers of emotional
experience. Many patients prefer not to mention them explicitly to
the analyst because they fear to expose something they feel is too
personal. Hans Küng (1979), the theologian, has referred to religion as the last taboo. People are no longer as bashful as they used
to be about their sexual experiences, wishes, and thoughts because
in this post-Freudian era sex has claimed its place in the public
market. Not so with religion. Analysts have no training in under-

standing the specific psychodynamics of religion. Very few insti-
tutes in the world address in their courses the dynamic components
of their patients' religious beliefs. Religion is still taboo in many
training analyses. The end result is that many analysts have no
personal experience in exploring the dynamic components of their
own religious beliefs or lack thereof. If the analyst is willing to listen
to the analysand's dealings with God, he or she must be able to
suspend disbelief in this area as required in any other realm of
analysis. The analyst must be ready to ask necessary and adequate
questions, however silly they may seem. If a patient is complaining
bitterly, as one of mine used to, about how God had selected him
for punishment, it is necessary to credit God with the same psychic
existence of any other object brought about by the analysand. In
the case of that patient, I had to ask him what had prompted God
to select him, and later, how was it that God had chosen a particular
punishment. The answers to such unlikely questions frequently
bring to focus past embroilments with parental figures and narcissistic, if paradoxical, selection for punishment. Complex and
deeply hidden libidinal, narcissistic, and oedipal issues emerged in
the case of my patient. In his case, God provided buffering by
assisting him in modulating his rage at his parents while directing all
the blame to God's assumed responsibility for the patient's predicament. The understanding of the patient's relationship to God
requires that God receive in the analysis "equal employment
opportunity" as a psychic object that deserves attention and dynamic understanding.

Does God really help?

This is what I have learned directly from patients. The
majority of the patients in my research concurred in saying that
what they liked most about God was that "He is always there." This
is perhaps God's oldest and most significant psychic help at many
levels of development. At the most primary level of early awareness
of being, God, as a derivative representation, may serve the maternal function of "being there" for us to go on living, knowing that
God never leaves us alone in this world. It has its shortcomings in

relation to a budding superego, because after the children experience separation from their mothers, normal youngsters learn that
they can deceive her. Not so with God. One of the character traits
and the power of most gods humanity has created is their ability to
read the thoughts and intentions of human beings. There is no
hiding from God. Burdensome as this exposure may be, it has its
psychic advantages too. By indefatigably watching the believer's
inner world, the deity not only provides company but also the
possibility of certain dialogue, a companion who can, as the patient
cited above described, "recognize when I am in trouble." Analytically speaking, we may consider this aspect of God as a component
of the superego. I have no problem with such understanding as long
as we keep it as our theory and do not superimpose it on the
experience of the patient who considers God as the companionship
of someone who knows her.

At the narcissistic level, at the moment of phallic narcissism,
when the representation of God and the sense of oneself are being
consolidated while the first oedipal stirrings confront the child with
exclusion from the privileged parental relationship, God may offer
other varieties of help or interference. I believe that I can make this
point come alive by presenting at length analytic material of a
young and competent woman, Susan, who entered analysis as a
declared and convinced atheist by firmly asserting: "The stark
evidence is there. There is no God." She marveled at the people
who could believe, and she considered them inferior to her.

CLINICAL MATERIAL

Susan had difficulties in accepting any of the many men who were
interested in her, and came to analysis because her friends told her
she was neurotic about it. She had a mixed neurosis and was gifted
with a most vivid fantasy, populated by extreme representations:
either very beautiful landscapes and places full of people and
exuberant life, or vivid sadomasochistic, self-maiming fantasies of

an overt sexual nature. She also had a way of keeping her mind very busy with many thought activities all at once as a way of not attending to more emotional thoughts. The death of her father after a relatively short illness when she was in her middle teens had contributed to the consolidation of her childhood neurosis. She had felt rejected by her father and had been unable to mourn him. Her mother was capable of tenderness and care but was somewhat unpredictable and very much in love with the father. The family had not offered any religious education, and the parents discouraged references to religion. The material I present here covers three sessions. The second is six months after the first, and the third is nine months after the second. Susan deals explicitly with her "private religion," as she herself called it, and with her predicament about a God she didn't know she had. She alternatively called God "God," "the Power," or "the Powers."

In the July session, Susan tells a fantasy she had on the way to the session. She saw and heard an ambulance and imagined that I was in it and that "something terrible" had happened to me. She connected it to having spoken harsh words to me and believed my death would be her punishment for it. I would die and she would be all alone. I remarked that her hard words seemed to have a terrible power to harm me.

Patient: Someone is there listening to my thoughts and words to punish me. . . . My private God is always ready to punish me for my thoughts, wishes—always ready to punish. Ridiculous! But I believe it.

Analyst: A pretty grouchy God!

Pt.: And pretty contemptuous of all my feelings.

A.: God won't make any room for you!

Pt.: That's the whole message. It sounds like my father. The thing is that it's *me* who punishes. There is no God.

A.: You seem to want to believe there is no God while on the other hand you believe God is always attentive to your thoughts, contemptuous, punitive, grouchy.

Pt.: Father won by dying. Had I died [first] I would have won! Had I died, maybe I would have gotten my father's attention. He may have had a few sentimental thoughts about me. He would have felt something about what he had missed [by not loving her]. He would have loved me, felt pain. It would have been my revenge.

A.: He avenged himself by dying on you.

Pt.: Right! If I love someone I get punished. There is pain in that person's absence. Pain of losing the battle, he died first. For some reason I'm afraid to live. I buried myself with him. God doesn't like me to feel, love, have feelings. Even if I like a person, enjoy the person, enjoy beauty, I will be disappointed. God is doing it. Showing his contempt. I'm afraid of knowing all that's wrong with what I feel. It's all in my fanciful imagination. Fanciful. I hate that word, it's silly, trivial, superfluous.

A.: It seems to me that you're as good or as bad as your God [in the way you treat yourself].

Pt.: I said a few minutes ago that God is me. I have that feeling. Being God is to be contemptuous.

Here are excerpts from a December session. The patient tells the story of a book she had read of a father who seemed to have been dead for ten years and then came back to the family. Susan reflected about her own situation:

Pt.: [When my father died] I was very young. I was always wondering where he was. It's a mystery where my father has been all these years. . . . Sometimes I have thoughts and fantasies that my father is watching me. He can see what I'm doing, what I'm thinking. So strange. I repress it.

A.: Can you describe what he sees?

Pt.: Sometimes he knows I think terrible things about him. He makes me feel guilty. At other times I feel sorry for him. Other times when I'm really suffering, he's watching how neurotic I am and how he made me that way. At other times he may see how successful I am and be proud of me. If I'm masturbating he may see me.

A.: One could say that in a subliminal way you live continuously in your father's presence.

Pt.: I'm not sure it's true. You said, "in a subliminal way . . ."

A.: You seem to live for him. ... *to give you meaning, a SELF (+/-)*

Pt.: [After becoming distracted with other things for several minutes] I certainly lived for him as a child.

A few months later she had entered into a new analytic phase and was actively trying to understand her situation and to find a way out of it. She was astonished at the discovery of her own unconscious and at the power of her unconscious convictions and wishes. *- in my V.P. ontologically*

Pt.: It's a big problem. My wishes and motivations make it impossible for me to live. This is a quasi-religion. Whatever you want to call it, in my unconscious it's so real and alive. It's no academic stuff. It's alive. How do I stop myself from being grounded by it? The religion, God, and me at the bottom of the pile, having nothing for myself, no significance, no right to anything. That's the *nature* order of things. Being punished for wanting love. My father being killed [by God] as a punishment for me. I hated him [father]. That was the real crime. What a punishment to take him away! I didn't appreciate him enough. The Powers took him away. That would show me!

A.: What?   *egocentric + referential*

Pt.: What it's like not to have a father. . . . The Powers are focused on me as the sadistic side of my father was focused on me. The way I think in my unconscious is religious. Probably it's part of human nature. Everybody is that way in the unconscious. If you indoctrinated them early in life [with religion], it shapes it. That unconscious would get organized. That could be pretty positive and useful. It's quite a connection!

I never understood how people could believe in God. If they can connect it [religious indoctrination] with their unconscious system, God can be a benign force. They're lucky. That's something I've never understood, how all those people were talking about God. For them it's a benign father. How do I stop that [God's punishment] in me? I feel I should be punished.

Later in the session Susan expressed her feelings of closeness with me and feared she had provoked the Powers.

Pt.: I feel close to you. I feel touched by you even when you don't touch me. It feels good being with you . . . feeling accepted. . . . I feel I should be able to express myself better than I do, not being so scared of being punished.
A.: By?
Pt.: The Powers through you . . . you get scared and disgusted. The Powers would bring harm to you. I am violating the order.

These clinical moments with Susan graphically illustrate the dynamic components that go into the formation and maintenance of a self-created God whose constant dominance over her is a core element of her neurosis. This type of God is a variation among many other dynamic configurations of the God representation: kinder Gods, Gods formed with more maternal elements, Gods connected to the transformative effect of experiences with organized religion and its representatives. What is particularly interesting about Susan is that it is the patient herself who discovers several of the sources contributing to the formation of what she calls the unconscious God she cannot stop believing in.

Susan's God obtains his dominant traits primarily from her experience with the rejection of her father but also from her identification with his sadistic traits. God's "order of things" is her interpretation of her father's behavior as well as her own self-punishment from the unconscious guilt of believing she had killed her father with her wishes for love and revenge. Behind that is the violation of the order of things she really desired: to win her father for herself and show him he should favor her because she was better than her mother. There is also a disguised libidinal element that keeps her living in the watchful presence of her father and her God, the manifestation of a masochistic attachment to both. In another respect, God is also partly herself, that aspect of her that is attached to and identifies with the father, regardless of the pain she feels he inflicts on her. The psychic construction of her God representation illustrates what is true for *all* God representations: they contain in a dialectic form the essential components of the object(s) and of the self in a particular form of emotional relatedness.

What Susan cannot do is to "exalt" her father to a more protective God. She frequently recognized that her father was a good man, but she could not feel it. The profound double fixation of her desires, to be loved by her father and to obtain narcissistic revenge on him as well as reparation from him, kept her unable to find an oedipal resolution. Such resolution could have permitted her to integrate repressed positive maternal elements to the more frustrating paternal imago to form a more accepting postoedipal God not intent on destroying her life and keeping her in a living death without love and without a loving man.

SOME REFLECTIONS

The critical question is: Why did Susan, who had no religious education or pressures from her cultural milieu, unconsciously form a representation of God? Why did she exalt the most painful aspects of her relationship to her father to the level of a Power or Godhead? My research has convinced me that the motive is different in each case. When what is exalted is, as in the case of Susan, what is most painful in the relationship with the father, the motives seem twofold: The first is to displace the cause of suffering onto a being "above" the parent in order to preserve what is salvageable about the parental actions. If the order of things exists, the father is part of it and therefore not directly responsible but only submitting to that order when he made the patient suffer. The other motive is to keep hope for love open, a hope that dominates Susan's desires: that father could love her, come back from death some day, and make up for the suffering he inflicted on her. If there is no god, there is no father either, because then the father is really dead. She knows that her waiting for her father's return is totally irrational but she cannot help hoping for it.

Susan's God has been organized around the narcissistic injury of her oedipal failure in the context of actual rejection. The dominant affects pertain to the narcissistic realm. On the side of father and God there is revenge, humiliating punishment, putting her down at the bottom of the pile for her longing for love, showing her what she really deserves. On her side there is a desperate wish for narcissistic reparation of her having been rejected, the wish for a revenge that would force her father to love her and recognize her value. Having God and father there, even if looking at her contemptuously, gives her the narcissistic satisfaction of remaining the focus of their attention, having their watchful eyes fixed on her.

Susan's God came to exist psychically as her own creation to sustain in paradoxical ways some narcissistic balance and to keep a pathological modicum of hope for reparation. Her psychic difficulty consisted in her inability to accept that she had failed to force her father to love her the way she wanted to be loved. This failure made it impossible for her to mourn her father and go on with her life. God contributed to the perpetuation of her misery by repeating the trauma.

Other Gods have much more to offer. Some bring the peaceful feeling of a person kindly watching over us. Other Gods are "great" and bring the excitement of childhood experiences of parental admiration, while others are a bit like a faithful but undemanding friend who can be neglected for a long time and

often b/c an object (inter-subj) of present to assist them ...

summoned back to psychic life when urgent help is needed. All
these and many other variations of a private God present the basic
emotional components that organized the early God representation
preoedipally and oedipally. As Susan said, humans seem to need to
have an official God when they are confronted with the impossible
dilemmas of childhood. Freud (1927) hoped that if we stop teaching religion, God would melt away: "I think it would be a very
long time before a child who was not influenced [by religious
education] began to trouble himself about God and things in
another world" (p. 47). Speaking in this manner Freud was ignoring the power of his own discoveries, the intensity of the child's
needs and wishes, and the need to transform and exalt the parental
imagos as a way of preserving life-sustaining psychic exchanges and
giving them cosmic power to create an order of things that goes
beyond the visible and the tangible. The early emotionally and
dynamically formed God representation of each individual child
takes place too early to be deeply affected only by the much later
formal religious education Freud was talking about. It is not
uncommon, however, that religious teachings about a kind God,
presented by teachers who relate emotionally to the child, may
contribute to modulating and questioning the starker dynamic
features of some private Gods.

the unresolved

relational exch; have; self-sust. (of life)

When the child's intellect matures in early adolescence, the
larger question about God as an existing being and the maker of the
universe confronts the child's private beliefs with the knowledge
acquired in school and in the world and may force the growing
individual to search for an integration of internal experience with
religious doctrine and scientific knowledge. This integrating task
remains necessary as long as life confronts human beings with
suffering or knowledge incompatible with their God representation. For those who pursue it, this task lasts as long as a person lives.
The task of integrating the emotional sources of the private God
representation with a God presented by official religion requires a
continuous process of self-examination and revision of dynamically
motivated beliefs. True seekers of a God they believe exists must

wrestle to the end with the tensions between their own homemade God and a God they believe transcends it.

DOES GOD HELP?

After a long detour I am ready to answer the question of this conference: Does God help? Yes and no. The answer—whether yes or no—must be divided up in order to explore the many aspects of God's help. There seems to be a childhood psychic need to exalt parental figures and to believe in a larger order of things than the visible order. The psychic function of such exaltation is to create a supernatural reality, that is, above the visible and natural everyday life. After children have experienced that they can hide from their parents, they also feel the fear of not being seen by them. An exalted parent made into a God has by definition the capacity to "see" everything internal and external, from actions to thoughts, thus guaranteeing that the child and the adult as well are never completely alone. Benign Gods are like Winnicott's "good enough" mother—one can play alone in her presence. Punitive Gods, such as Susan's, also provide this function by keeping their presences through a punishment that not only maintains the emotional relatedness but also sustains in a paradoxical manner the hope for some better reward from the actual parent or even God himself. It is a finding of my research that a large number of subjects explicitly said that what they like the most about God was that "he is always there." Such unwavering presence has, as in Susan's case, the power to not only perpetuate its punitive actions but also enlarge her childhood drama with her father to such a cosmic proportion that she cannot live her life. A domestic misery is now a divinely imposed destiny. It doesn't matter that she knows it cannot be true. She can't help but believe it.

Children who have attended religious services with their believing parents frequently find great satisfaction in watching their parents deferring to God. If the children are on good terms with the parents, the sense of jointly belonging to a wider reality offers comfort and sometimes a sense of pride. If they are in conflict with the parents, they may hope God may either straighten out the parents' behavior (this is a frequent prayer of children of troubled parents), help, or punish the offender. In either case, children find some satisfaction in believing that there is a higher authority above the parents. If youngsters feel that the parent is unjust or dishonest, they may experience rage at the parental hypocrisy and secretly hope God would punish the parent in a way that gives the children satisfaction. I have learned about these instances from the communications of my analytic patients. These childhood experiences reveal that, once God exists as a psychic representation to which actual existence is attributed by parents and child alike, a new theater of events is created of which the child can become, to a certain extent, the stage manager or the helpless victim or anything in between.

a self-sust.

a theatrical drama

Belief in God's existence usually brings with it the creation of an extraterrestrial space to locate the deceased. Knowing as we do that, as a psychic reality, the object is immortal, we all have to do something with the dead. Human beings have found basically two solutions to the location of the dead. A vast number of human groups have created through their religions many different abodes to locate their dead in a place where they find their Gods. The great masters of all times were the ancient Egyptians with their vast monuments and their deep commitment to the deceased. The second option is to keep the dead alive in our memories. Most people need both—the internal memento and the celestial abode where the dead can be safely located and found. My most impressive experience in this respect was a young professional woman who had been raised by militant communist parents. They forbade her to ask anything about religion. She felt desperate about it because she needed a God to give her the sort of company her parents could not offer her. At the age of 7, she invented a ritual. She locked the door of her room, threw herself to the floor, and prayed fervently: "Please, let there be a God." When her mother

? the living dead

died she became depressed and was unable to mourn. The mourning process began after she had a critical dream. In the dream, her mother was sitting on an oriental carpet flying to heaven. When the mother on the flying carpet passed by the patient who was on the ground, she said in a friendly way, waving her hand: "'Bye dear, I'm going to heaven!" The young woman, like an ancient Egyptian, felt that she had finally located her mother in the place where she should be, and the knowledge that her mother was in heaven permitted her to mourn her. As an analyst, I have come to call this phenomenon the "geography" of significant objects. I believe that this is the same need that prompts many patients to want to know where analysts go when they go on vacation. It has to do not only with object constancy but also with the need to be able to imagine an absent object in a concrete place.

BACK TO THE CLINICAL SITUATION

God may enter psychoanalytic treatment in many forms. God may be used as a defense against the transference, secretly displacing onto God, in prayers and rituals, feelings and wishes that may appear frightening if overtly expressed to the analyst. God may be used as a resistance, when the patient insists that s/he cannot talk about certain matters. God can be used also for satisfying one's own wishes without having to feel guilt.

> I have reported elsewhere (Rizzuto 1996) the analytic moment when Louis, a young man deeply conflicted about his relationship with women, enacted with his pastor and his analyst a compensatory moment of oedipal victory in the transference. At the time of the analyst's first vacation, Louis was frantic and terrified of his feelings, voiced in gruesome, fairytale metaphors. He dreamed of being castrated by his mother and indicated that he would kill himself if nobody loved him. During the analyst's absence, he went to his pastor

and repeated to him that if nobody loved him he would kill himself. The pastor, Scriptures in hand, insisted that God loved him. Louis felt much comforted by the pastor's words and asked the pastor to call his woman analyst. The pastor did call, expressing his concern for Louis and his well-being. The patient considered the entire event a proof of God's love for him. In the next session a good mood came upon him, and without transition, he fantasized being naked next to his mother and ready to have sex with her. He experienced no guilt and behaved as though God had given him permission to have sex with his mother. His mood lifted, and the analysis returned to a more habitual collaboration between patient and analyst.

i.e., did away the father (a caring, protective phallic father, not the pastor).

At this point Louis remained unaware of his sexual wishes for the analyst and the interconnections among God, pastor, mother, and analyst. It was too early in the analysis to interpret it directly to him. What was significant was the repetition of his childhood manipulation of his parents, now mediated by the need to be told by the pastor that God (in his hearing, the mother-analyst) loved him in spite of his angry and sexual wishes. In commenting about the case I wrote:

> The cleverness of unconscious processes is shown in its economy of means. In these few hours Louis unconsciously orchestrated a magnificent demonstration of how to keep your God, your mother, your analyst, and your pastor/father, while fulfilling in fantasy the double satisfaction of sex with his mother and narcissistic triumph, without any conscious guilt. All this he could achieve because God was his secret accomplice (as his mother had been) under the Scriptural certification provided by his pastor.
>
> In due time the analysis discovered that the mother, who supplied the representational elements for the God representation of these hours and was the source of Louis's intense despair, had overstimulated him as a small child with her physical games. She

too, he believed, had condoned their sexual involvement. [Rizzuto 1996, p. 428]

This illustration shows that the analyst must not be concerned with the confusing and, sometimes, unexpected emergence of these aspects of the God representation. It is only through an unimpeded exploration of all these elements that the analysand can work through the fixation to parental figures as well as aspects of God created during childhood at the service of psychic compensation or defense. For these reasons the analyst must follow the patient wherever his associations bring him. The rage of God, his love, neglect, sexuality, favoritism, curses, sadism, or any other belief must be taken with the utmost seriousness. It is only with such analytic freedom that the analysand can fully feel the complexities of his relation with his personal God. In so doing he may acquire a new mode of believing that is devoid of its old psychological burdens.

KEY →

To achieve this desirable goal it is *indispensable that the analyst never make any pronouncement about God or religion.* Technically, such pronouncement disrupts the working through of the personal representation of God and of personal belief. It also conveys to the patient that the analyst knows God for sure, and has the right to demand that the analysand submits to the authority of the analyst. This goes against the aim of the treatment, which is to help the patient find maximal autonomy and internal freedom. It is not the responsibility of the analyst to help the patient find the "true" God and religion. His responsibility is to help the patient to find God and religion in the context of his past life history and present circumstances. [Rizzuto 1996, p. 429]

This strong recommendation does not mean that the analyst cannot talk about God, or Scriptures, or religious topics with the patient. It means that the manner of talking remains within the dynamic content presented by the patient's personal and psychic reality, as I did with Susan in talking about God or the Powers. The analyst does not introduce his/her own knowledge, ideas, or convictions about these matters.

Other aspects of religious affiliation concern not only intra-psychic dynamics but aspects of one's own identity in the community. When the family has a religious denomination, issues of identification, ethnic and religious, as well as systems of overt or preconscious self-valuation, come to play a role in the developing child's sense of identity, which in turn may affect aspects of the transformation of the God representation and beliefs about God's special relation to the religious groups the child belongs to. The end result may oscillate from openness to others and to life to a paranoid stance either of grandiose superiority or paranoid fear of those outside the group. Well-publicized national events such as the Branch Davidians' deaths illustrate the intensity of emotions evoked in the group and in secular authorities when intense differences and actively messianic activities pit a small group of adamant believers against the culture at large and its beliefs. In situations of compulsory belief, enforced by strict group regulations and surveillance, a growing child has minimal freedom to elaborate more personal versions of the community's God, and yet such an unconscious process can never be fully inhibited.

The transformation of the United States into a country of numerous minorities with their own religious backgrounds gives further relevance to the religion and God of immigrants as one of the most powerful means of keeping personal and group identity at a moment in which immigration causes a major disruption of all points of reference for one's identity. My clinical experience suggests that a large number of immigrants seek out their churches and revitalize their religions not only as a means of keeping continuity of experience in new circumstances but also as a revival of the need for protection by God that Freud spoke so forcefully about. Supervising therapists working with Latino immigrants has brought home this point. Patients bring up some of their religious experiences early in the treatment and expect the therapist to understand the nature of their concerns. A team of therapists at the Children's Hospital of Boston has prepared a manual for the staff describing the different cultural and religious beliefs and practices of various minorities. It became evident to the team that when parents bring sick children for medical treatment they come with renewed prayers to and belief in a God who can help them and their children.

Prayer is a universal component of belief in God. Years ago at an exhibit at the Metropolitan Museum of Art, I read the 5,000-year-old prayer of a man, written on a stone, petitioning God to guide and help him cross to the land of the dead. Prayer may range from pleas for magical and miraculous intervention to the would-be mystic's supplications to know God and to be united with God in a shared communion of love. In each case, be it from the unrealistic magical prayer to the highest level of mystical contemplation, the examination of the prayer itself gives a glimpse about the psychic structure and desire of the petitioner and the kind of God being invoked. Prayer, more frequently than not, involves verbal exchanges with a God whose existence is taken for granted. The prayer may create grave conflicts, as happens with severe obsessives, due to their great ambivalence toward God and the contradictory desire to obtain something from God, while trying not to express to God deep anger and contemptuous feelings. This can become an endless process of doing and undoing. In other cases, prayer may provide the opportunity for self-objectivation and articulation of desires in the presence of a good-enough God, who can tolerate confusion and wishes for clarification. There are other people who find God the most desirable being in the world and choose such a God as the privileged interlocutor in their life journey. An extensive mystical literature in the Islamic, Jewish, and Christian religions, frequently poetic, reveals in inspired lines deep experiences with inebriating divine love. I had the opportunity to treat some contemporary mystics who were suffering from minor pathologies. I was able to trace such experiences, insofar as their genetic and dynamic roots were concerned, to greatly admired loved and loving parental figures who offered the child a sense of intrinsic value and to which the child added early heroic and grandiose fantasies, narcissistic in nature, but well integrated with everyday reality. My limited experience cannot be transformed into a general rule. But what is important for these persons and for other committed believers is the conviction of belonging to a deeply meaningful order of things governed by a loving and trusting God. They derive great sustenance from such conviction and may be moved to carry out activities in everyday life to bring to others what they consider their greatest riches. The difference in structure and meaning of this order of things from that of Susan's is striking; nonetheless, it reveals the totalizing tendency to encompass all reality, when God acquires psychic significance.

How does this brief description of prayer connect it to the question of whether God helps or not? The answer is similar to other aspects of belief in God. Prayer may be of great help to those who find a God they trust and feel related to. It may bring continuous anxiety and worry to those who doubt that a God they believe in has good intentions toward them, such assumed intentions being either a projection of their ambivalence or related to the type of God they have. Finally, prayer can become a nightmare of obsessions, doubt, and muffled hatred, capable of creating a battle of submission and defiance that never ends. In short, God's help in relation to prayer varies along the lines of the type of God that is being prayed to, as well as the character structure and the psychic dynamic situation of the one who prays.

Public liturgical prayer brings with it as many complex personal experiences as any of the private dealings with the divinity do. As a communal celebration, it offers the possibility of feeling integrated into a community of believers, which in turns evokes the double experience of belonging to an earthly group of believers as well as to a vaster world of ancestors and other beings all united in the visible and invisible network of worshipers of a shared divinity. The experience may arouse feelings of belonging and of being part of a meaningful universe. It may also bring up feelings of shame and entrapment, together with wishes to defect, when the believer is a member of a group considered inferior or even despised.

We may ask how all these experiences related to God and religion are integrated in psychic structure. The God representation finds its source and emotional value in the primary and later objects contributing to its formation and transformations later in life. It carries with it aspects of the libidinal attachments evoked by them as well as their prohibitions and approvals. To these must be added the affects and meanings emerging from actual religious experiences with their own repetitive or transformative influences of preexisting aspects of the God representation and the self representation in dialectical relations with the believed divinity. This means that either in a completely unconscious way—as happened with Susan until she came to analysis—or consciously or preconsciously, the God representation influences all the agencies of the mind, from unconscious libidinal attachments, to reinforcement of the superego's approving or reprimanding injunctions, to ego syntonic or dystonic experiences of self-identity, belonging, and being connected or separated from a God that one consciously believes exists or doubts may exist—as it was with Susan. It may also offer, as a benign superego does, sustenance for the ego ideal and the ideal self, or, on the contrary, it may become a persistent accuser and persecutor. It may be understood that this language is figurative because representations cannot do anything on their own. There are no "things" in the mind, but extraordinarily complex mental processes carried out by the individual himself (Rizzuto 1979).

In concrete everyday life, God exerts different types of influences according to the personal history, character structure, and religious belief or unbelief of the person who at one time formed a God representation. For many, God is a completely silent and unobtrusive psychic presence who demands no attention. Others have managed to repress or split off disturbing God representations and, while the defenses work, they are unaware of such a presence. There are still others who, based on the emotional sources of their

God, call upon the divinity only in moments of distress or moments of transition such as birth, death, or marital commitment. Finally, there are those who take God in all seriousness and consciously try their best to follow the recommended path offered by their particular faith in order to find deeper acceptance and love from the divine being.

CONCLUSION

My final answer may sound simplistic but I believe it is essentially correct: God helps those who can be helped by the God they have formed and transformed in the course of their lives. God does not much help those who are stuck with archaic and persecutory God representations. Paradoxical as it may seem, this type of persecutory God, as Susan's was, perpetuates pathology in the service of keeping open desires we are not able to renounce.

[handwritten marginalia: Kohutian; mourn; give up an self-defeating object tie; Blos...]

REFERENCES

Freud, S. (1887–1904). *The Complete Letters of Sigmund Freud to Wilhelm Fliess 1887–1904*, trans. J. M. Masson. Cambridge, MA: Harvard University Press, 1985.
———— (1910). Leonardo da Vinci and a memory of his childhood. *Standard Edition* 11:59–138.
———— (1913). Totem and taboo. *Standard Edition* 13:1–161.
———— (1927). The future of an illusion. *Standard Edition* 21:5–56.
Jacobson, E. (1964). *The Self and the Object World.* New York: International Universities Press.
Küng, H. (1979). *Freud and the Problem of God.* New Haven, CT: Yale University Press.
Rizzuto, A.-M. (1979). *The Birth of the Living God: A Psychoanalytic Study.* Chicago: University of Chicago Press.
———— (1996). Psychoanalytic treatment and the religious person. In *Religion and the Clinical Practice of Psychology*, ed. E. Sahfranske, pp. 409–432. Washington, DC: American Psychological Association Books.
Schafer, R. (1968). *Aspects of Internalization.* New York: International Universities Press.

3

THE GOD REPRESENTATION AND THE INNER DIALOGUE AS TRANSITIONAL PHENOMENA:

Discussion of Rizzuto's Chapter,
"Does God Help? What God?
Helping Whom?
The Convolutions of Divine Help"

Ruth M. S. Fischer, M. D.

This is good; read.

Ana-Maria Rizzuto explores the ways in which an individual's relationship with her/his God representation reflects the earliest relationships in life. Thereby, she notes the relevance of psycho-analysis and separation–individuation theory to a belief in God.

It was Freud who originally made this object relation observation. It was he who connected the psychic representation of God with the relationship to one's father, thereby bringing religion under psychoanalytic purview. However, he then dismissed it from serious consideration as he viewed God as merely a representation of the exalted father of childhood. Our turning to him was understood as a childish act that was to be outgrown or analyzed away. It is interesting that this childlike dependency on the father noted by Freud to be present in the relationship with God is echoed and elaborated on in Margaret Mahler's idea of the child's union with and separation from the symbiotic mother.

With time, we have developed a deeper appreciation of the child's needs and wishes that empower the parents and secure the child. And we have developed a much greater appreciation of the role of the mother and of others in this process. But first, there was Freud's dismissal of this "childish need" and a veering away of psychoanalytic interest from the topic of God. In her research, in her writing and in this presentation, Rizzuto brings God back into psychoanalytic discourse and brings psychoanalytic understanding back into belief in a divine being.

I see this renewed analytic interest in God as part of the ever-widening scope of psychoanalysis. We are opening our eyes and our ears, our hearts and our minds to issues of preoedipal development, the importance of the mother, the importance of the father, the role of adult development, neurobiological contributions, gender, sexuality, culture, countertransference, and the impact of the analyst. Of course, one of the earliest pioneers into this widening scope was Mahler herself, with her focus on the earliest years of life and the development of relatedness.

Rizzuto's focus is a truly psychoanalytic one. She does not concern herself with confirming or denying God's existence. Rather, she is interested in the understanding of the individual's subjective experience of her/his own personal God. She is concerned with making sense of it, not in doing away with it. The focus is on the form and the determinants of the belief (or lack of belief), not on its validity. At the same time, she reminds us that this belief in God is a belief that must be respected. Understanding its origins, attributes, transformations, and psychic uses is no different than analyzing any other aspect of the life of the individual. It is to be explored, not challenged. In this way, she calls attention to an important aspect of our technique.

EXPERIENCE OF GOD
WITHIN THE DEVELOPMENTAL CONTEXT

The word *help* in "Does God help?" is understood as an interaction. It is appreciated that helpful interaction is essential for growth and development. As development occurs within the mother–child orbit, it is within this realm that the interaction must take place. Here Rizzuto notes the fundamental role of the other in the life of the child, an idea that is central to Mahler's work as well as the work of Spitz, Winnicott, Emde, Stern, Brazelton, and many other "baby watchers."

The God representation evolves out of the relationships that the child enjoys with the important people in her/his life. The interactions with these individuals determine the relationship with the God representation. This is not determined solely on the basis of the actual interactions with the important others in the child's life, but also on the fantasized interactions and other life experiences.

KEY

The experience of the nature of God's help is determined by the experience of the nature of the help of the primary caregivers. There are many ways in which God may help, reflecting the many ways in which the individual experienced interacting with the original caregivers. As the maternal presence, the God representation may provide a sense of belonging, of security, of inclusion, of union. As the paternal authority, God maintains superego demands and reinforces strivings of the ego ideal. The God representation may also be alienating, demanding, demeaning, and intrusive. The nature of the experience of the interaction with the original caregivers, the nature of their help, and the subsequent vicissitudes of life are what determine this. "Does God help?" is directly related to "Do parents help?" with the understanding that we are not limiting ourselves to the actual parents and the actual interactions.

Paula Heimann

Similarities are noted between God's help, the analyst's help, and the help of the primary objects. There is a basic human need for attachment to and relationship with a reliable other. People need to be heard, to be seen, and to be understood. They need love and acceptance. They need trust and respect and safety in a relationship that they, in turn, can trust and respect. Herein lies the help of the parent, of the analyst, and of God.

TO BE ... TO COME INTO THEIR OWN...

Exploring a patient's conflicts in the context of a respectful relationship has the power to help. It is impossible to separate out the curative element. Is it the interpretation, that is, the words, or is it the relationship? The words have limited meaning without the understanding that comes with respect and affective attunement. Feeling is conveyed along with the words in the timing and the cadence of the voice and in the smile and the seriousness of the tone. The help and the helper are one. And so it is with God and with parents.

Rizzuto presents the case of Susan to illustrate the components that go into the formation and maintenance of the God representation. The presentation, in a way, is a prototype. It contains, as Rizzuto tells us, "in a dialectic form the essential components of the object and the self in a particular form of emotional relatedness." There is an interaction here between the self representation and the God representation. The interaction is a helpful one. The particular kind of help offered is the essence of what it is that needs to be understood. It is here that Rizzuto clearly makes her case for the presence of a God representation, the need to appreciate its presence, its evolution out of the early interaction with the primary objects, its developmental vicissitudes, and the need to deal with it analytically.

She also presents us with an intriguing developmental construct. She postulates that in the course of development, along with the establishment of representations of the self and the other there is the formation of a God representation. She is suggesting that this is a universal phenomenon on a par with the establishment of the self and object representations. It is clear how this idea evolves out of her clinical material. It is strikingly present in the case of Susan, a young woman who claims to have no belief in a God, yet clearly has developed a God representation out of her early object relations. Although I find this an intriguing idea and I appreciate the clinical material from which this idea emanates, I prefer to withhold judgment about its universality. I am more comfortable seeing it rather as one of many possible internal representations of self and object in interaction.

It is the interaction itself that I find intriguing. Separation-individuation theory is essential in pursuing these ideas. It is particularly pertinent to a consideration of the interactions of the representations of the self and object. I will consider the relationship to the role of the God representation shortly.

Mahler, in her research and in her writing, made it impossible for us to ignore the profound importance of the earliest interpersonal interaction—that between the mother and her infant (Mahler et al. 1975). As the mother and child smile and coo at and with each other, they are in the process of becoming a unit. The child will become a person as she/he separates and individuates out of this union. It is not on the separation and individuation that I would like us to focus, but rather on the early interaction in which mother and child are developing their particular union. They are in the process of creating their own unique dialogue. It is this dialogue that I find pertinent to our topic.

It is this dialogue that draws the child into an emotional engagement with the mother. It is with this dialogue that the mother attracts her child's attention, excites him, and soothes him. It is with this dialogue that she draws him into the world. It is here that the child learns about interacting, touching, being touched, and being in touch kinesthetically as well as aurally, visually, and emotionally. It is this dialogue that sets the stage for the subsequent interactions that will develop with important others in the child's life as well as setting the stage for the development of the interactions of the child's internal representations. All of these interactions, internal as well as external, in some way will reflect this early dialogue.

The dialogue is significant both in the founding of the union with the mother and in the separating out from it. It is in the separating out that the internal representations of self and other are formed with the possibility of an interaction between them. The establishment of the dialogue leads to the formation of a specific bond with the mother. This has two opposing outcomes: a new sense of security and a new sense of vulnerability. The bond establishes a connection to and a dependence on the mother, thereby providing a place of security out of which the child can grow. However, as the child becomes aware of the importance of and the dependence on the mother, she/he is now left with a new sense of vulnerability to loss.

As the bond brought with it a sense of security and the possibility of vulnerability, boundary development also evokes this double response. There is a new sense of security of self and a new sense of vulnerability about connection. Discomfort over separateness leads to attempts at restoring the earlier pleasurable bond. This is accomplished by making use of the dialogue. The child turns to the general patterns of behavior so well documented by Mahler: the mutual cueing, perceptual refueling, looking back to mother, leaning against her. And there is the very individual imprint as each dialogue is unique for the particular mother–child unit.

As the perception of mother and self becomes more differentiated, the need to dialogue across the barrier of separateness is increased. When faced with the unfamiliar, there is a need to turn to that which is reassuringly familiar. This is accomplished via the dialogue. That which is reassuringly familiar is the dialogue. This phenomenon is not limited to infancy or even to childhood. It is an important aspect of establishing comfort at any age and under a multitude of situations. The checking back, the refueling, the establishing the dialogue allows for a feeling of safety while retaining independence.

With the establishment of object constancy, the object, the mother, is now a constant in the psyche of the child. Her actual physical presence is no longer required to regain the sense of oneness with her in order to feel that all is right with the world. The dialogue can now take place internally between internal objects. An internal representational structure has been established within which the dialogue occurs. The child is freed from the need for the actual presence of the external object for refueling.

Slowly, the child develops the ability to re-create the relationship as a dialogue within, in the absence of the external object, so that when the inner equilibrium is upset, the child can return to a feeling of comfort by turning to her/his particular dialogue.

Many different forces may upset the inner equilibrium and evoke the dialogue. Drives, internal conflicts, or external disturbances may be the culprit. A need and a wish for safety are aroused. The wish contains mental representations of the self and the object in interaction. This is the dialogue. It is evoked in order to bring about a return to the state of comfort. Comfort can now be attained independently through turning to this internal dialogue.

Susan's case points to the complexities that may present themselves. Her comforting dialogue contains discomfort as well. Her father's sadism and rejection were an important part of the interaction between them. The comfort comes via the familiarity of the dialogue and the sense of his presence. The discomfort comes from the sadistic nature of the interaction. ... *but one comes to the other...*

When the inner equilibrium is upset, an internal dialogue may be set in motion. But comfort may also be attained through an external dialogue. Frequently, someone is sought out to play the required role to restore the more familiar, secure scenario. There is a tendency to seek people in the real world onto whom one can externalize aspects of internal objects. An attempt is made to evoke object-related role responses that belong to internal object relationships. This is a type of refueling, of regaining the early, comforting, unique dialogue.

Childhood relationships may be repeated without much alteration or they may be defensively disguised. This is strikingly noted in the transference. The analyst is experienced as supportive, critical, demanding, argumentative, distant, punitive, and/or seductive as needed. Under the stress of the analytic process the old familiar form of relatedness as well as its defensive expressions are evoked. The analysand seeks comfort in reaching for the early interaction. *not only comfort; also delays growth... disavowal of difference*

Here we make note of the analysand who experiences the analyst as contemptuous with every developmental step taken or another who feels the analyst to be distant as greater closeness is *persists.*

approached and needs to be defended against. Even more striking is
the analysand who evokes an argument whenever he becomes
aware of some significant period of emotional growth. All of these
situations are experienced as threatening to the analysis and to the
analyst as they were, no doubt, experienced as threatening to the
primary objects.

For Susan, the externalization of the internal dialogue in the
transference is quite clear. She reports that on the way to her
analytic session she had a fantasy. She saw and heard an ambulance,
imagined that the analyst was in it, and that something terrible had
happened to Rizzuto. The death of the analyst leaving Susan
feeling abandoned was her punishment for the harsh words she
expressed in anger. She had externalized one aspect of her internal
dialogue and experienced Rizzuto as the punishing abandoning
father.

At the same time, there is an internal dialogue as she feels that
someone is present with her, listening to her thoughts and ready to
punish her for them. This was another part of her dialogue with her
father, who she wished would be attentive to her thoughts and
whose contempt, anger, sadism, and abandonment she endured. It
was endured for the sake of the comforting sense of his presence.

At times, the dialogue is not expressed directly with the
analyst, but rather indirectly with a third person. This was the case
with Louis, who was able to engage his pastor in an enactment that
unconsciously involved his analyst and fairly directly expressed the
early important triadic interaction.

And finally, the dialogue may be experienced with a God
representation. Here we see Susan experiencing a relationship with
her God that has all of the elements, both real and wished for, of her
relationship with her father. Her God is contemptuous, punitive,
grouchy, vengeful, abandoning, guilt provoking, and cruel. He is
also omnipresent and attentive, as she wished her father to be. This
young woman, who claimed to be an atheist, was having an
internal dialogue with her Powers, whom she experienced as her
father, as a God representation, and as her own self.

Clearly, the dialogue is modified as the child grows and develops. Interactions with important others leave their imprint. This is strikingly noted in Susan's case. The impact of her oedipal conflict is abundantly in evidence in the dialogue presented in the transference and clarified in the analysis. It is all about interactions with her father, both in reality and in fantasy. She is loyal to him. She accepts no other suitors. She maintains her tie to him by not mourning him and feeling forever in his presence. But then she fears punishment from her omnipresent, omniscient father who knows her every thought and action. She experiences him as contemptuous, vengeful, rejecting, guilt provoking, and powerful. The sadistic aspect of her relationship with him has become internalized as an important element of their dialogue.

The feel of the oedipal conflict with her father is clear in the interaction. The Powers will bring harm as she is violating the order of things. She is being punished for wanting her father's love. Her father's death, as that of Rizzuto in the fantasy, is her punishment. She is also punished for hating her father as well as for her anger, that is, her harsh words with Rizzuto. Father was taken away as she loved him too much and didn't appreciate him enough. And the Powers are her father himself who focused his sadism on her.

The dialogue with her father is so loud that we are unable to hear any other dialogue that may be present, such as that with her mother. We can only assume that it is there somewhere underlying the interaction with the internalized father. I suspect that there are important similar components in the maternal dialogue on which the later dialogue is based.

But where is the earlier version of this dialogue, the one with the preoedipal mother? Rizzuto suggests, "The profound double fixation of her desires, to be her father's first love and to obtain narcissistic revenge on him and reparation from him, kept her unable to find an oedipal resolution that perhaps could have permitted her to integrate repressed positive maternal elements." I believe that there was an earlier version of the dialogue, the one with the preoedipal mother. And I believe that this was the original double fixation. This was her wish to be her mother's first love and her rage and revenge against her.

Of the few things that we are told about the mother, other than her inconsistent availability and her distance, is that she was very much in love with the father. Possibly, this is Susan's longing, her seeking of people in her fantasies, her business to fill the void of mother's absence, her sense of rejection, her anger, and the origin of her sadomasochistic dialogue with her father. The Powers had determined that obtaining mother's love and gratification was not to be. It was not the order of things. This is not to be her dialogue, so that when she feels close with Rizzuto, touched by her, feels good being with her and accepted by her, she fears that the Powers will bring harm. We must be open to the possibility that the dialogue with her father to which she turns for comfort contains within it elements of an earlier dialogue with her mother.

Clearly, a dialogue has multiple determinants. One should be able to ferret out both maternal and paternal components, as both parents were important people in her early years. It is suggested by the presentation that her mother was inconsistently available and somewhat emotionally distant. This may explain Susan's seeking the more alive, consistent dialogue that her father offers despite its sadistic nature. This may be her way of avoiding the void that may be one aspect of the dialogue with her mother. This is hinted at in her need to keep her mind busy with activities and vivid fantasies. The sadomasochistic dialogue with her father, then, may be reinforced as it defends against experiencing the void in the maternal dialogue.

In summary, then, when the inner equilibrium is upset, the dialogue is evoked. This may be an internal dialogue between self and object representations or an external dialogue with an object upon whom aspects of the internal object are externalized. The object may be real or fantasy. The God representation may be the fantasized other to whom the individual turns for dialogue. And this is clear with Susan's Powers who were maintaining the order of things, whether we understand them to be solely a representation

NB: the soothing dialogue is not subject to the vagaries of real life since all internal aspects of the self = control

of her oedipal father or whether we include the imprint of the earlier mother–child interaction.

There is another option that I would like to suggest: we are dealing with an intermediate space between an external and an internal dialogue when we consider the God representation.

GOD REPRESENTATION
AND THE TRANSITIONAL SPACE

I am suggesting that the dialogue with the God representation falls into the category of Winnicott's (1953) transitional phenomena. These are phenomena used by the child in dealing with stress when emotionally separate from the primary love object. By displacement from the original love object, they function as a substitute providing the illusion of the presence of the comforting mother when she is not available. This is the dialogue with the "blanky." There is an interplay here between the child's inner and the outer worlds, between the experience of the me and the not-me and between primary and secondary processes.

the reciprocal minuet to and fro

Winnicott's idea was that the illusion of symbiosis is evoked at a period of development in which self and object representations are only partially separated and individuated. I am suggesting that this dialogue is evoked whenever the sense of separateness is threatened by the wish for union. The transitional object, in this case the dialogue, reestablishes the union while maintaining a sense of separateness.

KEY

The God representation as presented has elements of transitional phenomena. Susan is confused about whether she is speaking of God, her father, or herself. God seems both herself and not herself, her me and her not-me. She turns to him in times of stress and she projects onto him aspects of her parents. I say "parents," as I cannot exclude her mother. The early mother–infant relationship and the unique dialogue that they develop between them are, after all, the infant's earliest way of being in the world.

dasein

Under vocabulary/ concepts the desc. paradox: God is me + not-me both: condensed

The dialogue is key. It is expressed in the transference. It may have its painful aspects, but it is familiar, and familiarity is comfort. Here we have Susan's fantasy of the analyst's death. She is abandoned. This is punishment for her hostility as well as for her wish for closeness. It is also her revenge. It allows her to leave before she is left. It controls the leaving. It is a compromise formation of her actual and fantasized relationships with her father, what she longed for from him and what she defended against, and it includes her punishment. It is so many things. And it is familiar and therefore sought out for comfort. The dialogue is expressed in the transference as aspects of it are externalized onto the analyst.

What I want to emphasize is that the dialogue that she establishes with the God representation, her use of it in times of stress as well as its soothing potential, is the same as that established in the transference. It is the all-important dialogue with the caregiving other sought out in times of emotional disequilibrium. It originated in her relationship with her parents. We assume the existence of an internal dialogue between self and object representation comparable to that which we see externalized onto the relationship with the analyst. And we see its repetition in the relationship with her God representation.

I am suggesting that this reflects a transitional phase between relatedness to primary objects and an inner dialogue between self and object representations. In this transitional phase, internalization has occurred but separation and individuation are not firmly anchored and regression occurs. The God representation serves as a transitional object with whom to dialogue: a me, not-me object; a mother, not-mother object sought out in times of stress.

I find it helpful thinking of the God representation as a transitional stage in developing object relations. It seems to occupy that potential space of mutual creativity between mother and child of which Winnicott speaks. It is within this space that there is interplay between inner and outer, which leads to the capacity for symbolic play and creative and esthetic experience. Certainly, herein lies religious experience.

When I began preparing for this presentation, it struck me that I had had very few analysands who had spoken of their interaction with their God. I wondered if this was because I was not open to hearing this material or was it that the individuals whom I analyzed were in some way different from those who came to see Rizzuto. Possibly, it had to do with a religious difference. It turned out that both seemed to be the case.

As I was busy pondering this puzzle, as so often happens under these circumstances, I began to hear about God. However, I found it noteworthy that the subject appeared in the material of adolescents and young adults whose separation-individuation experiences were sticky. There was an ambivalently loved mother, a difficulty delineating the boundary between the self and the world and/or a difficulty wresting control of their lives from the parents in order to establish autonomy. *KEY*

This brought to mind that under certain circumstances transitional objects become more urgent in the child's development than under other circumstances. The importance escalates when the process of separation-individuation is at risk. This is because of the important transitional role the transitional object plays as an intermediary between the mother and the self, between autonomy and dependence. And it was in just these arenas that these particular analysands were troubled.

In different ways, they had been robbed of an opportunity to slowly differentiate from their mothers within a close proximity to her. Thus they did not have the luxury of the gradual development of internal representations to carry with and to refer to in times of need. *,To EVOLVE IN ITS OWN TIME*

We have not focused on the importance of the time that is needed for this process to slowly evolve. We appreciate the need for the development of the bond between mother and child. We are increasingly aware of the intricacies of its development—at birth, in the neonatal period, and, more recently, prenatally—with studies of fetal and infant responses to maternal and paternal voices, words, and cadences. We appreciate the importance of the kinesthetic—of touch and of body movement as well as smell, sound, and visual stimuli. We see the impact of the infant–mother pair on each other and the dance they do as they develop their unique bond. We are beginning to appreciate the influence of the infant–father relationship on this bond as well as that of the mother–father bond. The lifelong importance of the bond is evident in the child's developing pattern of relatedness and expectations from relationships. It touches and determines every aspect of the child's and the ensuing adult's life. We see this in Susan's dialogue with herself, with Rizzuto, and with her Powers.

It is not only the establishment of the bond that we appreciate. We know the importance of the separation and individuation out of the bond. Mahler's studies of infant development have outlined for us the child's road to object constancy. Here again, we note the mother–child interaction at each phase of development and the impact of this interaction on all that ensues. Ultimately, it becomes a lifelong pattern. Anni Bergman beautifully illustrated this in a case presented at the 27th Margaret S. Mahler symposium entitled "Autonomy and the Need for the Caretaking Other" (Bergman and Fahey 1997). Here was a mother who was most comfortable when her child was autonomous and a son who had the ability to comply with his mother's need for his independence. This became their dialogue and his lifelong modus vivendi.

What we have not fully appreciated and very much need to focus upon is the timing, that is, the impact of a premature or too sudden or too definitive rupture of this bond with the mother. This is not a new idea, but it is one that needs our greater definition.

The reasons for a too early disruption to the connection are manifold. They run the gamut from maternal withdrawal to infant withdrawal and include external disruptions. Each of these possibilities will have multiple determinants and effects. Of course, the cause and degree as well as the underlying infant strengths will determine the outcome. However, no matter what the cause, the child is left struggling with the need to individuate without the time necessary to establish well-grounded internal representations

depend / hunger

with which to dialogue in times of need. It is here that we see the
children who desperately hang on to their transitional objects and,
even more unfortunate, those who are unable even to establish
transitional objects.

☆

CLINICAL ILLUSTRATIONS

Case 1

Margaret began treatment as she was entering high school. She was
quickly caught up in an eating disorder. She was weighing and
measuring, exercising, and endlessly counting calories. Two recent
events stood out. The first was her escalating anxiety as she
contemplated starting high school. She complained that her anxiety
was keeping her from living. It was not allowing her to be at school,
have sleep-overs with her friends, go to parties, go to camp, even,
at times, go to the movies. The second was her grandmother's
terminal illness. To her, these events meant loss and the passage of
time.

Her development had been marked by great success, as she
was precocious, bright, talented, charming, attractive, and sociable.
And it was marked by short episodes of anxiety that left her unable
to leave the house and/or her mother. As a child, she had been
preoccupied with Dorothy in *The Wizard of Oz*, who was separated
from her aunt and uncle by a tornado.

Because of her precocity, she developed quickly and handled
many adult tasks. She considered herself an equal partner with her
parents, as frequently did they. With the advent of high school, the
facade crumbled and the underlying emotional vulnerability became apparent. There were other important factors at play, such as
conflicts over aggression both in the realm of self-assertion and in
the expression of hostility. She was very nice and very careful to
avoid hurting anyone's feelings. She feared some terrible result
were she to express any anger. All of her niceness, however, did not

devil
↑
not even

love/hate
↙

too much
on the road
to death
= unavailable

prevent her grandmother from dying or her own entrance into high school.

An extended period of analysis allowed her to experience her dependency needs and come to terms with her vulnerability and her status as a child. As she gained comfort with her hostility, she allowed herself the expression of some anger at the injustice of it all and she became more self-assertive. She spoke with comprehension and great feeling of the passage of time and of generational differences.

It became apparent that her early precocity had led to accomplishments way beyond age expectations, thereby promoting early closure of the separation-individuation experience. She was left with object constancy but vulnerable to its loss. There was not enough opportunity for the establishment and integration of the intermediate stages, the transition, the play between the me and the not-me. Differentiation out of the mother–infant bond had occurred, but it was too precipitous, leaving her prone to anxiety and unable to make the final step in differentiation during the second individuation process in adolescence. Her analysis offered her this opportunity.

Case 2

Robert, at 17, was very quiet and was becoming increasingly withdrawn, sullen, sleep deprived, slovenly, and unable to concentrate. Conversation was difficult to elicit. Obsessive doubting followed almost any comment. Some of his thoughts were becoming bizarre. As high school progressed, he became less able to function. His anger and despair were palpable.

He too was a very bright, precocious, talented child who performed well beyond his age level academically and within the family setting. He asked little of his parents, usually preferring to handle things himself.

When he was a toddler, his parents went through a stressful time, resulting in his mother's emotional withdrawal with the consequent need for him to do things himself, to not bother his mother, at times to be his mother as well as himself. And he was very sad and very angry. He had a vivid memory of willingly and with great bravado giving up his pacifier and experiencing great sadness. His thought was that he was a big boy now.

As he dealt with all of these issues in his analysis, he developed a profound, close, and meaningful relationship with his dog. This allowed him some degree of closeness, warmth, dependence, and soothing. Gradually, he turned to his peers.

He, like Margaret, had had a protracted period of differentiating himself from his primary objects. It related to his precocity, but it also related to his parents' strife and their consequent lack of availability. This resulted in a significant degree of pathology.

DISCUSSION

Clearly, these are merely thumbnail sketches of complex situations. I note them to draw our attention to the importance of not prematurely foreclosing the individuation experience and the role the transitional object plays in this process. These two patients did not seem to have an adequate internal dialogue with which to soothe themselves. Under stress, Margaret required her mother's actual presence. Robert's situation was more extreme. He could rely only on himself. As we explored some of his difficulties, he turned to his dog as a transitional object indicating progress in the process of relatedness and individuation. For him, God was non-existent, though perhaps, as the analysis continues, we will discover his God representation, as Rizzuto found its presence in the atheist Susan.

Margaret intermittently spoke of her confusion about God. Her feelings related to magical thinking. She would appease her God with nightly prayer that followed a specific order, special self-protective rituals at school, and an avoidance or negation of negative thoughts. These diminished in importance and intensity as

as separation-individuation got under way

her analysis progressed. They ultimately disappeared, as does the transitional object that the child outgrows.

In returning to Susan and wondering about her early relationship with her mother, a number of aspects stand out: her contempt for need, her difficulty with aggression, and her problem with closeness—all of the same significant issues present in these two adolescents who experienced premature closure of the separation-individuation experience. Even the feeling of living in her father's presence suggests more than an oedipal wish. To me, it suggests the possibility of an underlying autonomy conflict. I hear this in her inability to live, love, or feel. I suspect that her fear of living is a concern about separation.

I wonder if Susan too had not been shortchanged when it came to slowly differentiating out from the early bond with her mother. Needs, wishes, and conflicts would then have been transferred onto her relationship with her father, resulting in an oedipal conflict overloaded with feelings derived from the earlier autonomy conflict and heavily laden with the anger of the conflict of ambivalence with her mother. All of this would intensify the sadistic component of her internal dialogue.

It is here that the transitional object and the internal dialogue come into play. If the child has had an adequate opportunity to experience the dialogue, to play with it, to have a back and forth with the mother and later, within herself, it will be firmly established and will be comfortably evoked in time of need. Adolescence, the period of development in which the child reexperiences the individuation process, is such a time of need. It is a time when the strength of the internal dialogue is put to the test. It is often at this time that we see the lack of solidity of the dialogue indicating the incompleteness of the individuation process. It is also at this time that we note strong religious preoccupations and involvement and interaction with a personal deity.

I am suggesting that the dialogue with the God representation may be an important part of the individuation process, a transitional

Excellent.

step along the road to object constancy and to taking one's place in the world.

REFERENCES

Bergman, A., and Fahey, M. (1997). Autonomy and the need for the caretaking other: data from a longitudinal study. In *The Seasons of Life: Separation-Individuation Perspectives*, ed. S. Akhtar and S. Kramer, pp. 23–50. Northvale, NJ: Jason Aronson.

Mahler, M. S., Pine, F., and Bergman, A. (1975). *The Psychological Birth of the Human Infant*. New York: Basic Books.

Winnicott, D. W. (1953). Transitional objects and transitional phenomena. In *Playing and Reality*, pp. 1–25. New York: Basic Books, 1971.

4

SO HELP ME GOD!
DO I HELP GOD OR
DOES GOD HELP ME?

William W. Meissner, S.J., M.D.

I would like to protest the title proposed for this symposium—"Does God Help?"—because I find it problematic and troublesome. So much of any possible answer depends on what we mean by the pivotal terms *God* and *help*. The focusing of the issues in the subsidiary terms *faith* and *belief* carry their own burden of uncertainty, and inexorably draw us into murky areas of controversy and theoretical debate, even if we pass over more practical and clinically relevant issues that lie close to hand. In the first instance, the terms are theological in intent and meaning, but the many centuries of theological debate have not had a great deal of success in figuring those terms out and presenting them in clear and unequivocal language. One of the unfortunate aspects of our topic is that it plunges us willy-nilly into the crux of the difficult and often contentious dialogue, or should I say debate, between psychoanalysis and religion.

I can explain what I mean a little better by providing some context. Early in my career in psychoanalysis, my interest was drawn to the study of psychoanalytic aspects of religious experi-

ence. But what I found was disappointing and disillusioning. I saw
clearly the limitations, interpretive and historical misapprehensions,
and fallacious reasoning in Freud's view of religion. After some
years, I gathered enough courage to attempt a book about this
problem (Meissner 1984) in which I tried to set the Freudian
argument in perspective and suggest that that argument had out-
run its usefulness. An important aspect of that discussion had to do
with the personal psychic determinants underlying and motivating
Freud's late enlightenment and rationalistic attack on the meaning
of religion.

These same aspects have been documented exhaustively and
comprehensively more recently by Rizzuto (1998). She and I, it
seems, share the same dissatisfaction with the Freudian argument,
but our approaches to an effort to get beyond it have followed two
somewhat divergent, but I believe mostly parallel, paths. The
direction of her thinking, following on her groundbreaking study
of the development and functioning of the God representation
(Rizzuto 1979), was toward a deeper and more detailed understanding of religious belief and the meaning of the God representation within the psychoanalytic process.

My own tack diverged to a slightly different direction. I found
myself increasingly engaged with issues more directly related to the
interaction and integration of psychoanalytic perspectives with
religious forms of understanding and belief systems. In other words,
if we assume, for the sake of discussion, the truth value or validity
of religious beliefs—and I am referring here not to the idiosyncratic
and highly personal beliefs of individual believers, but to belief
systems espoused and promulgated by established churches and
religious communities—we are confronted with the challenge of
bringing the resources of analytic understanding to bear in ways
that deepen our grasp of the psychological meaning of such beliefs
and our appreciation of the motivating factor that enlivens and
sustains them. The program in this terrain is not the questioning or
reductive obliteration of religious beliefs and convictions, but
rather accepting the validity of such beliefs, to seek a deeper

understanding of the meaning of such beliefs and the motivational substructures that lend them power and significance for so many over the full extent of human history. So I would conclude that whoever thought up this title was certainly asking for trouble! But a provocative title deserves a provocative response.

The confrontation this title raises before us is between a psychoanalytic perspective focused on the psychological complex of meanings and motives we can discern in religious concepts and beliefs on the one hand, and the status of religious beliefs as enunciating profound truths about the meaning of human existence and the implications for man's relatedness to an existing creative and saving God on the other. This basic religious postulate is attended by other sustaining beliefs concerning the immortality of the soul, the reality and sustaining power of divine grace, the pervasive salvific will of God extended to all mankind, and so on. These propositions are not based on any empirical foundations other than the sources of revelation accepted by a given religious tradition. They are accepted solely on the basis of faith; they cannot be demonstrated or proven by appeal to any evidential source or confirming arguments. They are simply accepted as objects of belief, or they are not. To those who believe, they are potentially sources of profound truth and existential guidance. To those who do not believe, they are illusions and deceptive fantasies and wish fulfillments that fly in the face of reason and reality.

Such, indeed, was Freud's view of these matters, and I presume that of many other analysts. Freud was in this respect the heir of Schleiermacher and Feuerbach (Dollimore 1998, Meissner 1984). Feuerbach's construction of a materialist philosophy has had a profound influence on modern thought and particularly on Freud. As Dollimore (1998) explains, "In that philosophy, God is displaced by man. Or rather, God, having been discovered to be made in man's image, is taken back into man. This is the exhilarating argument of Feuerbach's *The Essence of Christianity* (1841); 'All the attributes of the divine nature are, therefore, attributes of the human nature.' Religion arises when man 'projects his being into objectivity, and then again makes himself an object to this projected image of himself thus converted into a subject' [pp. 33–34]" (p. 207). The echoes of this atheistic and agnostic approach to God are readily heard in "The Future of an Illusion" (Freud 1927). Those who do not believe are well advised to read no further—what follows will have no meaning without either a believing disposition or at a minimum a willingness to accept the belief of believers as having meaning and validity for them.

I propose to make a few comments about these troublesome terms—*God* and *help*—and then offer a reflection on the interplay of these issues in relation to religious faith, as proposed in the subtitle for this symposium. Finally, I will discuss some case material that demonstrates the implications of the intermingling of psychic and religious perspectives as they come into play in the psychotherapeutic context. In the course of this discussion, I will be seeking to explore the relationship between psychic forces and process on the human level and the putative view of God's graceful intervention in the human heart and mind. Needless to say, this discourse is one that lies well beyond the usual or customary circuit of analytic or psychological consideration, but it is one that forces itself on us by reason of the fact that among the patients who come to us for help there are many who are religious believers for whom the concepts and values of their religious tradition are fundamental and vital to their view of themselves and their important human relations. Whether we, as analysts, like it or not, whether we agree with their religious beliefs and convictions, they do believe, and it is our task to understand and to help them to understand, not to undermine or destroy their faith when it functions as a sustaining influence in their lives.

In the course of this reflection, I will be raising a number of difficult questions. I would like to be able to say that I could at least try to answer some of the questions I will be raising, but I'm afraid that for the most part I have little more to offer than questions. So with that stout caveat, let us plunge ahead.

THE PROBLEM

There are two pivotal terms in this topic. First, what do we mean by God? Thrust squarely in the middle of the debate, between psychoanalysis and religion, we face an inherent and pervasive difficulty that continues to haunt that dialogue: the participants attach different connotations to many of the same terms. There are significant differences and debates among the theologians themselves, for example, as to what they mean by *God*. There is the God who creates, the God who saves, the God who loves, the God who judges and condemns, God the supreme being, God who is pure existence, the God of the philosophers, the God who transcends all human considerations, the God of monotheism, the Trinitarian God, and much more. For some theologians, God does not exist. Tillich (1952), for example, speaks of a "transcending theism," a God beyond God who transcends all known forms of existence. Faith in such an unknowable God is thus an ultimate concern beyond the categories of classical theism (Schrag 1997). But we need not trouble ourselves about theological variants; I will settle, for the sake of this discussion, for the common understanding of the God of the Judeo-Christian tradition. There are enough differences and difficulties between the analytic and religious views to keep us well occupied on this score.

The differences that concern us arise in large measure from the different connotations of psychic vs. actual reality. The concept of God is one of these pivotal concepts. From the psychoanalytic side, we can say little or nothing about God; we know little or nothing about God; if the subject of God or any of his works comes up, our lips are sealed and our hands tied. That is, we know and can say nothing about the God of religion—that God, at least in the mind of the believer, is real, existing from all eternity, and constantly active as creator and salvific force for all mankind.

As analysts we know nothing of that God. The best we can offer is a commentary on what, thanks to Rizzuto (1979), we have come to call the God representation, that is, the mental representation of God in the mind of a human subject, whether believer or not, whether conscious or not. That imagery is saturated with infantile derivatives of object representations drawn from multiple levels of the developmental history of any given individual and reflects many of the dynamic influences within that history. The God representation is to this extent an intrapsychic mental creation reflecting many of the dynamic, defensive, conflictual, and structural influences in the mind of the person in question. In other words, the God representation tells us nothing about God. It speaks not to an actual reality existing outside the mind of the believer, but to a psychic reality existing only within the mind of the believer (Meissner 1984).

But this formulation of the meaning of God is relatively meaningless to the religious mind. To the religious believer, God is not just a representation, not even a transitional phenomenon; he exists. God is not just a mental configuration reflecting dynamic motivational influences; he is an active and creative force acting and causing effects in the hearts and minds of his people. That God acts not only in history, guiding and orchestrating the course of human history in terms of his salvific plan and providence for all his children, but also immediately and directly within the soul of every human being through his grace, guiding, urging, and suasively drawing each and every one of us to our destiny of loving communion with him in eternity (Meissner 1987). It is this God who is opaque to the analytic mind, but who is the object of convinced belief for the religious mind. But, to stay on the theological track for a moment, this God also acts within individual souls with complete respect for the way he created them—as endowed with intellect and freedom. Analysts would not find it difficult to envision variations on the theme of how individuals can wander from and resist the salvific action of a loving creator within them—resistances to the action of the analytic process might provide a suggestive analogue.

So, if we are to ask "Does God help?" what God are we referring to? The God of psychic reality, or the God of actual reality? As analysts, we have every reason to question how the God representation is formed developmentally, how it finds expression in various states of normal or abnormal development and functioning, even how it influences the course of therapy for good or ill. But we cannot go beyond the confines of the representation, its history, and its intrapsychic influence, because beyond that, beyond the limits of our methodology and beyond the reach of our conceptual tools, lies the God of the religious believer. We are left, seemingly, with an irresolvable ambiguity. But .

What about the other term, *help*? "Does God *help*?" From the side of the God representation, we can ask some interesting clinical questions. To what extent does the God representation reflect its pathological origins in relation to primary or other objects? To what extent does it embody aspects of the patient's psychopathology? Here the projection of pathological superego dynamics onto the God representation is common coin. In what sense and to what degree does the God representation reflect transference dynamics? To what extent does the God representation offer itself as a preferred target for therapeutic intervention or interpretation? Are there instances when the God representation can be worked on directly with therapeutic benefit, more advantageously, let us say, than less direct interpretive interventions dealing with the originative relationships? Does the God representation serve then as a convenient object of displacement or does it offer itself as a preferred and primary target for intervention? If so, when and how?

On the other side of the equation, the religious side, there are also some interesting questions. These questions, however, do not register unless we address them in a context of religious belief and acceptance. The question "Does God help?"—by which I mean "Does the real God help?"—has no meaning unless we accept the proposition that there is a real God and that he—or she as the case may be—really acts in some way. Does the real God, then, play a role in development? In therapy? Some religionists would assert that he does through his ever-present and ever-active grace. To be respectful, we must acknowledge that there is mystery here. Theologians struggle to explain or understand how the presence and action of God is possible within the human soul. But they assert on the basis of revelation and belief that it is so. How it is so is harder to say, but that it is so they generally agree.

FAITH AND THE RELATIONSHIP TO GOD

In terms of the above perspective, the faith that we are concerned with is the faith of religion, the faith that saves, the faith that Paul wrote to the Romans about, the faith that accepts and assents to a religious belief system, the faith that theologians regard as a theological virtue. We are not concerned with any of the possible pale analogues of faith that involve psychic processes only, such as the "faith" a patient must have to some degree in the therapist in order that the therapy have any effect; this "faith" I would regard as synonymous with trust. Religious faith involves more than trust. Part of what it involves is due to the influence of divine grace. The issue before us, then, is how are we to understand the psychic correlates or underpinnings that relate to the capacity for religious belief and contribute to its motivational impact.

The understanding of religious faith has been a major problem at all stages of man's religious history. Abraham was the archetype of faith in the old dispensation, and for Paul, standing at the threshold of the new, it became a major theme of his preaching. And at the birth of the Reformation, the divisive rending of Christendom took shape around the issue of faith. Was man saved by faith alone, or did salvation require in addition good works? The preoccupation of philosophers and theologians throughout this long history has been primarily ontological—questions asked in an ontological perspective are questions about the nature of faith, about the metaphysical definition of faith, about the relation of faith and grace, and so on. Another traditional focus for the concerns about faith is the epistemological. What is the proper object of faith? How is assent possible without evidence? How do we achieve certitude, or what kinds of certitude do we achieve, in the act of faith?

I mention these traditional concerns for two reasons. First, to make it clear that my intention in this discussion differs quite considerably from the concerns that dominated traditional approaches. My approach here, and our concerns, are specifically psychological. We are focusing explicitly on the motivation, genetic, topological, structural, and dynamic aspects of faith. We seek to explore its relations to the structures of the mind and examine its motivational functions within the psychic economy. Such an approach has a quite different formality from the theological, ontological, and epistemological concerns of the religious mind. Faith is, after all, a human response to a revelation, and therefore has a psychological aspect related to the ordinary spectrum of human psychological functioning. We can explore and ask questions about the psychology of faith and thereby further illumine its structure and intelligibility. At the same time it is well to remember that, by limiting ourselves to a psychological perspective, we are prescinding from the further complexities of faith that belong more appropriately to the religious context.

The second reason for setting this present consideration off from more traditional concerns is simply that the psychological consideration of faith, while it is formally distinct from and independent of more traditional approaches, must in many ways depend on those approaches. The rich content of traditional formulations provides the material on which the psychological consideration can base itself. Moreover, it provides a considerable number of insights that can serve to direct the psychological inquiry. Thus, a true psychology of faith cannot work itself out in isolation from a theology and an ontology of faith. It must depend on them and seek their guidance through an uncharted country. But it can and must prescind from their conclusions where the conclusions do not materially affect the psychological consideration. The theological significance of the act of faith, for example, its relationship to grace, and its necessity for salvation have little to do with its psychological

understanding. Conversely, psychological understanding has little
or nothing to contribute to the theological significance or understanding of faith. This aspect of the methodology of this inquiry
into the psychology of faith diverges radically from the usual
analytic approach, which is directed exclusively to exploring the
subjective meaning and derivation of the object of belief in the
patient's mind.

Another discriminating emphasis in distinguishing the psychological from more traditional perspectives is that psychology
and psychoanalysis are fundamentally empirical disciplines. Their
formulations take the form of generalizations, and their perspective
emphasizes extension rather than intention and the varieties of
interindividual variation. It focuses on men rather than on human
nature. The more traditional philosophico-theological approaches,
however, work with abstractions, natures, universals. The formality
of statement is in terms of natures and properties, intention rather
than extension. Thus, where the tradition can speak of the nature of
faith and the nature of man as substantial and universal concepts, the
psychologist can speak only of faith as a phenomenal range of
experience that has an inner diversity as well as generality. It is an
experience that men share involving shared meanings and symbolic
elements, but remains an experience that is unique to each one of
them. It is within this context of diversity that the psychologist
seeks the more common elements and their inherent variation and
tries to relate them to known psychological principles.

The term *faith* can have a diversity of referents. The history of
the theological and philosophical arguments over faith is a sage of
diversity in definition and concept. We are concerned with faith as
a disposition in the human psyche. But the problem is to clarify
what we are encompassing in such a disposition. There has been
a tendency in the Christian tradition to intellectualize faith and
conceive of it as an intellectual act, an assent to revealed truth, an
assertion of revealed truth as true. The act is also related to its
disposing virtue or habit. The focus in this perspective is decisively
on the act, as the primary character of the drama. The drama is, in

fact, a dramatic monologue, and little else enters into the play. Other aspects of the human response are regarded as either preparatory or consequent to this central intellective act, but they in themselves are not faith. The Lutheran argument over faith and works seems to have been at its roots an issue of whether faith was only the central act or included more. From a psychological point of view, to isolate a central element (an intellectual element at that) and consider only it as relevant is to invite sterility.

While there can be little argument with the centrality of the intellectual dimension in faith, as a human response faith also embraces the totality of man's psychic life. Man's intellect does not function as a disembodied phantom. Man's intellectual response, particularly in the act of faith, is an expression of the whole man, of the rich complexity, motives, needs, instincts, defenses, and capacities, and the constellation of these that is uniquely his. Faith, then, even if one seeks to isolate and analyze an intellective element, derives from and reflects other aspects and levels of the psychic organization. When we speak of "faith," therefore, we will have reference to an organized sequence of acts deriving from various levels of the mind and integrating the diverse functions of these various structures into a complex experience. We can call such an organized sequence a "process," thereby emphasizing that the organization involves sequence, that it cannot be conceived of as static, frozen in a moment of time, and that it is a dynamic activity.

To speak of faith as process and to assert that the process is dynamic implies further that the organization and integration inherent in it are relative terms. One can think of degrees of integration and/or organization and that at any given point in time the process in any individual is more or less organized and more or less disorganized. The system is dynamically in flux, approaching and receding from an ideal state of maximal integration—and perhaps never quite reaching it. If we could envision that end point of total integration as perfect faith, we would have to think of faith as a graded phenomenon. However we formulate the total integration of the "fullness of faith," the process in the believer concretely represents some degree of that faith. Faith, therefore, is a range, a spectrum, that reaches from the lowest degree of mere assent and minimal involvement all the way to total conviction and an unreserved totality of commitment in which faith fuses with charity. Faith is a complex process whose richness is the richness of man's capacity to reach out for something beyond himself.

Faith and Reason

The problematic of faith has always cast faith in terms that set it off as an act in a different order from ordinary human experience. Within the context of its ontological and theological involvements, there is reason to regard it as a unique act and experience. It involves a firm assent to and acceptance of religious truth and reality without the usual props of intellectual conviction. One cannot ascribe reasons or provide arguments or point to compelling evidences; the believer is "rationally vulnerable." As a consequence, faith is set off from and opposed to *reason*. Reason arrives at its convictions and certitudes by a process of investigation and argument and proof. Faith, as a psychological process, arrives at its convictions and certitudes by an appeal to nothing outside itself. And so believers believe because they have faith, and disbelievers disbelieve because they have no proof. (or lack faith)

No thinker has better captured the absurdity of faith than that remarkable preanalytic "psychoanalyst", Søren Kierkegaard. His ruminations on the faith of Abraham and the challenge to that faith in the command to kill Isaac, his only son and the fruit of his old age, the promise of his heritage, serves to open up for us the complexities of faith and the fitting of it into a broader context of human existence (Kierkegaard 1941). Faith involves and depends upon a particular relation to the divine that dispenses with every form of intermediary, whether community, state, church, or tradition. The individual thus enters into an immediate and absolute relation to the Absolute. Abraham's faith was a paradox, because his belief was a belief in the absurd. One is reminded of Tertullian's "*credo quia absurdum.*" Faith reaches beyond the illumination of reason into the darkness of paradox.

The last outpost of reason was what Kierkegaard called "infinite resignation." Faith presupposes the resignation of all finite goods and dissociation from all wish-fulfillments. One who has not made this resignation has not faith. It is only in such an infinite resignation that man begins to catch a glimpse of his true validity, and only then does it become possible for him to grasp his existence by virtue of faith. One must stand at the edge of the precipice if he is to leap into the dark chasm. Thus, faith is not an emotion precisely because it requires resignation. It is not an instinct of the heart, but a paradox of life and existence. Faith is not a suspension of reason, but a reaching beyond it. The paradox is rooted in the antithesis between God and man. It is a submission to God requiring ethical maturity and the capacity for resignation, leaving man no recourse but the impossible.

At this point we encounter the absurd. And the paradox is that man, by reaching through a veil of dread into the emptiness of the absurd, finds a relation to God stripped of all the trappings of the finite and in which man finds his own highest self-realization. And the further paradox is that beyond resignation man is enabled to live once again in the finite, but by virtue of a faithful relation to God that derives in no sense from understanding. Faith is, therefore, for Kierkegaard, the highest human passion—touching life at every point and containing the entire reality of man's essential existence, transcending the calculations and illusions of worldly wisdom, grasping and immersing itself in the finitude of life (beyond the withdrawal from the finite in resignation), and triumphing over the dread that permeates the experience of man's finite existence.

The process of faith, then, embraces both resignation and belief, loss and restitution. The psychological insight into this sequence is profound. It pivots around the issue of the absurd, for this constitutes in a sense the borderline between resignation as a function of reason and the movement beyond resignation in faith. It is important to emphasize that faith does not dissolve or resolve the absurdity. If the absurd ceases to be absurd, faith ceases to be faith. Theologians are wont to emphasize the certitude of faith. But certitude has little place in a psychological discussion. Psychologically speaking, nothing is ever certain. Psychologists can deal with probabilities, but not with certainties. But it should also be added that there is no inherent inconsistency in permitting psychological probabilities to stand side by side with theological certainties.

Psychologically speaking, then, the more significant aspect of faith is its uncertainty. Faith is a category of life and existence rather than a category of thought. Human life is filled with uncertainties and conflict. Faith provides illumination, direction, and meaning to life. Faith is an affirmation of encounter and relation between God and man. But within this affirmation, which is after all a human affirmation, there lie the shadows of self-deception, projection, denial, illusion, doubt—in short, uncertainty. But in Kierkegaard's terms these are categories of the finite, and they must be resigned before true absurdity and authentic faith can be achieved. The resignation, however, does not eliminate the shadows. Nor does faith, in passing beyond resignation, eliminate the finite and its shadows.

We cannot think of faith as a static stance at which one arrives and into which one settles comfortably once and for all. Faith is a dynamic, living process. It takes place through time and has a history. Its realization is never total and final like the casting of a statue. Rather it is a vital reality always in flux. Its grasp upon the certainties of its assertion is unstable and precarious. Abraham believed in the virtue of the absurd, but his belief did not dispel once and for all the absurdity. The continuance and persistence of faith are impossible without the persistence of the absurd. And while faith in a sense triumphs over dread, it cannot annihilate that dread. Rather its threat persists, modulated and surpassed no doubt, but persisting nonetheless as a constant reminder of man's fragility.

When considering the act of faith as such, it is neither unreasonable nor surprising that it should be set off from reason and contrasted with it. Focusing rather on the process, it becomes reasonable to shift the emphasis in two ways. Rather than conceiving reason in narrowly intellective terms, reason can be thought of in terms of all of the levels of psychic structure and organization that determine and contribute to the process of faith. Therefore, it becomes possible to explore faith less in terms of its divergence from or contrast with reason, and more in terms of its continuities with reason. This is no more than to insert faith back into the living reality of human existence and to try to envision it as it really is, not as a static abstraction of an ideal, but as an imperfect and fragile, dynamic, and vital process that is (as Kierkegaard would have it) man's highest passion.

This does not explain faith in any sense, but it gives us the opportunity to explore the implications and derivations of faith. In so doing, we are not understanding faith so much as we are setting it in relation to processes and functions that we can understand. And if it is fair to say with Kierkegaard (who echoes a substantial Christian tradition) that faith cannot be understood because it transcends the categories of understanding, it is also fair to say that faith is after all a human process with a history and a psychology that do not transcend understanding.

Regression in Faith

If faith endeavors to reach beyond reason, to go beyond the limits of infinite resignation, and to leap into the darkness of the absurd, there is in this impulse of faith a deviation from the intellective standards of reason. The reaching beyond the limits of logic and reason poses a problem. How are we to conceive such obvious deviance? Is it a deviation in a downward direction, that is, a retreat to more primitive and less developed forms of thinking that might be found in primitive cultures or in the alogic of children? If so, we could consider it as a form of regression and thereby seek its explanation in terns of wish-fulfillments and instinctive motivations. This was the direction Freud (1927) took in his analysis of religious beliefs; they were for him illusions, and their illusoriness and power stemmed from the powerful wishes that they were meant to gratify.

The deviation, however, may take an upward turn, that is, an advance beyond the limits of reasoned thought and the capacities of logical process to attain a unique apperception of revealed truth that cannot otherwise be attained. Thus Kierkegaard points out that faith is unique in that the particular transcends the universal, whereas all other particulars are understood in terms of the universal. These are the Hegelian categories of reason, and faith escapes understanding precisely because it breaks out of these categories (Kierkegaard 1941). We have an analogous problem with creative insight in science. Is intuition a form of regression, or is it a grasp of inherent intelligibility that lies beyond reasoning capacity? In science, the ultimate test is still based on evidence and reason; whatever intuition may provide must submit to the arbitration of test and experimental confirmation. But in faith, it is not so easy.

It should be said immediately that regression does not necessarily imply pathology or impaired psychic functioning. It does imply a relaxation in the organization of psychic functioning that permits greater cognitive flexibility and freer expression. There are many creative and productive aspects of human activity that in fact require a capacity to retreat from the confinement of strict logicality and permit the emergence of aspects of mental functioning more attuned to primary motives. This is presumably what happens in dreaming activity, and recent dream research suggests that this may serve an essential function in the preservation of normal psychic functioning. A similar regressive moment seems to occur in the experience of artistic creativity. The artist regresses to permit unconscious fantasies and images—a freedom of expression that he is then able to direct to new creative purposes à la Kris's (1952) "regression in the service of the ego." It is very likely that all truly creative thinking enjoys such a moment of regression by which it refreshes itself from sources of its own unconscious dynamics.

As I will discuss more fully later on, we can probably find something of this nature in faith. Faith is not framed in terms of secondary process, and correspondingly reaches back to the most primitive levels of its originative experience and dynamic power. It embraces those infantile residues, and finds in them a source of motivational power. But this regressive moment captures only one partial aspect of faith. While faith reaches downward, in the same movement it also reaches upward. Consequently, while unconscious and instinctive roots are identifiable in the process of faith, the organization of faith is not dependent altogether on such motivational sources; nor is it completely describable as driven by the purposes of wish-fulfillment. Therefore, we can argue that faith has a regressive moment and that it can be at least partially accounted for in primary process terms; but these terms touch only fragments of it and do not characterize its most significant dimensions.

Kierkegaard is only partially correct in his insistence on the infinite resignation. Faith must effectively resign infantile wish-fulfillments before true faith becomes possible. Yet it is part of the paradox of faith that in its progression beyond finitude it simultaneously regresses to the most primitive levels of that finitude. In resigning all wish-fulfillments, faith revives and revivifies the most fundamental human wishes and finds their fulfillment in virtue of faith. Thus wishes are fulfilled, but wish-fulfillment is not the motive force in faith. We must distinguish, therefore, between wish-fulfillment in virtue of basically human desires (expressed in primary process terms) and wish-fulfillment in virtue of faith. In the former, wishes are fulfilled and provide the motive force. In the latter, wishes are fulfilled, but the motive force comes from elsewhere.

The regressive moment in faith, then, may involve the classic Freudian regression in some aspects of the process. It may also show some of the characteristics of regression in the service of the ego. But the ultimate characterization of regression in faith cannot be left in these terms. While the regression reaches back to and draws upon basis instinctual motivations, it concurrently transforms them and reorganizes them into a new synthetic integration. They are resigned as such, but are also reassumed into a new configuration of psychic components through faith. The regression, then, is a reaching back, but not a return, to more vital strata of experience and motive power. But the reaching back is both recuperative and restorative and at the same time constitutes a creative reemergence on a new level of psychic organization. The new level of organization is dependent on neither instinctual motives nor secondary process, but is something totally other. As Erikson (1958) commented, "If this is partial regression, it is a regression which, in retracing firmly established pathways, returns to the present amplified and clarified" (p. 264).

Instinctual Basis of Faith

In its regressive moment, the process of faith reaches back to, touches, and somehow embraces the fundamental instinctual dynamics of man's nature. In this insight there lies a rich psychology of man's religious development. Freud (1927) had spoken of religious beliefs as follows:

> We turn our attention to the psychical origin of religious ideas. These, which are given out as teachings, are not precipitates of experience or end-results of thinking: they are illusions, fulfillments of the oldest, strongest and most urgent wishes of mankind. The secret of their strength lies in the strength of those wishes. . . . Thus we call a belief an illusion when a wish-fulfillment is a prominent factor in its motivation, and in doing so we disregard its relations to reality, just as the illusion itself sets no store by verification. [pp. 30–31]

Freud called them illusions to underline the element of wish-fulfillment he recognized in them. And thus his genius focused on what is probably an essential and significant feature of the psychology of faith.

Freud attributed the motivation of faith to the terrifying

effects of infantile helplessness that aroused the need for protection through love. The continuance of such helplessness throughout life made it necessary to seek a protective father. The benevolent rule of divine providence, the care of an omnipotent father, protects us in the face of life's dangers. While Freud's account was highly rationalistic and reductionistic, and his account of faith did not reach much beyond such infantile wish-fulfillment, his fundamental insight has been extended in somewhat more sensitive analyses. Particularly, the evolution of the psychology of the self gives us better resources to formulate the basic insight.

A fundamental component of this dynamic is narcissism. Narcissism plays a central role in the drama of childhood. The child's early narcissism, which makes him the center of the universe and gives him the feeling of self-centered omnipotence, is eroded gradually by two forces. The first is the child's unavoidable dependence on his parents for the satisfaction of his needs, which highlights the indispensability and high value of the parent. The second is the confrontation of reality with the fantasies and wishes of omnipotence. Consequently, the elevated sense of self-esteem is reduced and reversed into esteem for an object. The high valuation placed on the parent gradually becomes associated with fears of abandonment and loss. The burden of childhood fears is eased by an evolving sense of trust (see below) and an emergent belief that there will be one who cares and who will be present. Mahler and her co-workers (1975) have explored these processes in terms of separation-individuation.

The vicissitudes of childhood narcissism are basic to the psychology of loss and restitution. Rochlin (1965) argued that the cycle of loss and restitution begins in early infancy and extends to the very end of life. Significant losses throughout life are often regarded as not only inevitable, but also adventitious, painful, and primarily injurious to the individual's well-being. Personal deprivation produces a saddening aftermath of loss that obscures the fact that losses, whether real or fantasied, serve as catalysts of change and bring into play the mechanisms of substitution and sublimation.

They thus play a critical role in psychic development, particularly in that most exalted human capacity for creativity. The losses man suffers are many: loss of love, loss of self-esteem, limitations, deprivations, disappointments, frustrations of wishes, abandonment and loneliness, illness, and ultimately death. Central to them all are a loss of a sense of well-being and a diminution of self-esteem.

The sense of loss and diminished self-esteem are equivalently attacks on the fundamental narcissism at the root of our emotional lives that must be resisted. Loss, therefore, calls into operation restitutive efforts by which the person strives to recover the loss and reconstitutes the sense of self-esteem. Self-esteem is a fragile vessel, perishable and unstable, but indispensable. Its preservation requires care and constant effort in the face of the continual inroads of life's deprivations and losses (Rochlin 1965). Man's ultimate loss and most dreaded abandonment is in death. While the restitutive moment of faith answers to this loss more than any other, it is not the only loss that underlies it or the only deprivation that it answers to. Man is unwilling to die; his death, taken as an end to his existence, is a diametric affront to his fundamental narcissism. Religious belief restores to him the promise of life, beyond death and overcoming death.

Yet faith is not simply this. In the context of loss and restitution, human faith answers to more than the loss and abandonment of death. Man's inner integrity and his sense of self-esteem, not merely with his face turned inward but with his face turned outward to the universe of his experience, call for a sense of meaningful completion to that existence. Man seeks for a sense of meaningfulness to complete and fill out his sense of identity as it opens out upon the universe. He seeks for a sense of meaningful fulfillment to complement his own inner sense of esteem. As Martin Buber (1959) put it, man's *I* calls out for an absolute relation to an eternal *Thou*.

I would regard the exigency for faith as rooted in narcissism, answering in a profound sense to man's most basic needs. The loss of personal meaning and the threat of the meaninglessness of

existence lie at the heart of that dread that is rooted in existence. It
is to this that faith answers primarily, but that answer reverberates at
many levels of man's existence. It touches also the unconscious and
infantile dread of loss and fear of abandonment. At this level, then,
faith is more surely and distinctively a wish-fulfillment. As Erikson
(1958) wrote, man "forgets that he achieved the capacity for *faith*
by learning to overcome feelings of utter abandonment and mistrust" (p. 112). In this sense and to this degree, faith derives its
strength from the motive power of these instinctive desires. But it
is also plain that the function of faith transcends mere wish-
fulfillment, and that to this degree the motive power of narcissism
is integrated through faith with other powerful motivational
themes that are channeled into the creative and integrative commitment of faith.

Faith and Trust

In his excellent little work on faith, Buber (1961) distinguished
between two fundamental kinds of faith: "There are two, and in the
end only two, types of faith. To be sure there are very many
contents of faith, but we only know faith itself in two basic forms.
Both can be understood from the simple data of our life: the one
from the fact that I trust someone, without being able to offer
sufficient reasons for my trust in him; the other from the fact that,
likewise without being able to give a sufficient reason, I acknowledge a thing to be true" (p. 7). The lack of reasons is not a matter
of defective intelligence, but rather flows from the relationship to
the one trusted or the thing acknowledged as true. The believing is
not a matter of rationality, but engages one's whole being. It is
more than rationality and more than feeling. Buber goes on to say,
"The relationship of trust depends upon a state of contact, a contact
of my entire being with the one in whom I trust, the relationship of
acknowledging depends upon an act of acceptance, an acceptance
by my entire being of that which I acknowledge to be true" (p. 8).
For Buber, the faith of trust is characteristically Jewish, and the

faith of acknowledgment characteristically Christian. But the process of faith cannot be adequately conceived without embracing both trust and acknowledgment. The intellectualistic emphasis of Christian theology works itself out in the context of living trust in the revealing God. If the faith, which was born in the patriarchal migrations, took shape in the tradition of guidance and covenant, and expressed itself as a perseverance of trust in that guidance and in the promises of that covenant, the later doctrinal emphasis on acknowledgment does not abstract itself from the psychological roots that vitalize all faith. And as Buber (1961) himself commented, the belief of the patriarchs was simple trust, as Abraham trusted God, but "when anybody trusts someone he of course also believes what the other says" (p. 35).

The implications of trust reverberate within the deepest structures of the mind. The capacity for trust is an expression of one's whole self; it engages one's total being. As Buber (1961) observed, "But the realization of one's faith does not take place in a decision made at one definite moment which is decisive for the existence of him who makes the decision, but in the man's whole life, that is in the actual totality of his relationships, not only towards God, but also to his appointed sphere in the world and to himself. A man does the works of God accordingly in proportion to the effectiveness of his faith in all things" (p. 40). Faith, therefore, is not an isolated act standing apart from the context of the believer's life cycle. It is rather a process that has a history and a genesis and that represents a fundamental disposition of human existence.[1]

On the psychological side, Erikson (1959) has tried to illumine the continuities between faith and trust:

The psychological observer must ask whether or not in any area under observation religion and tradition are living psychological

---

[1]See my more extended discussion of the developmental aspects of faith in Meissner (1987).

forces creating the kind of faith or conviction that permeates a
parent's personality and thus reinforces the child's basic trust . . .
in the world's trustworthiness. . . . All religions have in common
the periodical childlike surrender to a Provider or providers who
can dispense earthly fortune as well as spiritual health; the demonstration of one's smallness and dependence through the medium of
reduced posture and humble gesture; the admission in prayer and
song of misdeeds, of misthoughts, and of evil intentions; the
admission of inner division and the consequent appeal for inner
unification by divine guidance; the need for clearer self-delineation
and self-restriction; and finally, the insight that individual trust must
become a common faith, individual mistrust a commonly formulated evil, while the individual's need for restoration must become
part of the ritual practice of many, and must become a sign of the
trustworthiness of the community. [pp. 64–65]

Faith implies a capacity for trust. It is receptivity, an openness to
God, a willingness to accept his word. It involves a basic trust in
God, a sense of confidence in his love and saving power. It involves,
moreover, a sense of confidence in one's self and in one's capacity
to make the commitment of self that is necessary to bridge the
chasm between the security and self-reliance of reason and the
absurdity and other-reliance of faith.

   The capacity to trust in any adult human being is not a
property to be taken for granted. It is rather a precarious achievement that has undergone a history of developmental vicissitudes.
According to the Eriksonian schema of development, important
and often decisive influences are brought to bear on the infant at the
earliest stages of his life experience that contribute to the direction
of his future growth in personality. One of the primary polarities
that accompany the child's initial contacts with the world around
him is the tension between basic trust and basic mistrust. Along
with an emergent sense of self as dissociated from surrounding
objects through separation and individuation (Mahler et al. 1975),
there arises the basic issue of the quality of the relations between self
and objects. For both the inner developmental timetable in the

child and the biological requirements from nutriment, the most significant object in the child's environment is the mother, and the basic orientation by which the child is most sensitively related to his environment is oral. The classic "situation" in which the child begins to resolve the primary crisis of trust versus mistrust is the feeding relation at the mother's breast (Erikson 1950).

It is this basic disposition, then, upon which faith rests. for it is precisely in faith that trust finds its unique expression. As Erikson (1958) observes, "The ratio and relation of basic trust to basic mistrust established during early infancy determines much of the individual's capacity for simple faith" (p. 255). Upon the basic disposition of trust depends the capacity in man to turn to God a trusting face. The openness to God in faith, the confidence in God in faith, the trusting in the trustworthiness of God in faith, the confidence in one's own trustworthiness before God in faith, the basic trust in one's own sense of judgment and capacity for self-commitment in a faithful leap into the darkness of the absurd, these are impossible without basic trust. It requires, moreover, a developmental history that has preserved those infantile residues and successfully prolonged them into a fundamental capacity of the adult and mature personality.

Faith, therefore, is in this sense a recapitulation of infantile determinants. Its trusting is a reaching back to those decisive moments of childhood trust. We are again faced with the dilemma of whether this is a regression or not. If the reaching back is also a return to childhood trust, it is thereby a regression. One can argue that in the unconscious this is exactly the true state of affairs. But then one who possesses a measure of basic trust is always unconsciously returning to the infantile sources of trust. It may be fair, then, to say that faith carries within it an unconscious regressive moment. But faith is not merely a return, conscious or unconscious; it is a recapitulation, a reorganization, a reintegration, a synthetic process within the self that summarizes and reasserts basic trust. Its assertion is not merely reassertion; it is a creative assertion of something beyond trust and far more significant. Its regression is, if anything, recapitulative. It returns to trust in order to go beyond it. There is something here akin to what Kierkegaard grasped in the infinite resignation—man resigns all finite goods in order to find them again in virtue of faith. He must also in a sense resign the imperfection and finitude of basic trust in order to reach beyond it and thereby recapture it more profoundly and more meaningfully in faith. The creative moment in faith is unique and beyond understanding, and beyond mere regression and mere recapitulation as well. As Erikson (1958) has put it:

> Must we call it regression if man thus seeks again the earliest encounters of his trustful past in his efforts to reach a hoped for and eternal future? Or do religions partake of man's ability, even as he regresses, to recover creatively? At their creative best, religions retrace our earliest inner experiences, giving tangible form to vague evils and reaching back to the earliest individual sources of trust; at the same time, they keep alive the common symbols of integrity distilled by the generations. If this is partial regression, it is a regression which, in retracing firmly established pathways, returns to the present amplified and clarified. [p. 264]

Faith and Fidelity

Implicit in the notion of faith, there is an element of perdurance, constancy, the security of stable persistence, the assurance (to use a scriptural term from Hebrews 11:1) of God's continued faithfulness to his promises, a confidence in the finality and eternity of what one believes—in short, fidelity. There are a correspondence and a mutuality between the stability of one's belief and God's faithfulness on the one hand, and the psychological dimension of fidelity on the other. The commitment of faith is not, therefore, a commitment of transient and momentary assent. It is a trusting commitment of one's total being in an absolute and perduring relation to God.

We again owe to Erikson (1964) the illuminating exploration

William W. Meissner, S.J., M.D.

of the psychology of fidelity. Fidelity emerges with and from adolescence, "the ability to sustain loyalties freely pledged in spite of the inevitable contradictions of value systems" (p. 125). Fidelity is a major component of the emerging sense of identity that receives its inspiration from confirming ideologies. Identity and fidelity are necessary but not sufficient components of ethical strength. Each generation must provide for the ready loyalty of its youth a worthy content. For youth selectively extends its fidelity to the conservation of what it feels to be true and brings its energy to bear on the correction or destruction of what has lost all regenerative significance for it. Each generation, then, must find again and regenerate the sources of its belief.

Cultural institutions in general provide the ideologies that shape the individual's sense of identity in the cultural matrix and enrich and rejuvenate themselves with the energies of youthful commitment. Erikson (1958) spoke of ideology as "an unconscious tendency underlying religious and scientific as well as political thought: the tendency at a given time to make facts amenable to ideas, and ideas to facts, in order to create a world image convincing enough to support the collective and individual sense of identity" (p. 22). Religion serves a cultural role, then, insofar as it provides an ideology for the emergent need to create not so much a "world image" as a meaningful framework of existence. The religious ideology, if we may speak of such, has a breadth and depth and significance that outreach all others. It is no wonder that one finds in young adolescents a preoccupation and a searching, even doubting, inquiry into religious beliefs.

The emergence of fidelity and its correlative need for commitment is a developmental phenomenon. It requires a degree of maturation in personality and the development of specific component capacities that bring the evolving individual to a point at which the genetic exigencies call for an alignment of basic needs, significant identifications, and formative experiences into a more or less definitive constellation. The realignment underlies and contributes to the ultimate self-definition of identity formation. The formation of identity takes place in the intrapsychic realms, but its action is open on all sides to the extrapsychic realm of social and cultural interaction.

Adolescence is a developmental period of peculiar sensitivity and vulnerability. The emerging adolescent is confronted by the upsurge of powerful motives and urges, libidinal and aggressive, that create turmoil and disorder and threaten his own fragile sense of personal integrity. He is challenged to find new and sanctioned channels for the expression and control of these powerful and disruptive impulses. He is beset by strong regressive pulls that draw him back to previous more infantile, if adaptive, configurations. These too must be resisted. In addition, new social and cultural demands are placed upon him, new perspectives of society and culture open before him reaching far beyond the confines of the home, the family, and the neighborhood that provided the context of his childhood perspectives. If the adolescent is to come through all of this and achieve a new maturity of adjustment, which effectively turns him from the things of childhood to the things of adulthood, it is essential that the ego develop a capacity to pledge and receive fidelity.

Faith is not the only source or receptacle of fidelity. But it is an important one insofar as its scope and its assurance of truth and meaning reach beyond all other ideologies that claim man's fidelity. We can conclude, therefore, that faith serves a culturally useful and psychological function. Although fidelity has its greatest developmental significance in the adolescent stage, its implications are not limited to adolescence. While fidelity is a developmental necessity in adolescence for the emergence of a secure sense of identity, it remains a continuing psychological necessity in the entire course of the life cycle. Human life and existence demand meaning and a sense of belonging.[2] The sustenance of identity depends upon

---

[2]The achievement of a sense of belonging is an aspect of what I have previously conceptualized as the "paranoid construction" (Meissner 1978).

the continuing identification with significant institutions and the meaningful commitment to convincing ideologies.

Thus authentic faith has a psychological capacity to sustain the individual sense of identity. But beyond this dynamic and positive aspect there lies a danger. Commitment to an ideology tends to be exclusive, as ideologies themselves tend to be intolerant of each other. The danger in any commitment is overcommitment. The history of religious faith is a rich legend of such overcommitment. The pity of it is that overcommitment, or overidentification, really distorts the significance of the ideology that made commitment a necessity to begin with and gave it strength and purpose. Its outcome is not only a distortion of ideology but a fault in identity. Turning it around, it is also true that the fault in identity underlies overcommitment. The implicit incapacity in the self provides a channel for the expression of raw aggressive and libidinal motives, legitimized in a sense by a perverted ideology. The result is a blend of sadism, sanctimoniousness, and moralism against which true religious faith must wage an endless struggle.

Such overcommitment, then, is inconsistent with true faith just as it is inconsistent with true identity. In a sense, we would have to say that the essence of faith lies beyond fidelity, although it is impossible to translate that essence without putting it in terms of fidelity, or in terms of trust for that matter. Fidelity is, after all, a finite good that—if we remain true to Keirkegaard's insight— must be resigned if we are to have faith. But the resignation is a moment beyond which absurdity and absolute relation become possible. To be able to pass beyond fidelity requires a strength surpassing mere ideology. And to reach beyond fidelity is para-doxically not to surrender it, but to find it again, enriched, more profound and more meaningful in virtue of faith.

Integrative Function of Faith

These aspects of the psychological process of faith, each of which has rich implications for the psychic economy, can be recapitulated and integrated into a more general view of the function of faith within psychic life. I have reconstructed piece by piece a mosaic within which we can discern a portrait of faith as a psychological process. Faith is a dynamic process involving and expressing man's total existence. It embraces a reaching back to the basic wishes and needs characterizing man's most primary and primitive experiences and are subsumed into and unconsciously operative in his subsequent evolution. The reaching back is both regressive and recapitulative, but it returns to infantile sources only to reorganize and revitalize them into a new psychic alignment. It finds a source of power and reconstitutive creativity in the basic motivational forces of narcissism and the dynamic cycle of loss and restitution. Thus faith has its rich and powerful roots in the vital stratum of man's psychic actuality.

At another, more complex, level of psychic organization, faith functions as derivative from and as a dynamic extension of basic capacities within the individual that have emerged from the total course of his developmental history. It requires and depends on, as well as enlarges and enriches, the basic sense of trust with which the infant emerges from his earliest developmental experiences. Further, the relation of basic trust and faith is both dynamic and reciprocal. Faith builds upon trust, but it also builds trust. Trust is always imperfect, carrying within it the shadow of mistrust. So in all belief there is a shadow of unbelief, just as in all unbelief there is a shadow of belief. The believer and the unbeliever are closer to each other than they realize. But faith is impossible without basic trust, yet in faith trust becomes more than it was—it is enriched, recovered, and the shadow of mistrust is diminished (if never abolished). Whatever may have been the structure of trust in the psychic economy, it is altered and transformed in virtue of faith.

Faith in addition embraces and builds upon man's inner need for fidelity. Faith is, therefore, a phenomenon of psychological maturity. It must wait upon the emergence of fidelity and a sense of personal identity. And as it touches them, it transforms them.

Fidelity becomes no longer adherence to an ideology, but is enlarged and enriched in meaning and purposefulness in virtue of a relation to the absolute that is both personal and perduring. And identity itself is profoundly affected, since in faith man finds the true and authentic validity of his existence. Faith is in these terms a transforming process that touches all levels of the psychic structure and reorganizes and integrates them into a more mature and effective pattern and level of functioning. Faith, therefore, has an integrative function in the psychic economy. True faith is thereby restorative, recuperative, and transforming.

To this assertion we must immediately add that true faith rarely achieves all these teleogical functions, or it achieves them only partially. There are many ways to understand this impoverishment of faith. The fullness of faith rests on many cornerstones. As a process it endures many vicissitudes, and if it survives at all, it may not survive them unimpaired. One can ask pertinently whether all believers really have faith. Kierkegaard was sure that few did. It is perhaps better to say that most do have some minimal degree of faith—and even minimal faith can sustain and assuage in the face of personal tragedy and conflict. But the fullness of faith is rare; it requires great psychic strength and capacity that few possess.

The integrative function of faith, therefore, is often impaired. This should not mask our appreciation of the function, however, nor should it blind us to its psychological perspective. To the extent that the integrative function of faith is realized, it enlarges and intensifies the sense of personal identity that is the hallmark of mature psychological adjustment. In faith, man realizes more fully his psychological potentiality, and this in turn enlarges his capacity for autonomous, conflict-free function, for spontaneity, and for freedom from impulsive gratifications and restrictive compulsions.

Faith takes place in relation to a community of believers and in relation to institutionalized religions. These provide the context of social integration by which the faith of the community confirms and supports the faith of the individual, while it rejuvenates and replenishes itself from the complement of individual faith. The faith of the community reinforces the faith of the individual. As Erikson (1958) comments, "It is clear that organized religiosity, in circumstances where faith in a world order is monopolized by religion, is the institution which tries to give dogmatic permanence to a reaffirmation of that basic trust—and a renewed victory over that basic mistrust—with which each human being emerges from early infancy. In this way organized religion cements the faith which will support future generations" (p. 257).

But the relationship is precarious. Faith is essentially a dynamic process. The institution of faith is cast in static dogmatic formulae and repetitious ritual and cult. The vitality of the process and the renewed significance of the objects of faith must be related. The personal act of belief and what is grasped in the act are distinguishable, but inseparable. *Fides qua* (the act of faith by which the believer believes) and the *fides quae creditur* (the propositional faith or the content of belief) form a totality. Belief is always belief in something. Yet the process cannot be cast in dogmatic terms since its very nature is radical openness. It is always an intentional and existential act. The further complexities of the relation between faith as an act of belief and faith as a content of belief belong to the theology of faith rather than to its psychology. Yet it seems reasonable to say that the reaffirmation of trust, the enrichment of fidelity, and the clarification of identity are somehow stabilized by participation in the shared meaning of shared beliefs.

Faith, whether individual or communal, is a dynamic, integrative, and, therefore, positively adaptive force in the psychic economy. It is not enough to think of it merely in restitutive terms. There is no question that the process of faith draws its dynamic power of change from fundamental, even instinctual, motivations. The cycle of loss and restitution and the derivation of faith from narcissistic sources of motivation serve the defensive and restitutive aspects of psychic functioning involved in faith. But faith requires in addition creative potentials that serve the creative and integrative capacities of the self as it reaches beyond the limits of defense, restitution, and adaptation through the veil of infinite resignation into the darkness of the absurd.

Faith and Grace

The process of faith, even within the limited purview of its psychology, touches and intertwines itself with many significant aspects of the theology of faith. Faith is operative analytically in a sort of borderland where psychology fades into theology and, vice versa, theology into psychology, and the line between them is sometimes obscure. The Christian theological tradition teaches that faith requires the sustaining and conforming strength of God's grace.[3] The action of divine grace remains mysterious but its effects can be more or less adequately considered on the psychological level in terms of the support and reinforcement of what we might regard as certain ego capacities and relational dispositions. We can conceive of grace, psychologically speaking, as operating to sustain the capacity of the self to mobilize its own inner resources and to carry out more effectively those ego functions underlying regulation of instinctive motives, reinforcing the orientation and adaptation to reality, organizing and directing executive functions, and most significantly those that carry on the dynamic processes of synthesis and integration within the personality. The overall direction and focus of these influences is on those psychic processes that culminate in greater ethical maturity and adaptation and that reinforce and sustain the value system inherent in the believer's belief system (Meissner 1987).

On these terms, then, the recuperative, restorative, and integrative functions of faith become more understandable. If faith requires basic trust and fidelity, it also creates them. The ego's

---

[3]I have previously attempted an exploratory and tentative analysis of the psychological aspects of grace, especially in its sanative function (Meissner 1987).

capacity for trust may be developmentally impaired, and thus the movement to faith becomes more difficult. But the motivating capacity of grace can intervene to shore up the self's impaired capacity and renew those basic sources of trust in and through faith. Thus grace and faith, through the renovation and functioning of basic psychic capacities, touch every stratum of the mind and affect the functioning of all parts of the psychic organization. The psychological impact of the action of grace is profound and psychologically enriching, potentially changing, transforming, and in some sense reintegrating psyche capacities.

DOES GOD HELP?

With these somewhat exploratory and tentative suggestions in hand, I return to the main topic of our symposium—Does God help? To bring my previous considerations to a focus in relation to our work as therapists, what can we say about this topic and its implications in therapy? If we accept, as we might as an aspect of faith, that God is present and active in the heart and mind of both therapist and patient, acting surreptitiously within the inner and internal worlds of both to move them motivationally or inspirationally to do what is best for them in their human lives, to facilitate and accomplish the mutually compelling goals and purposes of the therapy, and to lead them progressively toward more fulfilling, purposeful, and religiously meaningful lives, then the divine action through grace may well have a place in therapy.

I should clarify my use of the expression "religiously meaningful." Therapists, to my way of thinking, are not in the business of proposing, advocating, or in any way promoting religious behavior or thinking. But to the extent that the patient's life and behavior become more mature, more responsible, and more socially and personally adaptive—all legitimate therapeutic objectives—they become by that token more in tune with the religiously meaningful ideals and purposes of whatever religious tradition they embrace; if they embrace no religious tradition, they become more in tune with what most established religious traditions would find religiously meaningful.

But, getting back to the question of therapy, such grace-related influence, given the inviolability and persistence of human freedom, is not efficacious, but rather no more than suasive. Grace, as I have argued above, can be conceived of as operating in and through psychic functions and as such can be no more than unconscious (Meissner 1987), meaning that if we accept the idea that God's grace is operative we would never be able to identify it as such and that it would find expression in psychic actions or behaviors that were quite adequately explainable or understandable in exclusively human or psychological terms.

To take an example, a patient who clings to bitter resentments and hatred of her mother for childhood deprivations and abandonments inflicted on her by a depressed and relatively unavailable mother, comes in the course of therapy to comprehend better the contexts and circumstances related to her mother's conflicts and limitations, and thereby reaches a level of resolution of her resentments sufficient to allow her to forgive her mother and reestablish a degree of satisfying communication with her. To a point, we can relate these changes to progressive developments in the therapy, to a degree of insight, to changes within the therapeutic relation, especially the transference, to developments within the alliance, the resolution of conflict, and so on. As analysts, we would have no need to appeal to any other causal connection.

But can we argue that grace was not involved? I think not. Then can we argue that grace *was* involved? Again, I think not. I do not know any empirical grounds on which I could either draw such a conclusion or reject it. The question is irresolvable. There is just as much reason for the nonbeliever or analyst to reject the proposition as for the religious believer to accept it. If it is to be accepted, it can be so only on the basis of faith involving trust in God's providence and the hope that God's loving intervention is for our good and directed to our ultimate salvation. There is, of course, a profound paradox in such a position. To anticipate my later discussion, the best resolution I know of that paradox was offered by the great St. Ignatius of Loyola, who said, "Pray as though everything depended on God, but act as though everything depended on you."[4]

This principle has profound implications for therapy. Any number of religiously oriented and based therapies have arisen, in which grace or divine intervention is called on as a therapeutic aid. Patients are urged to pray, to make retreats, to rededicate their lives to the love and service of God, and so on—all riding on the supposition that if patients were to somehow correct the religious deviations in their lives, the psychopathology would be eliminated. In their rush to put a religious spin on things, some therapists of an overly religious persuasion overlook the efficacious steps inherent in the therapeutic process and tend to divert it into religious channels. Other religious counselors, particularly professional pastoral counselors, many of whom are sufficiently well trained to avoid such obvious traps, still struggle with the issue of how to integrate their religious beliefs with their therapeutic praxis. I have no easy answers to this problem, except to note it as a problem. Functioning in my own career as an analyst, I have leaned in the direction of trying to do my best as an analyst, and, believing as I do in God and his grace, leaving those effects and the patient's responsiveness to grace between that patient and his God. My job is to help the patient to analyze as best I can.

Religious questions and feelings in this context come up, but only when the patient brings them up. My responses are calculated to be exploratory of the patient's beliefs and religious attitudes, and I try—with some exceptions, as will be seen below—never or almost never to introduce my own religious views or beliefs. At the same time, the range of interpretive devices is wide indeed. I refer to literature, movies, fairy tales, poetry, humorous stories and jokes,

---

[4]See my development of this paradoxical principle in Meissner (1999).

and a variety of personal experiences to make my point. I have even at times quoted scripture in making an interpretation. So I cannot claim that religious elements do not have an integral part in my therapeutic armamentarium, but the focus and purpose has been, I hope and trust, always analytic.

THE CASE

The question of whether God helps cannot be directly answered, but my purpose here is to focus on the role of a patient's belief, presumably sustained and reinforced through grace, in the therapeutic context. Martha was in her early sixties, physically tall, rawboned, and sturdily built. She often wore print dresses down to the ankles, lace collars, straw hats with a flower on them—looking like something out of a Dickens novel. She was struggling as far as I could see with a good bit of depression and episodes of rather severe anxiety. Her anxiety and internal struggle were obvious from the start. Telling me anything but the most mundane things about herself was accompanied by anxiety and conflict over what to tell me, what could she tell me, what should she tell me, what was safe to tell me.

She was the only girl in her family among her four brothers— two older and two younger. She had never married, never in fact dated as far as I could tell, or had any meaningful or romantic relationship with a man. After her two older brothers had married and moved out and after her father had passed away, she continued to live with her mother and two younger brothers. The two brothers finally moved away, so she was left with her mother. From her high school days, Martha had worked. She had held her present job for over forty years. She was employed as a shipping clerk for the telephone company and worked in a warehouse with all male fellow workers. The job often required heavy lifting and she carried her share with the best of them. She got along well with the men, as she had with her brothers, and they respected her, kidded with her, shared their worries and concerns with her, and treated her as a good friend and counselor. I never heard a word about sexual or romantic involvement with her co-workers.

The problem area centered around religion. Martha was an extremely devout Irish Catholic. She attended mass regularly, and spent a good bit of time at her prayers and spiritual reading. When she came to my office, there was usually a rosary dangling from her purse and often when I met her in the waiting room she would be engrossed in some sort of spiritual reading. In her early perturbation in unfolding her story, she would at times refer to me as "Doctor" and at times as "Father." She was obviously confused in her own mind as to what the quality of our relationship was to be. As she gradually calmed down and edged closer to the core material, I heard less "Father" and more "Doctor." By the time we ended our work together the "Father" had disappeared altogether.

The kernel of the problem was that Martha was plagued by obscene thoughts and images that came upon her when she was attending mass or during her prayers. When she looked at Jesus hanging on the cross, she had thoughts about his sexual organs and images of him hanging naked and exposed, even with an erection. Other sexual images crowded her mind along with obscene phrases and thoughts that caused her a severe degree of turmoil and distress. When these thoughts and images came upon her, she was over-whelmed with feelings of anxiety and guilt and was convinced that she was committing mortal sin and that she would be condemned to an eternity of pain and torment in hell. The erotic character of these intrusive thoughts and images, I thought, was entirely con-sistent with her rather obsessional character structure. My early impression was that her extreme religiosity and her obsessional defenses were serving as a barrier against unresolved sexual conflicts and that these had probably been a source of conflict and distress for her for most of her life. It was not clear to me why they had taken this symptomatic turn at this point in her life.

But I was to learn that there was more to the story. As she became more comfortable in discussing these matters with me, I began to hear some of the historical details of her experience with her spiritual adviser. As a young woman, she was experiencing difficulties with her sexual feelings and impulses and was greatly in fear that she was committing sin by having such desires and impulses. She sought spiritual advice and counsel from her confessor. These sessions occurred on regular occasions in which she would discuss her sexual anxieties and concerns with him. To a certain extent, as far as I could gather, the priest did offer some reasonable advice—Martha would from time to time cite some comment he had made to her that had a ring of appropriate pastoral concern and direction. But the sessions unfortunately deteriorated and became increasingly eroticized. Before long they were being conducted in the nude, with a good deal of touching and fondling along with the spiritual advice. As far as I could tell, touching and fondling was as far as it went. Martha never indicated or hinted that there was ever any intercourse.

This information came out in painful bits and pieces. I could sense the intense shame and guilt connected with all of this in her mind. As it unfolded the recounting had a confessional quality— Martha confessing her sins and presumably seeking some kind of absolution. That was not the answer, obviously, since whatever guilt was involved for her had been thoroughly confessed and absolved already. In view of the obsessional quality of her self-doubt, any absolution would have to come from within, from an easing of her superego severity and its replacement by ego-based reasonability. But I had difficulty negotiating this passage with her. In retrospect, part of the problem had to do with her image of me and her expectations of what sort of help she was looking for—did she come to me as priest, looking for spiritual consolation and relief, or did she come to me as doctor, looking for a more humanly therapeutic benefit? My operating assumption was that her involvement with Father X had resulted from a mixture of naive trust and simple submission to the seductions of this revered religious figure cloaked under a guise of pastoral concern and spiritual direction. But the experiences must have been sexually arousing and titillating, and in the untutored mind of this young woman the line between what was spiritually good and pastorally commendable and what was erotic, seductive, and sexually forbidden was not at all clear. The experience had been traumatic and abusive and had put her trusting religious dependence in conflictual jeopardy. The perplexity and doubt must have bothered her conscience ever since, and she never found adequate surcease or resolution of the titer of shame and guilt.

There was a problem for me in deciding what to do with this material. I had formed the tentative hypothesis that, whatever the degree of naïveté and misguided trust, there may have been an element of guilt connected with the degree of sexual arousal and excitement she must have felt. I reasoned, perhaps somewhat naively myself, that a primary task was to alleviate her guilt. But how was I to do that? My first tack was a good one—I just listened quietly and empathically to her story. As she gained some reassurance that I was not going to be disapproving, condemning, or castigating, she became more comfortable talking about these matters. After a while I decided that I might begin by trying to bring more clearly into focus the failure and fault of her wayward spiritual guide. But I ran into trouble there. If I made the slightest hint that Father X's behavior had been reprehensible, or that he had behaved in a manner ill-suited to his role and function as a priest, Martha would become quickly upset and agitated, her voice trembling and her speech impaired. I gathered that however conceptually correct that tack might have been, it was not going to work very well. It created too much anxiety and threat for her. There was some need in her to preserve the integrity of her view of him as a priest and an unwillingness to accept his behavior for what it plainly was. I did not feel that any attempt on my part to add to her psychic burden on this account would be very helpful. She seemed to be bearing as much as she could without my adding to it. So I was stumped.

I searched my mind for any scraps of psychoanalytic lore that might help. But I kept running into dead-ends. Part of the problem was that this was once-a-week psychotherapy, and that limited my options, particularly the option of waiting for more unconscious material to become available, as I might have done with an analytic patient. The problem, as I saw it, was how to alleviate her guilt without pouring oil on the smoldering embers or casting the blame on the errant priest—this last alternative, for reasons unclear to me at the time, seemed to be even more disturbing to her. It might simply have been her need to preserve an unsullied image of the priest in the face of all evidence to the contrary as part of preserving her religious outlook and her somewhat naive dependence on religious figures for spiritual support and solace. Those motives were partly involved in her coming to my office. I would presume that she came to me at first more as priest than therapist, and only gradually came to relate to me more as therapist than priest.

So, faced with the impasse and the fact that my analytic resources were proving of little avail, I grew increasingly frustrated and began to cast a wider net to see what I could catch. I cast about for anything that I thought might carry the weight of my putative interpretation and would be in tune with her perspective and point of view. I thought of literary material, but she was relatively unschooled and unread in such matters. She was not a moviegoer, so that did not seem very helpful. What material would help us find common ground on which to understand each other? The answer, once asked, came quickly—she and I were both Catholics, raised in the Catholic tradition, and sharing at least superficially the same belief system. I also knew that she was familiar with spiritual books and was a regular reader of the Bible. So my mind turned away from concepts analytic to concepts spiritual. It didn't take long before I had my inspiration.

One day when she was recounting one of her agonizing episodes of intrusive sexual thoughts, I inquired, "Martha, do you know what a temptation is?" She stopped and looked at me for a minute, as though I had suddenly stopped speaking Swahili and started to speak a language she understood. I went on to explain that when the devil wanted to tempt good souls who were living a good life, his tactic was to cause them to be distressed or disturbed, and that he used whatever device he could get his hands on to pull it off, to interfere with their good works or their tranquillity of soul. Might it be that she was such a case, I wondered. If old Satan could toss a rock through the window of her peace of soul, he would have scored a victory. Her reaction was interesting. When I mentioned the devil, her eyes lit up. We had identified the enemy, the cause of all the trouble.

Now you might say, "Well really! Does such talk about the devil belong in any respectable therapy?" Was I functioning no longer as psychotherapist and was I now playing the part of spiritual guru? In fact, the devil does not play much of a part in my religious outlook. In my view, the figurative language in which he (or she) is portrayed is metaphorical at best, a personification that embodies and expresses a principle of evil embedded in the core of human nature. From a theological perspective, what remains valid is that human nature involves a principle of inherent disorder and sinfulness. The disorder, however, is within man; the elaborate fictions about the devil, whether produced by poetic imagination or the overactive fantasies of religious adherents, are something else again. But the issue here is not what I might think about the devil; the point is that she believed in the devil and knew exactly what I was talking about. My comment had given the problem a local habitation and a name. What had been disturbing, confusing, and incomprehensible to her before was now relocated in a context that was familiar, comprehensible, and therefore manageable.

Now I must confess that my inspiration was not entirely original. The idea comes straight out of *The Spiritual Exercises of St. Ignatius* (Ganss 1992), particularly in his "rules for the discernment of spirits." The spirits in question, cast in terms of medieval metaphor and imagery, are the good and evil spirits that try to influence men to seek for or stray from God and the path of salvation. The evil spirit was the devil. Something similar, I think, can be found in C. S. Lewis, especially in his *Screwtape Letters* (1962), where old Screwtape, a highly regarded senior devil, advises his nephew Wormwood, a comparative novice in the deviltry business, on ways to disturb good souls who are at peace in the love of God—a sort of supervisory relationship not unlike that between training analyst and candidate.

Martha and I could come to a meeting of minds on this issue. But if we accepted the hypothesis, the question then became what was one to do about it? Digging deeply into my somewhat limited theological expertise, I first added a proposition to the effect that, as far as I knew, God allows temptations to those he loves in order to strengthen them in the face of spiritual adversity, and that when he allows temptation he always provides sufficient grace to the tempted soul to help it overcome the temptation and thus gain even more of his love and grace. This seemed to be another eye-opener and seemed to set the stage for the rest of our work.

Staying within the Ignatian paradox—pray for God's grace, but take action and responsibility yourself—we had a number of options to discuss. The first thing that one did *not* do was to get bent out of shape over such temptations. One was better off if you could maintain some perspective about it, not to let it get to you and throw you off stride. One could distance oneself from it, or find it amusing, or even interesting. One could even experience it as an interesting phenomenon worth thinking about, examining, and trying to understand what it was about and where it was coming from. When an intrusive thought came into her head, she didn't have to react with fright, turmoil, or panic. She could think about what she was experiencing no matter what the subject or content might be. If in the midst of her devotions she were to begin to think about Jesus' penis, that need not be so upsetting, but might be something that she could think about, try to understand what it meant and why she might be having such a thought at that particular time. Appeal to the devil was useful since he provided a convenient fall guy for explaining the causality.

The reader might complain—and rightly so—that I was instigating or at the least confirming a projective defense and helping the patient to avoid dealing with underlying sexual conflicts. Psychoanalysis this was not! And I hasten to add that I bring this experience up, not as recommended psychotherapeutic practice—any decent therapist could not help but have reservations—but as a vehicle for addressing the subject of our meeting: Can we think of God in any meaningful sense as helping in the work of therapy or analysis? In any case, putting the matter in these terms led to a number of important by-products; one such consequence was a degree of mobilizing of her psychic resources to begin to deal more objectively and adaptively with these experiences and enabling her to take charge of her inner life in a way that she had not done for years. She had lived her life in large measure as the victim, helpless and uncomprehending, of her sexual needs, impulses, and desires. She became increasingly accepting of her sexual impulses, and even more tellingly, I thought, accepting of the idea that she had some control over such impulses and could in fact begin to exercise her capacity to understand and buffer herself against such onslaughts. Seeing the disturbing sexual thoughts as temptations located them in a category in which they were no longer sinful and guilt-inducing phenomena that condemned her to damnation and the eternal punishment of hellfire, but could be seen as challenges to be overcome, and which indeed she could overcome with the help of God's grace. Instead of carrying the burden of sin and guilt, they became opportunities for spiritual challenge and growth.

As time went on, she became much freer in her self-expression and social activities. During the course of our treatment, she retired from her job of over forty years, with great demonstrations of affection and regard from her fellow workers and her employers. She quickly developed a circle of women friends of similar age and situation whom she enjoyed and with whom she shared various activities. And before long she had found another job to supplement her income. She became the part-time cook in the rectory of a local church. In the later stages of her time with me, she would come in and regale me with anecdotes and amusing observations about her experiences with the priests in the rectory, enjoying every minute of it—and, as I gathered, the good fathers enjoyed her being there as well.

Things were going so well that we decided to gradually cut back the frequency of our meetings. Toward the end I saw her monthly, usually with the same pattern of joviality and good-natured kidding. She repeatedly expressed in various ways her appreciation for what we had accomplished together and for my role in it. I then stopped seeing her on any regular schedule, but at intervals of several months she would call for an appointment. Usually, after a half hour or more of banter, she would bring up something related to her basic problem, some recurrence of the "temptations," or some related concern. We would discuss it briefly and she would leave in great relief and cheerful spirits. The calls dwindled over time. For some years I received a card, usually along with a spiritual bouquet, at Christmas time, at Easter, and—how she found this out I do not know!—my birthday. These too finally stopped.

DISCUSSION

The questions posed at the beginning of this chapter seem to me to overshadow this case. How much of the outcome can I attribute to my own inspired interventions, and how much to the hand of God? If I can review for a minute my contributions as a therapist, the first piece I would put in place is the therapeutic alliance. I have broken a few lances in defense of this aspect of the therapeutic relation, and I regard it as an essential component of that relation along with the ubiquitous transference and countertransference and the real relation (Meissner 1996). Martha and I had developed a solid therapeutic alliance based on mutual trust, respect for her freedom, complete openness and honesty, her slowly emerging autonomy and initiative, and her ultimately taking responsibility for the therapeutic outcome and applying herself to its achievement.

Further, my demeanor was calm, even, accepting, nonjudgmental, and nonpunitive. Part of her transference was a view of me as confessor and judge, but my refusal to respond to her invitations to play that role was for her in part a disappointment, but then also in part a relief. My demeanor and acceptance was in itself reassuring and in some sense absolving. I did not trample on her anxieties—or better, if I had made any moves in that direction, her perturbation and turmoil served as a signal that even if I had been right, she was in no position to hear or accept what I might have to say. One way to see this was that she might have been helping me to keep from putting my foot into another countertransference trap, that of enacting my judging role, as I would have by any attempt to relate her symptoms to her own sexual drives. Rather than alleviating her guilt, I felt that approach would only increase it and put me in an uneasily judgmental position as she would have experienced it, regardless of my intentions. Interpretations are, whether we like it or not, or mean it or not, forms of judgment.

I was puzzled for a time by her seeming need to protect the offending priest from my condemnations, but I reasoned in retrospect that this response was overdetermined. From one perspective, her need to preserve the religious integrity of the priest-seducer was strongly connected with her need to preserve her devout appraisal of things religious and reflected the depth of her need to cling to the essentials of her belief as sustaining her own sense of identity and as giving value and meaning to her existence. For me to attack and undermine her adherence to the idea of the priesthood and the church would have had devastating effects. One could argue with some justification that my approach served only to reinforce her defenses and allow her to disown any responsibility for her impulses by projecting them to the devil as an external agent. In other words, I would have been supporting a "The devil made me do it!" defense. Maybe so, but in my own defense, that may have been the best I could manage under the circumstances. Given other options and circumstances, I might have done better. But, to clarify any misapprehensions, the appeal to temptation does not relieve the sinner of guilt. Even if it arises from an external source—and devils are not the only external source—the sinner remains responsible for the sin. Temptations are not sinful, but yielding to them becomes sinful. Only then is the question of responsibility or guilt relevant.

But the objection gives rise to another troublesome question. Does the putative effect of ascribing causality to an external source, thus relocating the source of difficulty and putatively relieving, as some would think, the onus of guilt, differ in any significant way from ascribing causality to putative infantile drives that serve as sources of causal efficacy beyond the scope of the patient's conscious awareness? The drives are not facts; they are hypotheses, however devotedly we might cling to them to help us understand our patients. When we attribute a patient's symptoms to the operation of such drives—part of what Freud called "our mythology"—do we not have in mind, at least in some degree, to relieve the patient of the burden of guilt or shame?

But what is critical to the therapeutic outcome, in any case, is what the patient does with such influences. We assist the patient to become more consciously aware of the meaning of such impulses, but the process does not stop at mere awareness. The patient must determine a course of action to modulate, regulate, redirect, or otherwise manage such often peremptory impulses. In the course of such ego engagement, we typically find that the intensity and disruptiveness of such "drive" effects diminish, become less conflictual, and can be more readily integrated with the rest of the patient's experience. Bringing Satan into the picture had, as far as I could tell, a similar effect. It allowed Martha enough leeway and distance from her turmoil and distress to begin to gain some perspective on what she was experiencing and to allow her ego to take hold and begin to deal with these impulses more adaptively and constructively. Where id was ruling the roost, ego had asserted itself. Freud himself had suggested that our task as analysts was to bring about those conditions in which the patient's ego was better able to do its job. I think whatever else may have occurred, Martha and I at least accomplished that.

And lastly, I managed to come up with a formulation that made sense to her, that proved to be nonthreatening, that offered a context of meaning that she could recognize and accept within the framework of her belief system. Viewing the situation from the vantage point of temptation, I would assume, removed her disturbing experiences from the category of sin and damnation, allowed her to regain her footing on more familiar ground, and allowed her to begin to assert herself and attain a degree of self-mastery and mastery of her symptoms. In other words, instead of relying on my psychoanalytic belief system, my psychoanalytic mythology, I called her belief system into play, or perhaps more specifically the belief system in terms of which we could relate and develop some consensus. This to my mind reflects a triumph of ego over superego and id. Freud, I think, would have approved of that.

But, giving myself all due credit, or fault as some might suggest, we are still left with the haunting question of whether God was in the act or not. To what extent was my own inspired interpretation the result of some graceful effect in me? Was Martha's attunement to what I had to say to her, and her remarkable ability to put it to work for herself in what seemed to be an effective and enduring way, in some part attributable to the effects of grace, working silently and unseen from within her own psychic capabilities to reinforce and sustain her capacity to deal effectively and adaptively with her symptoms, to achieve good therapeutic results, and to recover her tranquillity of spirit and peace of soul? Was God helping both of us to accomplish the good work of relieving her of the burden of guilt and bringing her to greater peace of soul and closer to him? Or could I imagine that I was helping God out by bringing one of his beloved creatures closer to him and enabling her to be at peace with herself and her relation with him? I wish I knew. But, at a minimum, if we are to engage with any degree of seriousness and purposefulness in the dialogue between psychoanalysis and religion, we must allow room in the discussion for all of these questions. They are questions that are intelligible and meaningful to many of our patients who in one manner or other are religious believers.

As therapists we owe it to our patients to begin by accepting their belief systems, certainly to the extent that it is helpful to them in living their lives and dealing with their psychic difficulties. By the same token, we also owe it to them to find a way to rethink or correct those aspects of their beliefs that are pathologically distorted and contribute to their difficulties (Meissner 1992). Martha's footing in her religious faith was to a degree fragmentary and uncertain. Her faith was in that sense incomplete, riddled with superstition, and cast in terms of popular, if theologically unsound, persuasions. Her conscience was overburdened with harsh and punitive super-ego influences that distorted her simplistic and childlike view of the devil and his wiles and of her understanding of God. Martha had developed a God representation that did a disservice to herself and to her religion—a God who judged, condemned, and punished, rather that a God who loved and wanted to be loved, and who was constantly at work to gain her love and facilitate her peace of mind and heart. Did the therapy have any effect on her God representation? Or should we allow ourselves to think that God had a helping hand in her therapy? I guess God only knows!

However, were we to allow ourselves to think along these lines, we might set foot on a new path of discovery and understanding of the religious dimension of human experience. Given the substance and validity of religious belief, we might ask what further understanding can the analytic perspective bring to the meaning of religious beliefs. To keep the focus on God and the religious meaning of the God concept, we might seek to understand the complex interweaving of unconscious fantasies evident in the sources of our religious revelation that speak to the nature and reality of God and his (or her) involvement in human affairs. We have only touched the tip of an iceberg of questions regarding the meaning of a God who loves and saves as opposed to a God who judges and damns, and I do not limit the scope of inquiry merely to how such concepts come into existence in the mind of individual believers. Rather the question is how do such concepts arise in the belief system of any given religious group and how do they achieve the status of religious doctrine. Why is it, for example, that Christian teachings about God and his nature are Trinitarian, and Judaic concepts of God are essentially monotheistic?

Does psychoanalysis have anything to contribute to the understanding of how and why such beliefs came into being, and what motivates and sustains our belief in such concepts? And if we extend the scope of our inquiry to aspects of belief in God's presence and action in human affairs—including doctrines pertaining to grace, providence, and salvation—I can envision a new era in the sometimes troubled and fragmented history of the dialogue between psychoanalysis and religion. But, to end where I began, we see the kind of trouble the question posed by this symposium gives rise to and why I felt I had to complain about it. Perhaps we would be better off ignoring any questions about God and sticking to issues of how we and our patients experience God. That would keep our noses closer to the analytic grindstone, and leave the theologians to speculate, but without benefit of any analytically informed understanding. Perhaps it's better that way!

REFERENCES

Buber, M. (1959). *I and Thou*. New York: Charles Scribner's Sons.
——— (1961). *Two Types of Faith*. New York: Harper & Row.
Dollimore, J. (1998). *Death, Desire and Loss in Western Culture*. New York: Routledge.
Erikson, E. H. (1950). *Childhood and Society*, rev. ed. New York: Norton, 1963.
——— (1958). *Young Man Luther*. New York: Norton.
——— (1959). *Identity and the Life Cycle*. (*Psychological Issues*, Monograph 1). New York: International Universities Press.
——— (1964). *Insight and Responsibility*. New York: Norton.
Feuerbach, L. (1841). *The Essence of Christianity*. New York: Harper, 1957.
Freud, S. (1927). The future of an illusion. *Standard Edition* 21:1–56.
Ganss, G. E. (1992). *The Spiritual Exercises of Saint Ignatius: A Translation and Commentary*. St. Louis, MO: Institute of Jesuit Sources.
Kierkegaard, S. (1941). *Fear and Trembling*. Princeton, NJ: Princeton University Press.

Kris, E. (1952). *Psychoanalytic Explorations in Art*. New York: International Universities Press.

Lewis, C. S. (1962). *The Screwtape Letters and Screwtape Proposes a Toast*. New York: Macmillan.

Mahler, M. S., Pine, F., and Bergman, A. (1975). *The Psychological Birth of the Human Infant*. New York: Basic Books.

Meissner, W. W. (1978). *The Paranoid Process*. New York: Jason Aronson.

——— (1984). *Psychoanalysis and Religious Experience*. New Haven, CT: Yale University Press.

——— (1987). *Life and Faith: Psychological Perspectives on Religious Experience*. Washington, DC: Georgetown University Press.

——— (1992). The pathology of belief systems. *Psychoanalysis and Contemporary Thought* 15:99–128.

——— (1996). *The Therapeutic Alliance*. New Haven, CT: Yale University Press.

——— (1999). *To the Greater Glory—A Psychological Study of Ignatian Spirituality*. Milwaukee, WI: Marquette University Press.

Rizzuto, A.-M. (1979). *The Birth of the Living God*. Chicago: University of Chicago Press.

——— (1998). *Why Did Freud Reject God? A Psychodynamic Interpretation*. New Haven, CT: Yale University Press.

Rochlin, G. (1965). *Griefs and Discontents: The Forces of Change*. Boston: Little, Brown.

Schrag, C. O. (1997). *The Self After Postmodernity*. New Haven, CT: Yale University Press.

Tillich, P. (1952). *The Courage to Be*. New Haven, CT: Yale University Press.

5

DOES GOD HELP ME OR DO I HELP GOD OR NEITHER?:

Discussion of Meissner's Chapter, "So Help Me God! Do I Help God or Does God Help Me?"

J. Anderson Thomson, Jr., M. D.

On the dogma of religion . . . all mankind, from the beginning of the world to this day, have been quarreling, fighting, burning, and torturing one another, for abstractions unintelligible to themselves and to all others and absolutely beyond the comprehension of the human mind.

Thomas Jefferson

William Meissner's title, "So Help Me God! Do I Help God or Does God Help Me?," reminds one of the old story of a famous rabbi who taught by only asking questions. Everything that came out of his mouth was a question. His students loved his teaching but became frustrated. They went to him and said, "Rabbi, why do you only speak in questions? Why is all of your teaching only in questions?" The rabbi thought for a moment and responded, "Why not?" My hope is to leave the reader with more questions than answers.

How many readers believe in the God Woton? Poseidon? Zeus? Apollo? Krishna? Allah? Why are most of us atheists when it comes to most of the gods worshiped by most people in human history? Why are we reluctant to take it one god further (Dawkins 1999)? Why are we all susceptible to religious belief?

Why, if we are believers, is the one and only true god the God of our parents and grandparents? The laws of the universe are the same in Nepal and Norway, in Tennessee and Tibet. Yet why are we prepared to accept religion as true, and specific religious beliefs as the geographical accident of birth (Dawkins 1994)?

If we put a transmagnetic stimulator over certain areas of our temporal lobe, why will we all sense we are having a religious experience? We will see God or the universe in a grain of sand. Why is it that some people suffering temporal lobe epilepsy become hyperreligious? Why is it that certain parts of the temporal lobe play a direct role in the genesis of religious experience (Ramachandran and Blakeslee 1998)?

Jefferson's puzzlement, cited above, is no longer warranted. Religious ideas are no longer beyond our comprehension. We have an increasing understanding of why people have religious beliefs. With a combination of psychoanalysis, cognitive neuroscience, and anthropology we can begin to answer the crucial questions: Why religious ideas at all? Why those religious ideas? Why widespread? Why recurrent features? Why attractive to human minds (Boyer 1994)?

PSYCHOLOGICAL MECHANISMS
UNDERLYING RELIGION

All religious ideas can be understood from the following perspective. They are the ideas in which we credit nature with a human capacity for symbolic action (Gutherie 1993). All religious ideas are basically human concepts with alterations. They are by-products of cognitive mechanisms that were designed for other purposes (Kirkpatrick 1999, Wenegrat 1990).

Let me illustrate with the human facility for writing. We have biological systems that were originally evolved for other adaptive reasons: eyes evolved for sight, hands for our arboreal past and picking fruit from trees, and a language acquisition device to communicate among ourselves. They combine to form writing. We are not biologically evolved for writing. It is a unique by-product of mechanisms that evolved for other purposes.

Similarly, we are not evolved for religious beliefs. Religious beliefs arise as a by-product of mechanisms that were designed for other purposes. They are then used, as writing is, throughout all cultures. This chapter cannot offer a comprehensive theory of religion, but some basic ideas will be illustrated. What are some of those psychological mechanisms that are utilized to form religious ideas? The attachment system is one (Kirkpatrick 1999). The attachment system evolved for ensuring proximity of caregiver and helpless infant. It is part of the adaptive solution to the problem of survival. The attachment system, as Fischer (Chapter 3) outlined in her discussion of Rizzuto's chapter, is easily utilized in religion. When there is distress, we turn to the caregiver to reestablish a connection and a dialogue. Meissner's description of a "spectrum of faith" reads as a review of the range of attachment styles.

We come into the world with numerous other mechanisms that are utilized by religion. We are biased toward reciprocal relationships, keeping track of them and measuring disturbances in them. Such reciprocity is almost invariably established between the believer and his or her gods. We pray for help and in exchange offer something in return, often the promise to be good. Or we explicitly pay for the help with a donation to the collection bowl as it is passed.

We all contain "natural kind" modules, which permit us to distinguish animate from inanimate objects. This ability to cognitively see the living essence of things easily slides into assuming that there is a living essence in inanimate objects (Kirkpatrick 1999). Animism is the sharpest example of this, but it is present in the more complex religious ideas that impute living substance to nonliving things and spaces. Such features of religion, particularly primitive religions, as animism are grounded in our universal experiences.

Animism helps explain data that stymie our everyday senses. For example, in dreams and trances we leave our body. We see our full reflection on the water. When someone dies, it is as if he loses an invisible force. Animism and religions incorporate such notions as the soul leaving the body or existing in inanimate objects (Pinker 1997).

 We also come into this world with a "theory of mind" module. We are born with the ability to read intentions and beliefs into behaviors. The absence of a theory of mind module is the fundamental defect in autism (Baron-Cohen 1995). In religions we assume an entity that has a mind responsible for behaviors in the world. Some have seen religions as, in effect, the theory of mind module run amok (Pinker 1997).

 The concept of transference is particularly useful in understanding aspects of religion. One must first ask why the capacity for transference evolved in the human mind. What adaptive function does it serve? Early relationship strategies form stable personality characteristics. Early relationships are the basis for conducting later relationships. One need only think what it would be like if we had to learn how to relate to people with each new relationship as our lives unfolded. Basing present relationships on past relationships is an accurate way of anticipating expectations. The capacity for transference evolved as a crucial aspect of the human mind (Nesse and Lloyd 1992). In our clinical work we see daily how disturbed early relationships distort present relationships. When that transference is repeated in psychoanalytic therapy, it becomes the arena for treatment. Just think of all the potential transferences that are mobilized in religions between believers and their gods—God the father, God the mother—and all that we may bring of our personal relationships with our fathers, mothers, and significant objects into religious beliefs. We are born biased to favor kin. Religions frequently hijack our propensities in this area. As Meissner notes, "We are all God's children."

One of the strongest mechanisms of the mind utilized by religion is man's tendency to anthropomorphize. This is a powerful strategy that pervades human thought and action and religion is probably its most systematic form (Guthrie 1993). When faced with uncertainty, we are biased toward betting on the most significant possibility. Human forms are the most important. If we are mistaken, we lose little. It is better to mistake a shadow for a burglar than a burglar for a shadow.

In the Judeo-Christian tradition we are taught that God created man in his image. The opposite might, however, be more true. We make our gods in human images. They often extend into our notions of hierarchies. We create attachments and reciprocal relationships with them. Gods are almost invariably associated with parental authority and utilize our inborn bias toward honoring dominant figures. In the real world some have greater rights than others to design rules and enforce them. Some are destined to be leaders, others followers. The routine human asymmetries in power and judgment are carried into religion. We are also born with psychological mechanisms to negotiate coalitions and dominance hierarchies. These are also called into play in religions (Kirkpatrick 1999).

God is a continuity of social units providing lasting intergenerational social contract. He/she serves as a renewable contract in reciprocity. The concept of God was associated with parental authority and dead ancestors, and the origin of divinity resides in the reverence toward deceased powerful ancestors. The concept of God was also likely to have been originally generated and maintained to further the interests of one group at the expense of another (Alexander 1987).

The afterlife utilizes our desire to continue our influence and to help relatives. Ancestor worship will be particularly important to those who are about to become ancestors.

Gods personify, control, and appease the unpredictable. Gods also induce a fear of higher authority and ensure subordination. People turn over the fruits of their labor to invisible gods, not just to the current king or tax collector. What happens to the dominant male in any social group if the group is successful and gets too large?

Must the group splinter? Over our long evolutionary history, group dissolution happened many times before a unique innovation arose that allowed larger groups to stabilize. That discovery was that there is greater safety in declaring oneself to be a mere messenger who represents the presence of a divine power. The messenger, God's vicar on earth, has authority without having to take the chance of full responsibility. The leader who accepts inferior status to a deity chooses a brilliant and cunning strategy. As every subordinate knows, one's commands carry weight when they are accompanied by the threat of a greater power (Dennett 1997).[1]

The move toward monotheism is a two-edged sword. The idea of justice for all creates a moral consistency, but such unity of belief leads to evangelism and enforcement (Alexander 1987).

It was often assumed that religions evolved because of their social uses and their influences on groups. They certainly have these qualities, but the social uses had to come after their individual use (Sperber 1996). The anthropologist Ruth Benedict describes religion as a "technique for success." Religions are very useful ways of acquiring resources, attracting mates, thwarting competition, redirecting loyalties, and even subverting families.

Meissner identifies himself as a Catholic. Christianity actually began among the disenfranchised of Roman society. Whereas alone they were powerless, individuals could acquire power through their collective influence (Alexander 1987).

The idea of subverting families may come as a surprise to those who think of religions as oriented toward family values. But the family is a danger to religion. Families are a rival coalition. They have the unfair advantage of being bound together by kin emotions. We favor and forgive family members before we do others. We are also more quick to seek revenge when our kin are harmed.

---

[1] This was illustrated at the Mahler Symposium when Parens introduced Meissner. Because Meissner is also a Jesuit priest, Parens added a genuflection of submissiveness when he referred to Meissner as an agent of a higher power.

The hostility to family values is nicely illustrated in the Bible. "I came not to send peace, but a sword. For I am come to set a man at variance against his father, and the daughter against her mother, and the daughter-in-law against her mother-in-law. And a man's foes shall be they of his own household. He that loveth father or mother more than me is not worthy of me: and he that loveth son or daughter more than me is not worthy of me" (Matthew 10:34–37). That was none other than Jesus.

Religions have also served as a cultural adaptation for facilitating war. They permit the takeover of groups by disenfranchised young males. Belief in an afterlife and a reward for dying in a holy war helps minimize the fear of death in the pursuit of conquests. Religious adherence turns off mechanisms of compassion, and turns on and maximizes dehumanization. Religions are very effective at guiding in-group morality and guiding out-group hatred. Religions provide their followers the ability to assess others' commitments to dangerous tasks and to maximize the commitment to those potentially lethal endeavors. Oaths have the imprint of psychic terror and serve as costly advertisements. They broadcast the superiority and commitment of those who swear allegiance. Religions often ensure warriors their share of the spoils, and religions are very useful in preparing for war to exterminate out-groups (Hartung 1995, Kriegman and Kriegman 1996). Meissner notes this tendency of religions, but sees it as an extreme to be resisted, and fails to see it as one of religion's very foundations and purposes. The body count of human history is the bloody proof.

Miracles create a market that would-be priests can compete in, and such priests succeed by exploiting our dependence on experts (Pinker 1997).

Many think rituals are exclusively a human phenomenon. In fact, they are fossilized versions of animal displays. Pigeons develop rituals when rewards are uncertain and unpredictable. Rituals help trigger emotions and make chaotic facts of life manageable and predictable. They also serve as hard-to-fake signals of commitment (Irons 2000).

The rise in the United States of creation science has further
clouded the issues. Creation science is actually on a par with the
idea of a flat earth. Creation science provides no empirical, experimental, or theoretical evidence. It is empty of intellectual reasoning
or persuasive argument. It closes minds and forces obedience. It
would return the world to a paradise that never existed. Creation
science upholds no explanatory power, offers no further applications, and in effect is a sterile concept (Berra 1990). Creation
science disguises the essentially religious nature of creationism. It
attacks selected particulars of science and pretends to be a separate
science of its own. We substitute blind faith for reason and in so
doing discard all modern biology and most geology, physics, and
astronomy (Berra 1990).

Science is a self-correcting method for seeking the truth. It
exists because of the evidence. Religion is based on faith and in
spite of the evidence. Science is pedantic, expensive, and subversive
(Pinker 1997).

The creator had no job to do and so might as well not have
existed. There is no need to regard consciousness as an intrinsic
complexity embellished by soul. Behavior is a complex organization of simple processes. The only immortal "soul" is the lasting
impression we have on other men's minds (Atkins 1996).

MEISSNER'S CONTRIBUTION

Meissner says that he will settle for the common understanding of
the God of the Judeo-Christian tradition. Does this leave out a lot
of religious people and their gods?

He states that as analysts we know nothing of that God. Along
with Rizzuto he insists that all we can focus on is the God
representation, a mental representation of God. With regard to the
existence of God, Meissner said, "Our lips are sealed." He insists
that "He exists. God is not just a mental configuration reflecting
dynamic motivational influences, he is an active and creative force

really acting and causing effects in the hearts and minds of his people." So Meissner closes off any discussion about the existence of God or the possibility that God is just a product of the human mind. This is the usual argument in the religion–science debate. Science is a self-correcting way of discovering the truth. Science proposes hypotheses and tests them. Religion proposes facts, "He exists," and closes them off for testing. They are to be accepted by faith, in spite of the evidence.

Meissner does some interesting intellectual jujitsu. He says God exists and then lays out some of the evidence that God is merely a product of the human mind:

> To what extent does the God representation reflect its pathological origins and relation to primary or other objects? To what extent does it embody aspects of the patient's psychopathology? Here the projection of pathological superego dynamics onto the God representation is common coin. In what sense and to what degree does the God representation reflect transference dynamics? To what extent does the God representation offer itself as a preferred target for therapeutic intervention or interpretation? . . . Does the God representation serve then as a convenient object of displacement or does it offer itself as a preferred and primary target for intervention . . . ?"

I submit these are excellent descriptions of some of the psychic mechanisms at work in the creation of religious belief. Meissner must then do an irrational leap over his own analysis to justify religious belief.

Meissner says that therapists to his way of thinking are not in the business of proposing, advocating, or in any way promoting religious behavior or thinking. Is Meissner true to this in his treatment of Martha?

In Meissner's discussion of grace he demonstrates one of the frequent arguments in the religion–science debate. He discusses a patient who clings to bitter resentments of her mother for childhood deprivations and who comes in the course of therapy to comprehend better the circumstances related to her mother's limitations. The patient consequently reaches a level of resolution of her resentment sufficient to be able to forgive her mother. Meissner says that these changes can be related to "progressive developments in the therapy, to a degree of insight, to changes within the therapeutic relation, especially the transference, to developments within the alliance, and so on." He further says, "We would have no need to appeal to any other causal connection." Why not? He thinks we can argue that grace was involved. "I do not know any grounds on which I could draw such a conclusion, nor do I know any grounds on which I could reject it. The question is irresolvable. There is just as much reason for the nonbeliever or analyst to reject the proposition as for the religious believer to accept it." This is one of the standard arguments in the debate about God. You cannot prove that God doesn't exist so that therefore you have to consider the possibility.

It is true one cannot prove a negative. We cannot absolutely prove that there is not an English teapot orbiting the planet Pluto. But since we can't absolutely prove there isn't, must we consider the possibility that it is with the same weight as the probability that it is not? Obviously not. The whole issue of probability is omitted from these arguments. We can't absolutely prove there is not a teapot orbiting Pluto, but we can say with a fair degree of probability that there is not (Dawkins 1999). We cannot absolutely prove that grace wasn't involved in the changes in that patient. However, with a fair degree of probability, we can argue that the changes that occurred in the patient were the result of the kind of therapeutic factors Meissner outlines. Similarly, we cannot absolutely prove that God doesn't exist. But there is a fair degree of probability, based on the evidence, that there is no God and never has been.

Meissner says the best resolution he knows of that paradox was offered by the great St. Ignatius of Loyola who said, "Pray as though everything depended on God, but act as though everything depended on you." This is a variant of Pascal's wager. You might as well believe because if it's true you get the kingdom of heaven. If you believe and there is no heaven, you don't lose much. It's a form of game theory brought to religion.

Meissner is very disarming in his presentation. He says, "I cannot claim that religious elements do not have an integral part of my therapeutic armamentarium, but the focus and purpose has been, I hope and trust, always analytic." What is the evidence for an analytic focus in the case that he then presents?

MEISSNER'S CLINICAL MATERIAL

All we know is that Martha was a woman in her early sixties who was struggling with depression and episodes of rather severe anxiety. How depressed was she? How severe was the anxiety? What is her past psychiatric history? What is the family psychiatric history? Was medication considered? What was her medical status? What was her hormone replacement status?

We have almost no developmental history. All we are told is that she was the only girl in a family among four brothers, two older and two younger. She never dated, never had any romantic relationships with a man, and never married. Her older brothers had married and moved away, and after her father passed away she continued to live with her mother and two younger brothers. The two younger brothers then moved away and she was left with her mother. It sounds as if something in this loss of the men in her life had to do with the intensification of her symptoms. There obviously were substantive losses there that don't seem to be linked in Meissner's mind with the onset of her worsening depression and anxiety. She has lost all the men in her life. She is now left alone with her mother. Is that contributing to her depression and generating some of her anxieties?

We learned that she had worked for forty years as a shipping clerk in a warehouse full of male workers. She lifted cartons with

the best of the men. It sounds like she became somewhat mascu-
linized in her adult life, but we know nothing about the dynamics.
Meissner insists, "I never heard a word about anything sexual or
romantic" in the workplace. Did he ask? He is going to tell us there
is a workplace full of men and one woman and there is nothing
sexual going on in forty years? Whose sexuality is Dr. Meissner
denying?

He says the problem centered around religion. We are told
that Martha is a devout Irish Catholic who attends mass regularly
and spends a good amount of time at prayers and spiritual reading.
He notes how she would initially refer to him as Doctor and at
times as Father. He notes the obvious confusion in her mind about
the nature of their relationship. He says, "As we edged closer to
core material I heard less Father and more Doctor." At the same
time that it sounds as if she is seeing him more as a doctor, he is
behaving more like a "father" (priest).

He says the kernel of the problem was Martha's having
obscene thoughts and images when she was attending mass and
prayers, including looking at Jesus on the cross and having thoughts
about his sexual organs. When these images came upon her, he says
she was overwhelmed with feelings of guilt and convinced that she
was committing a mortal sin and would be condemned to an
eternity of pain and torment. He says, "The erotic character of
these intrusive thoughts and images were entirely consistent with
her rather obsessional character structure." Might they also be
consistent with other things: the sexual abuse by the priest we are to
learn about or the only outlets she has for a long suppressed
sexuality? Even though he states that "her extreme religiosity and
her sexual defenses were serving as a barrier against unresolved
sexual conflicts and these had probably been a source of conflict and
distress for her for most of her life," he is uncertain why it took this
symptomatic turn at this point in her life, and he seems to do little
to explore what those unresolved sexual conflicts are.

He learns that when she was a young woman, and we don't
know the age, "she was experiencing difficulties with her sexual

feelings and impulses and was greatly in fear that she was committing sins by having such desires and impulses." In other words, was she having the same problems as a young woman that she is having at age 60? At that time she sought "spiritual advice and counsel from her confessor." Meissner learns that these sessions occurred regularly and she would discuss sexual anxieties with the priest. He says that the priest offered some reasonable advice, yet we don't know what this allegedly "reasonable" advice was. Meissner acknowledges that "the [pastoral] sessions unfortunately became increasingly eroticized. Before long they were being conducted in the nude, with a good deal of touching and fondling along with the spiritual advice. As far as I could tell, touching and fondling was as far as it went. Martha never indicated or hinted that there was ever any intercourse." Yet Meissner does not ask. Was there intercourse? Was there more than just fondling? Was there manual penetration? We do not know the full extent of the sexual abuse.

He notes that as part of the transference she was relating to him in a confessional manner, "confessing her sins and presumably seeking some kind of absolution." Puzzlingly he says that this was not the answer since whatever guilt was involved for her had been thoroughly confessed and absolved already. What? A more reasonable formulation would be that the sexual stimulation involved in the abuse continued to give her distress and guilty feelings and she was confused about this, an inevitable result with sexual abuse and one of its tragedies. The victims often feel guilt because of the pleasure that sometimes occurs in the abuse. This guilt confuses them to the extent that they lose sight of who the truly guilty party is—the perpetrator, in this case the priest.

Meissner says, "I had difficulty negotiating this passage with her. In retrospect, part of the problem had to do with her image of me and her expectations of what sort of help she was looking for—did she come to me as a priest, looking for spiritual consolation or leave, or did she come to me as a doctor, looking for a more humanly therapeutic benefit? My operating assumption was that her involvement with Father X had resulted from a mixture of naive trust and simple submission to the seductions of this revered religious figure cloaked under the guise of pastoral concern and spiritual direction."

Meissner seems to become confused and stops behaving like a doctor and starts to behave more like a priest. There is also the troubling "blaming the victim" type of statement, attributing her involvement with the priest to her "naive trust and simple submission." We don't know her prior history of sexual activity in the family, or abuse by others previous or subsequent to the priest. Even if she had not mentioned it, it has to be explored. But earlier abuse doesn't have to be present to explain the difficulties she was having.

Meissner notes, "The experiences must have been sexually arousing and titillating and in the untutored mind of this young woman the line between what was spiritually good and pastorally commendable and what was erotic, seductive, and sexually forbidden was not at all clear. The perplexity and doubt must have bothered her conscience ever since, and she has never found adequate surcease or resolution. . . ." He notes appropriately the possible arousing and titillating nature of the sexual abuse. He does not seem to connect it with her guilt and the need for treatment.

Meissner states, "I had formed a tentative hypothesis that, whatever the degree of naïveté and misguided trust, there may have been an element of guilt connected with the degree of sexual arousal and excitement she must have felt. I reasoned, perhaps naively myself, that a primary task was to alleviate her guilt. But how was I to do that? My first tack was a good one. I just listened quietly and empathically to her story. As she gained some reassurance that I was not going to be disapproving, condemning, or castigating [or sexually exploitive and abusive?], she became more comfortable talking about these matters."

It certainly doesn't seem to be naive that a primary task for the treatment of this woman would be to alleviate her guilt. And his first tack indeed was a good one, creating a sense of safety for her and countering her prior experience with a priest.

Meissner states, "If I had made the slightest hint that his [the abusive priest] behavior had been reprehensible, or that he had behaved in a manner ill-suited to his role and function as a priest, she would become quickly upset and agitated, her voice trembling and her speech impaired." What did Meissner expect?

He insists that "however conceptually correct that tack might have been, it was not going to work very well." How do we know? It does not seem he persisted from various angles to help her see that no matter what degree of sexual arousal she felt, and the guilt it induced, the perpetrator of the abuse, the priest, was the guilty party. Victims of sexual abuse by trusted ones in their lives will often idealize or fight desperately to keep a good image of the perpetrator.

He states, "There was some need in her to preserve the integrity of her view of him as a priest and an unwillingness to accept his behavior for what it plainly was. I did not feel that any attempt on my part to add to her psychic burden on this account would be very helpful—she seemed to be bearing as much as she could without my adding to it. So I was stumped." Is there the possibility that there was some need in Meissner to preserve the integrity of the former priest and an unwillingness for *him* to accept completely the behavior for what it fully was, sexually exploitive and damaging to a degree that it may have accounted for this woman's loss of a sexual life and a marital life, and for the symptoms now burdening her? Was the psychic burden that might be added on to Meissner the burden that one of his brothers in the priesthood had violated the trust of a young woman and sexually abused her and now she was coming to him, another priest to undo that legacy?

Most troubling is Meissner's comment, "I searched my mind for any scraps of psychoanalytic lore that might help. But I kept running into dead-ends." "Scraps of psychoanalytic lore?" What about the voluminous literature on the effects of abuse, of sexual exploitation by trusted authority figures? These are scraps? This is lore? What about psychoanalytic knowledge we have gained from

innumerable in-depth treatment experiences of those who have
suffered as Martha did?

Meissner states that the problem was

> how to alleviate her guilt without pouring oil on the smoldering
> embers or casting the blame on the errant priest—this last alterna-
> tive, for reasons that remain unclear to me, seems to be even more
> disturbing to her. It might simply have been her need to preserve an
> unsullied image of the priest in the face of all evidence to the
> contrary as part of preserving her religious outlook and her depen-
> dence on religious figures for spiritual support and solace. These
> motives were partly involved in her coming to my office. I would
> presume that she came to me at first more as a priest than therapist,
> and only gradually came to relate to me more as a therapist than
> priest.

What about the possibility that the reasons remain unclear
because they are located within Meissner? Might there have been
some need on his part to preserve an unsullied image of the priest?
In several instances he refers to the priest as merely "errant." That
priest's behavior toward Martha was more than just being late for
mass. Indeed, it was probably criminal. It is routine in dealing with
the legacy of sexual exploitation to have to help the victim give up
an idealized image of the perpetrator as a necessary part of alleviating her own guilt and shame. This approach is well documented
and would have been easily accessible to Meissner. Undoubtedly,
colleagues of his in Boston would have been familiar with the
treatment of victims of sexual exploitation had he chosen to consult
with them. In fact one of the authorities in the field of sexual
trauma and its treatment, Judith Lewis Herman, is in Boston, and
her book is neither scraps nor lore and is easily accessible (Herman
1992).

He justifies his ultimate intervention by saying that the patient
was not available for literary material, movies, and so on. But how
long did he search? He says, "The answer once asked came

quickly—of course, she and I were both Catholics, raised in Catholic tradition, and sharing at least superficially the same belief system." Is it possible that there was too close a countertransference identification with the patient that got in the way of a more analytic approach to this woman? Meissner seems to justify his unusual interpretation to the patient by saying,

> The patient stopped and looked at me for a minute—as though I had suddenly stopped speaking Swahili and started to speak a language she understood. I went on to explain that when the devil wanted to tempt good souls who were living a good life, his tactic was to cause them to be distressed or disturbed, and that he used whatever device he could get his hands on to pull it off, to interfere with their good works or their tranquillity of soul. . . . When I mentioned the devil, her eyes lit up. We had identified the enemy, the cause of all the trouble.

mon dieu!

Just because her eyes lit up and a suitable target of externalization has been discovered, does this mean it is the right interpretation?

Meissner goes on, appropriately, to ask, "Does such talk about the devil belong in any respectable therapy?" The reader of the case must judge. He asks further, "Was I functioning no longer as a psychotherapist and now was playing the part of spiritual guru?" Again, the reader must decide.

Meissner clearly believes that "she believed in the devil and knew exactly what I was talking about. My comment had located the problem, which had been disturbing, confusing, and incomprehensible to her before, and relocated it in a context that was familiar, comprehensible, and therefore manageable." If a patient is delusional and believes that she is the Queen of England, certainly if we addressed her as Her Royal Highness that would make her relieved and her eyes might light up. Does that make it right?

Meissner says that he also "added a proposition to the effect that, as far as I knew, God allows temptation to those he loves in order to strengthen them in the face of spiritual adversity and then when he allows temptation he always provides sufficient grace to the tempted soul to help it overcome the temptation and thus gain even more of his love and grace." In effect, Meissner tells us to respect a patient's religious belief. If we respect this patient's belief in God, her lifelong belief in God, how kind is it to her to tell her that God is tormenting her in her declining years?

It seems that one of the few helpful things Meissner did for Martha was to tell her that "the first thing one did not do was to get bent out of shape over such temptations. One was better off if you could maintain some perspective about it, not let it get to you or throw you off stride." He was indirectly, with the authority she invested in him, alleviating some of her guilt.

But, he insists, "Appeal to the devil was useful since he provided a convenient fall guy for explaining the causality." Again, the perpetrator of her abuse, and one of the sources of her symptoms, was let off the hook. Meissner raises the objection that any psychoanalytic reader would certainly raise. "Now you might complain—and rightly so—that I was instigating or at least confirming a projective defense in helping the patient to avoid dealing with underlying sexual conflicts." He certainly was reinforcing a projective defense and, in so doing, was he keeping the possibility of doing more appropriate work out of the picture? Indirectly he was saying that sexual thoughts were something bad ("temptations") that she would just have to endure. There is no exploration of the possibility that some of her sexual thoughts were normal. Jesus was one of the few attractive men left in her life.

Meissner says that he had helped mobilize her psychic resources to begin to deal more objectively and adaptively with these experiences and enable her to take charge of her inner life in a way that she had not done for years. According to him, she had lived her life in large measure as uncomprehending of her sexual needs and desires. And this interpretation again says she is merely the victim, in this case of the devil, helpless to fully comprehend her sexual needs, impulses, desires, and whatever contribution the legacy of sexual exploitation by the earlier priest had made.

Meissner notes that she retired from her job where she worked with all men and developed a circle of women friends of similar age. Before long she had become a part-time cook in the rectory of a church. "In the later stages of her times with me, she would come in and regale me with anecdotes and amusing observations about her experiences with the priests in the rectory, enjoying every minute of it—and, as I gathered, the good fathers enjoyed her being there as well." A psychoanalytically informed reader would wonder about, in effect, a transference cure. If she could bring stories to Meissner of safe and enjoyable activities with priests, she had turned the tables a bit.

The therapy was tapered off. He describes the sessions merely as "the same pattern of joviality and good-natured kidding." Yet even then he notes that she would bring up something related to her basic problem, "some recurrence of the temptations or some related concern. We would discuss these briefly and she would leave in great relief and cheerful spirits." In what manner were they discussed? He noted that calls dwindled over time. For some years he received a card along with a spiritual bouquet and birthday cards. These, too, finally stopped. One can only wonder what happened. Was she better? We certainly hope so. If she was, does that justify the treatment that was given? Was an opportunity missed, even in once-a-week therapy, to ease her suffering by a more standard approach to her symptoms? We will never know. In fairness, we must trust Meissner's report. He was there. We were not. And we can still have our doubts and questions.

Meissner discusses this case in terms of the question of how much of the outcome can be attributed to his interventions and how much to the hand of God. He insists that "Martha and I had developed a solid therapeutic alliance based on mutual trust, respect for her freedom, complete openness and honesty, her slowly emerging autonomy and initiative, and her ultimately taking responsibility for the therapeutic outcome and applying herself to its achievement." If there was "complete openness and honesty," how does that square with the ideas that he withheld from her?

Meissner says that part of Martha's view of him was "as confessor and judge, but my refusal to respond to her invitations to play that role was for her in part a disappointment, but then also in part a relief." But he ultimately did play the role of a priest, telling Martha that her symptoms were the fault of the devil.

He defends his actions, saying, "I did not trample on her anxieties—or better, if I made any moves in that direction, her perturbation and turmoil served as a signal that even if I had been right, she was in no position to hear or accept what I might have to say." Perhaps he, because of countertransference problems, was in no position to tell her? Victims of abuse are, by nature, fragile. The first task of treatment is to make them feel safe before such issues can be addressed. But ultimately such issues can be addressed. He says, "She might have been helping me to keep from putting my foot in another countertransference trap, that of enacting my judging role." So does Meissner hold her responsible for keeping him from judging the abusive priest in the manner that he might have?

He says, "Lastly, I managed to come up with a formulation that made sense to her, that proved to be nonthreatening, that offered a context of meaning that she could recognize and accept within the framework of her religious system." One could, within the context of her religious system, talk about a priest who is human who made a terrible mistake but who, nonetheless, was responsible. One could tell her that one of the consequences of abuse is often guilt over the pleasurable sensations it arouses, shame and guilt that make it hard for the victim to know what happened and to hold the perpetrator fully responsible. One could talk to her about the normalcy of sexual feelings and curiosity, even when they might manifest as thoughts about Jesus' genitals.

Meissner justifies his actions by saying, "Instead of relying on my psychoanalytic belief system, I called her belief system into play." Was it not also his belief system? Meissner has equated a

KEY

psychoanalytic belief system with a religious belief system. Certainly there have been those that have argued that psychoanalysis has overtones of religious belief. However, there is justification in psychoanalytic treatment for talking with the patient in direct terms about sexual exploitation. In a strange leap of logic Meissner says, "This to my mind reflects a triumph of ego over superego and id. Freud, I think, would have approved of that." I disagree.

CONCLUSION

Meissner and Rizzuto represent an unfortunate strain in psychoanalysis, those who want the benefits of its insights but who do not want to bear the cost of what it shows them about their religious beliefs. They acknowledge Freud's atheism and its grounding in his discoveries about the illusions that the mind creates (Freud 1927). But they then question Freud's rejection of God, even using his own tools against him (Rizzuto 1998); they defy logic to justify faith, for example, dynamically determined God representations separate of God; and, if that isn't enough, they reject further discussion: "psychological understanding has little or nothing to contribute to the theological significance or understanding of faith." They maintain a blind eye and a deaf ear to all the work in related disciplines that delineates the origins and structure of mankind's religious beliefs.

Mushy illogic prevails in the gyrations used to reconcile psychoanalysis with faith. Meissner says,

> In resigning all wish-fulfillment, faith revives and revivifies the most fundamental human wishes and finds their fulfillment in virtue of faith. Thus wishes are fulfilled, but wish-fulfillment is not the motive force in faith. We must distinguish, therefore, between wish-fulfillment in virtue of basically human desires (expressed in primary process terms) and wish-fulfillment in virtue of faith. In the

former, wishes are fulfilled and provide the motive force. In the latter, wishes are fulfilled, but the motive force comes from elsewhere.

Is this clear? "The creative moment in faith is unique and beyond understanding, and beyond mere regression and mere recapitulation as well." Meissner, a qualified psychoanalyst, again bars the door to any deep, rational inquiry, the fundamental process of psychoanalysis.

Justifying faith in the face of Freud's discoveries requires a little undoing on Meissner's part. "Man is unwilling to die; his death, taken as an end to his existence, is a diametric affront to his fundamental narcissism. Religious belief restores to him the promise of life, beyond death and overcoming death. Yet faith is not simply this." He has nailed down one of the functions of faith, but then undertakes an undoing.

At the close of his case discussion Meissner returns to the issue of whether God was involved. "To what extent was my own inspired interpretation the result of some graceful effect in me?" Or, how much was the wish to be a priest, not a psychotherapist, and absolve a fellow priest involved?

"But, giving myself all due credit, or fault as some might suggest, we are still left with the haunting question of whether God was in the act or not. To what extent was my own inspired interpretation the result of some graceful effect in me?" As he is aware, there is certainly some reason to give fault to his conduct of this treatment. Often in his chapter he writes as if acknowledging his possible error erases the mistake and absolves him. Hardly. And the haunting question of whether God was in the act or not becomes more interesting. Were the mistakes just Meissner's? Or were the mistakes also God's?

Meissner asks, "Was I helping God out by bringing one of his beloved creatures closer to him and enabling her to be at peace with herself in her relation with him?" In other words, was Meissner's wish to be a good priest rewarded?

Meissner says that we owe it to our patients to find a way to correct those aspects of their beliefs that are pathologically distorted and contribute to their difficulties. Yet does it seem that he accomplished this? By telling his patient it was the devil at fault and God's fault for allowing the devil to tempt her, was this physician and psychoanalyst correcting the pathologically distorted belief or reinforcing it? Does Meissner's treatment of Martha meet the standard of care of such a patient with our current knowledge? Did Meissner help God, did God help him, or was it neither?

REFERENCES

Alexander, R. (1987). *The Biology of Moral Systems*. New York: Aldine de Gruyter.

Atkins, P. W. (1996). *Creation Revisited*. New York: W. H. Freeman.

Baron-Cohen, S. (1995). *Mindblindness: An Essay on Autism and Theory of Mind*. Cambridge, MA: MIT Press.

Berra, T. (1990). *Evolution and the Myth of Creationism*. Stanford, CA: Stanford University Press.

Boyer, P. (1994). *The Naturalness of Religious Ideas: A Cognitive Theory of Religion*. Berkeley, CA: University of California Press.

Dawkins, R. (1994). "The "know-nothings," the "know-alls," and the "no-contests." *The Nullifidian* 1(8):10–12.

———— (1999). Snake oil and holy water. *Forbes*, October 4.

Dennet, D. (1997). Appraising grace. *The Sciences*, Jan./Feb.

Freud, S. (1927). The future of an illusion. *Standard Edition* 21:1–56.

Guthrie, S. G. (1993). *Faces in the Clouds: A New Theory of Religion*. New York: Oxford.

Hartung, J. (1995). Love thy neighbor: the evolution of in-group morality. *Skeptic* 3(4): 86–99.

Herman, J. L. (1992). *Trauma and Recovery*. New York: Harper.

Irons, W. (2000). *Religion as a hard-to-fake sign of commitment*. Unpublished manuscript.

Kirkpatrick, L. A. (1999). Towards an evolutionary psychology of religion and personality. *Journal of Personality* 67:921–949.

Kriegman, D., and Kriegman, O. (1996). *War and the evolution of the human propensity to form nations, cults, and religions*. Paper presented at the Association for Politics and the Life Sciences Annual Conference, Boston, September.

Nesse, R., and Lloyd, A. (1992). The evolution of psychodynamic mechanisms. In *The Adapted Mind*, ed. J. Barkow, L. Cosmides, and J. Tooby, pp. 601–624. New York: Oxford University Press.

Pinker, S. (1997). *How The Mind Works*. New York: Norton.

Ramachandran, V. S., and Blakeslee, S. (1998). *Phantoms in the Brain*. New York: William Morrow.

Rizzuto, A.-M. (1998). *Why Did Freud Reject God? A Psychodynamic Interpretation*. New Haven, CT: Yale University Press.

Sperber, D. (1996). *Explaining Culture: A Naturalistic Approach*. Oxford, UK: Blackwell.

Wenegrat, B. (1990). *The Divine Archetype: The Sociobiology and Psychology of Religion*. Lexington, MA: Lexington Books.

6

PSYCHOANALYTIC REFLECTIONS ON THE SACRED HINDU TEXT, THE *BHAGAVAD GITA*

Satish Reddy, M. D.

If the red slayer think he slays,
Or if the slain think he is slain,
They know not well the subtle ways
I keep, and pass, and turn again.

Ralph Waldo Emerson, "Brahma"

The *Bhagavad Gita (Gita)* is one of the most profound, sacred, and widely memorized texts of Hinduism. It consists of 700 stanzas and occurs in eighteen terse and dense chapters in the great Sanskrit Hindu epic, the *Mahabharata*. The *Gita* is a philosophical treatise, a religious document, and a practical manual for living. It outlines and explains in a highly condensed form the essential teachings of Hinduism. The *Mahabharata*, the longest epic in the world, is the story of a great fratricidal civil war between the five Pandava brothers and the hundred Kaurava brothers. The Pandavas are fighting to reclaim a part of their kingdom from their cousins, the Kauravas. The *Gita* is narrated in the form of a poetic dialogue by the bard Samjaya to his patron, the blind king Dhrtarastra, father of the Kauravas. The dialogue occurs between Arjuna, one of the

Pandavas, and Krishna, Arjuna's friend, charioteer, and god incarnate. Before the battle begins, Arjuna, the epic hero, hesitates and becomes despondent. Seeing his kinsmen, relatives, and teachers in both armies, his conviction and heroism fail. He refuses to fight and asks Krishna to help him. Krishna's advice and instruction to Arjuna constitute the content of the *Gita*.

This chapter uses the interaction between Arjuna and Krishna, which leads to the resolution of Arjuna's crisis, to show that a psychoanalytic situation and process occur in the *Gita*. Krishna functions both as Arjuna's friend and advisor—and I propose as his analyst. Krishna's analytic function is not primarily interpretive but more as an object that facilitates Arjuna's psychic development. The cardinal analytic techniques and principles of neutrality, abstinence, and anonymity are both observed and violated in the *Gita*. Indeed, it is the violation of the principle of anonymity, in the form of the human Krishna displaying his divine nature as God in Chapter 11, that leads to Arjuna's transformation.

THE CONTEXT

The *Mahabharata* consists of eighteen major *parvans* (books) subdivided into chapters. The *Gita* occurs in the *Bhishmaparvan*, the sixth major book, in a chapter entitled, the *Bhagavadgitaparvan (The Book of the Bhagavadgita)*. *Bhishmaparvan* is named after Bhishma, great-grandfather to both warring parties, and chronicles the killing of Bhishma by Arjuna. The central plot of the *Mahabharata* revolves around Bhishma's voluntary renunciation of the throne by an oath of celibacy so that his father might marry a low-caste woman. This renunciation leads to progressive problems in succession to the throne that ultimately climaxes in the great war. Krishna himself is an epic hero, a Vrisni prince, who is a cousin to both warring parties. In the epic, he oscillates between the human and the divine. To stay neutral in the war, he offers himself as a charioteer to one side with the condition that he will not fight and offers his army to the other side. Arjuna chooses Krishna, and the Kauravas opt for Krishna's army, with both sides consenting to the arrangement. Arjuna considers Krishna as his friend and is not consciously aware of Krishna's divinity.

ARJUNA'S CRISIS

The Book of the Bhagavadgita begins with the announcement by the bard Samjaya, to the blind king Dhrtarastra, that Bhishma has been killed. Dhrtarastra is stupefied by the news and questions Samjaya how this occurred. The *Gita* occurs midway in *The Book of the Bhagavadgita*. It is not coincidence that the *Gita* occurs in the *Book of Bhishma*, as it is the killing of Bhishma that occasions Arjuna's crisis. As van Buitenen (1980) notes, "The preamble tells us that Bhishma is dead, that Arjuna's reluctance to fight in this war was fully justified, and that consequently a need existed to override Arjuna's reluctance with a higher truth, so that in fact *that* will come about which we know is *already* the case" (p. 3).

War is about to begin. Arjuna instructs Krishna to position the chariot between the two armies. Seeing friends and relatives in both armies, he becomes depressed and loses his resolve. This is described beautifully, in poetic and emotive terms:

And to Krishna then, Arjuna spoke these words: "Stop my chariot in the middle of the two armies, Krishna, that I may behold these men standing there eager to fight, with whom I am to engage in this war. I want to see those who, about to fight, are assembled here desirous of accomplishing in battle what is dear to the evil-minded son of Dhrtarastra." Thus addressed by Arjuna, Krishna placed the best of the chariots in the middle of the two armies. And when they were facing Bhisma, Drona, and all the princes, he said: "Arjuna, behold the assembled Kurus!" Arjuna saw standing there fathers, grandfathers, teachers, uncles, brothers, sons, grandsons, companions, fathers-in-law, and friends, belonging to both armies. And

having looked closely at all these relations standing there, Arjuna
filled with the utmost sadness, and weighed down by his sorrow, he
said: "Krishna, seeing my own kin on hand and eager to fight, my
limbs become weak, my mouth dries up, my body trembles, and my
hair stands on end. Gandiva (the bow) slips from my hand; my skin
is also burning, I can scarcely remain standing; My mind is reeling."
[*Gita* 1:21–30]

Recalling Freud's (1923) statement that "the ego is first and
foremost a body ego" (p. 26), we see that Arjuna's ego and his
body are both failing him. He is overcome by sadness, and his
Gandiva bow slips from his hand. He is losing his grip, metaphorically speaking, both mentally and physically. Psychoanalytically,
Arjuna's distress and inhibition are precipitated by oedipal guilt,
specifically the killing of Bhishma. Of all the warriors in the
opposing army, it is Bhishma that Arjuna hesitates in killing. In the
Mahabharata, there are several instances where Arjuna hesitates in
killing Bhishma. Bhishma, though fighting on the Kaurava's side, is
revered and respected by both the Pandavas and Kauravas. Prior to
the enmity that develops between the cousins, the Pandavas and the
Kauravas grow up in the same house with Bhishma as the head of
the household. A special affection develops between Arjuna, the
child, and Bhishma. When prodded by Krishna to fight and kill
Bhishma, Arjuna says:

"How, Krishna, shall I fight in battle, with the venerable and aged
preceptor of the Kurus, the grandsire of accomplished understanding and intelligence. Krishna, while playing in the days of childhood, I used to soil the garments of the high-souled and illustrious
one by climbing on his lap with my body smeared with dust.
Krishna, in my childhood, climbing on the lap of the high souled
father of Pandu (our father), I used to say 'father.' 'I am not your
father, but your father's father, Arjuna' were the words he used to
say in reply to me. Oh how he used to treat me thus; how could he
be now slain by me." [*Mahabharata*, Book 6, Chapter 108, verse
90–93]

Bhishma, the supreme commander of the Kauravas, is powerful and unassailable. Without his death, victory for the Pandavas is not possible. Despite Krishna's exhortations, Arjuna's inhibitions run deep:

"Krishna, how am I to fight with arrows against Bhisma and Drona, both worthy of reverence? Surely it would be better to be even a beggar in this world than to have slain those mighty teachers. For having slain them, wealth desiring though they are, I would enjoy only blood-smeared pleasures here on earth. We know not which is better for us, to conquer them or that they should conquer us. For having slain those sons of Dhrtarastra standing there before us, we would not desire to live. My inmost being is stricken by this flaw of pity, for my mind is confused about dharma (duty), I ask you which would be better? *Tell me decisively, I am your pupil; Instruct me who have come to you.*" [*Gita* 2:4–7, italics mine]

ANALYST AND ANALYSAND

In the *Gita*, Krishna acts as Arjuna's analyst. He takes on this role at Arjuna's request when Arjuna asks for Krishna's help to resolve his grief and advise him on what he should do. Krishna, by accepting to help him, becomes his analyst. The relationship between Arjuna and Krishna occurs on several different levels in the *Mahabharata* and forms the basis for the transference and transference distortions that occur in the *Gita*. There are four notable relations that are relevant to the analytic process: (1) as close friends and companions, (2) as warrior and charioteer, (3) as the ancient divine warrior/sage pair Nara/Narayana, and (4) as devotee and god/divinity.

In The *Mahabharata*, Arjuna and Krishna are close friends and share a special camaraderie that is unparalleled in the epic. Karve (1991) notes: "Of the Pandavas, Arjuna was the same age as Krishna. He always bowed to Dharma and Bhima as his elders, and was, in turn, shown respect by the twins, but he always embraced

Arjuna as his equal. These two picnicked together, drank together, and were intimate friends" (p. 163). When Abhimanu. Arjuna's son, is killed in the war, Krishna consoles him. After the war, when Krishna dies, Arjuna cremates him (Karve 1991). As epic heroes, they burn the Khandava forest and kill all the creatures in it, at the request of Agni, the God of fire.

> As portrayed in the Khandava episode, the friendship of Arjuna and Krishna is easygoing and pleasant, a camaraderie that begins with quiet withdrawal from the other picnickers by the Yamuna river and cheerful conversation reminiscing over past events, and extends into a boisterous, almost childlike or ecstatic routing of the forest. Throughout the epic, the friendship of Arjuna and Krishna is so close that the two are often said to be aspects of one another, or even one and the same. . . . . Their closeness is brought out several times in the Khandava episode by the use of a dual phrase that recurs throughout the epic, calling them by the same name: "the two Krishnas." At the end of the episode (the burning of the forest), Krishna chooses eternal friendship with Arjuna as a boon from Indra (king of the gods in heaven). [Katz 1990, p. 83]

In the Khandava forest burning episode, an explicit reference is made to the fact that Arjuna and Krishna are the divine warrior/sage pair Nara/Narayana. When Indra is attempting to stop the burning of the forest, he is told by a voice: "You cannot defeat Krishna and Arjuna when they stand fast in war, Sakra, listen to my word! They are the two divinities Nara and Narayana, who are renowned in heaven. You yourself know well of their power and bravery. Unassailable, invincible in battle, these two ancient seers cannot be vanquished in any world" (*Mahabharata* 1, 219:15–17). "Nara" means man and Narayana is the name of Vishnu, the supreme godhead of Hinduism. Krishna, in the *Mahabharata*, is an incarnation of Vishnu, and has descended into the world in human form to uphold and protect *dharma* (righteousness). Krishna states in the *Gita*:

"For whenever there is a decrease in *dharma*, Arjuna, and a rise in *adharma*, then I send forth myself. For the protection of the good and the destruction of evil, for the purpose of the establishment of *dharma*, I am born from age to age. He who knows in truth this, my divine birth and actions, having relinquished his body, he goes not to rebirth but to me, Arjuna." [*Gita* 4:7–9]

In Vaishnavite Hinduism, Nara/Narayana expresses the relation of god in man and man in god and highlights the distinction between the phenomenal, psycho-physically conditioned self as opposed to the unconditioned nonphenomenal spiritual self (*purusha*/soul).

In the *Gita*, Krishna is Arjuna's charioteer. The Sanskrit word for charioteer is *suta*.

This role assumed by Krishna, because of the conventional cama-raderie between warrior and driver, provides the intimacy which makes exhortations possible and appropriate. Traditionally, the *suta* on the chariot of the warrior is witness to the warrior's triumphs and occasional lapses; in danger, he protects him. The triumphs of the warrior he celebrates in song, hence *suta* also means "bard"; the lapses, he condemns in private. [Van Buitenen 1980, p. 5]

The relations between Arjuna and Krishna in the epic not only form the foundations for the transference and transference distortions that occur in the *Gita* but also highlight the symmetry and asymmetry of the relations between Arjuna and Krishna. In the beginning of the *Gita*, there is a symmetrical relationship between them in the form of warrior and charioteer that is not conducive to the analytic process. We see Krishna, in Chapter 2, chastising Arjuna for refusing to fight:

"Whence came to you this weakness in this moment of crisis? It is ignoble, Arjuna, and neither leads to heaven nor brings glory. Yield not to such unmanliness, Arjuna. It does not befit you! Having relinquished this petty faintheartedness, stand up, Arjuna." [*Gita* 2:2–3]

Clearly, Krishna's stance is not analytic. In verses 9 and 10, asymmetry is established as the warrior/charioteer relation changes to a teacher/disciple relation. An analytic attitude is evident in the following verses:

Having so spoken to Krishna, and having said to Govinda, "I will not fight," Arjuna became silent. Then, Krishna, *as it were smiling,* spoke these words to him who was sinking into depression in the middle of the two armies. You grieve for those who are not to be grieved for, yet you speak words that sound like wisdom. The wise do not grieve for the dead or for the living. Never was there a time when I was not, nor you nor these rulers of men; and never hereafter shall there be a time when any of us will not be. [*Gita* 2:9–12, italics mine]

Krishna's smile is the beginning of the analytic process. The smile signifies both detachment from the situation at hand as well as empathy for the subject. As Loewald (1970) notes: "That the analytic relationship is an asymmetrical one, and that it has to be that if the analysis is to proceed, is unquestioned" (p. 48). The asymmetrical position continues in the *Gita* and reaches its zenith in Chapter 11, where it takes form as a relation between human analysand and divine analyst.

PSYCHOANALYTIC SETTING: THE BATTLEFIELD

In the original Sanskrit, the first stanza of the *Gita* reads: "*Dharmaksetre kuruksetre samaveta yuyutsavah mamakah pandavas caiva kim akurvata samjaya.*" The translation reads: "My sons and those of Pandu, what did they do, Samjaya, when eager to fight, they assembled on the field of the Kurus, the field of *dharma* (righteousness)?" (*Gita*, 1:1). As de Nicolás said in *Avatara* (1970), Arjuna's very human problem is identified in the first verse of the *Gita*. The "field of the Kurus" and "the field of *dharma*" are the same: "*Dharmaksetre kuruksetre.*" He tells us that Arjuna's crisis unfolds in the field of the Kurus—in the field of *dharma*. In Arjuna's mind it is not just the battle but his whole social and conceptual scheme, his whole life is at stake (de Nicolás, p. 179).

Kuruksetra is an actual place 100 miles north of Delhi, but for our purposes it is the battlefield where Krishna and Arjuna interact and engage in a dialogue, a sort of psychoanalysis. *Ksetre* means "in the field" or "on the field." It is significant that the *Gita* occurs in the battlefield, as *Kuruksetre* refers not only to the literal battlefield but also metaphorically to the intrapsychic and interpersonal battlefield. Freud (1940), in his *Outline of Psychoanalysis*, likened the analytic situation to a civil war:

> The ego is weakened by the internal conflict and we must go to its help. *The position is like that of a civil war which has to be decided by the assistance of an ally from the outside.* The analytic physician and the patient's weakened ego, basing themselves on the real external world, have to band themselves together into a party against the enemies, the instinctual demands of the id and conscientious demands of the superego. We form a pact with each other. The sick ego promises us the most complete candor—promises, that is, to put at our disposal all the material which its self-perception yields it; we assure the patient of the strictest discretion and place at his service our experience in interpreting material that has been influenced by the unconscious. Our knowledge is to make up for his ignorance and to give the ego back its mastery over lost provinces of his mental life. *This pact constitutes the analytic situation.* [p. 173, italics mine]

The *Gita* taking place in the middle of the battlefield is significant as the "middle" connotes neutral ground. It is in neutral space that Arjuna's interaction with Krishna occurs. I emphasize "interaction" because it is through the interaction in the neutral field, the analytic setting/space, that Arjuna's psychic development and reorganization as well as psychic transformation occurs. The dialogue between Arjuna and Krishna is not psychoanalysis in the conventional sense of the term. That is, Krishna (the analyst) does most of the talking while Arjuna (the analysand) does most of the listening. There are no interpretations of Arjuna's intrapsychic conflicts per se. Krishna's analytic function in the *Gita* is less as an interpreter of Arjuna's intrapsychic conflicts and more as an object that facilitates Arjuna's psychic development and maturation (see Winnicott 1971). Krishna's allowing Arjuna to use him as an object for his transformation is based on Arjuna's love and devotion for Krishna, not only in the psychoanalytic sense of a positive transference or transferential love, but, more importantly, by the Hindu notion of devotion called *bhakti*.

The *Gita* is psychoanalysis in that Krishna facilitates Arjuna's self-understanding by instructing him about the nature of his situation and his misapprehension about his reality and circumstance. The teachings form the philosophical core of the *Gita* and address, in part, Arjuna's identifications with his family and phenomenal self that lead to his crisis. These identifications constitute the "ego" or the experiential "I" of the psychic apparatus (*das Ich*) in psychoanalytic terminology. In the *Gita*, this ego is called *ahankara*, the ego function. Zimmer (1969), in his *Philosophies of India*, lucidly describes it:

Ahankara, the ego function, causes us to believe that we feel like acting, that we are suffering, etc.; whereas actually our real being, the *purusha*, is devoid of such modifications. *Ahankara* is the center and prime motivating force of "delusion." *Ahankara* is the misconception, conceit, supposition or belief that refers all objects and acts of consciousness to an "I" (*aham*). *Ahankara*—the making (*kara*) of the utterance "I" (*aham*)—accompanies all psychic processes, producing the misleading notion "I am hearing; I am seeing; I am rich and mighty; I am enjoying; I am about to suffer," etc., etc. It is thus the prime cause of the critical "wrong conception" that dogs all phenomenal experience; the idea, namely, that the life-monad (*purusha*) is implicated in, nay is identical with, the processes of living matter (*prakti*). One is continually appropriating to oneself, as a result of *ahankara*, everything that comes to pass in the realms of the physique and psyche, superimposing perpetually the false notion (and apparent experience) of a subject (an "I") of all the deeds and sorrows. [p. 319]

The *Gita* is also psychoanalysis in that Krishna analyzes (lysis = to cut) Arjuna's *ahankara* and shows him how and why it leads to unhappiness and misery. Krishna describes its structure, genesis, and interrelations with other parts of the "self" and shows Arjuna how to master and control it. The *Gita* is also psychoanalysis in the sense that Loewald (1970) conceptualizes psychoanalysis in "Psychoanalytic Theory and Psychoanalytic Process":

Psychoanalysis is an activity of the human mind which we as analysts exercise upon and in conjunction and cooperation with another person and his mental activity—whether we think in terms of "pure" psychoanalytic investigation or in terms of therapeutic process. [p. 54]

We become part and participant of and in the field as soon as we are present in our role as analysts. . . . For the purpose of study, we have to become an integral, though in certain ways detached, part of the "field of study." [p. 47]

When Arjuna asks for Krishna's help in the *Gita*, Krishna, by instructing and tutoring Arjuna, becomes Arjuna's analyst and part of the "analytic field." This analytic setting is Kuruksehtra, the battlefield; here, an existential encounter occurs between the human analysand, Arjuna, and the divine analyst, Krishna. In Chapter 13, Krishna says:

"This body, Arjuna, is called the field, and he who knows it, those who know, call the knower of the field. Know me, Arjuna, to be

the knower of the field in all fields; the knowledge of the field and
of the knower of the field: This I hold to be (real) knowledge."
[*Gita* 13:1–2]

ANALYTIC PROCESS IN THE *GITA*

By analytic process, I refer to the totality of the verbal, nonverbal,
and subject-object interactions that occur in the analytic setting. I
am following Etchegoyen (1991), who clearly articulates the difference between the analytic setting and process:

> When we begin to define the analytic situation as a relationship
> between two people who come together to carry out a particular
> task, we slide imperceptibly from the situation into the process. It
> could not be otherwise, because every task implies a development,
> an evolution in time, while the situation, if we are going to respect
> what the word tells us, is something that does not move. The
> difference between situation and process is basically, then, that the
> former has a spatial reference and the latter necessarily includes
> time. [pp. 488–489]

The *Gita*, as mentioned, occurs in eighteen chapters in the
form of a poetic dialogue between Krishna and Arjuna. These
eighteen chapters may be seen as eighteen analytic sessions that
constitute Arjuna's analysis. As in a sonata, there are three major
movements or phases in this analysis. The first is from Chapters 1
through 10, which outline Arjuna's crisis and Krishna's attempts at
resolving Arjuna's crisis. The second is Chapter 11, the pivotal
chapter in which Arjuna's transformation occurs. Chapters 12 to 18
constitute the continuation of Krishna's teaching, but now with a
difference. Insight has been gained in Chapter 11, and Chapters 12
to 18 may be seen as the consolidation phase of the analysis after
insight occurs. On another level, Chapters 1 to 10 comprise mainly
intellectual arguments, whereas Chapters 12 to 18 have a decidedly
more emotional and religious/devotional ambience to them.

The English word "to know" (knowledge) does not have the connotations and nuances that "knowing" has in other languages. In French, there are two words that refer to knowing: *savoir* and *connaitre*. *Savoir* is to know intellectually, as in a scholarly manner. *Connaitre* means to know intuitively, emotionally, or spiritually. This distinction between *savoir* and *connaitre* is useful in approaching Arjuna's level of self-understanding—that between intellectual knowledge and emotional knowledge. It is the latter that analysis endeavors to develop and foster in the patient.

The First Movement

The analysis begins when Arjuna asks for Krishna's help. Krishna's formal teaching begins in Chapter 2, when Krishna with a smile states that Arjuna should not grieve either for the living or the dead. Krishna states:

> "It is the contact with objects of the senses, Arjuna, that yield pleasure and pain, cold and heat. These conditions are not lasting. They come and go. Endure them, Arjuna. For he whom these do not disturb, the intelligent man who remains the same amidst pleasure and pain, he is fit for immortality. Of what-is-not, there is no coming to be; of what-is, there is no ceasing to be. The final truth of these is also known to those who see the truth. Know that that by which all this is pervaded, is indestructible; nothing can work the destruction of this which is imperishable. These bodies, it is said, come to an end. But they belong to an embodied one who is eternal, indestructible, immeasurable. Therefore fight, Arjuna. *Both he who considers this to be the slayer and he who considers this to be slain, fail to understand: this neither slays nor is slain.*" [*Gita* 2:14–19, italics mine]

Krishna goes on to explain the nature of the body and the soul that survives the body. He expounds the essentials teachings of Hindu philosophy and the three routes to salvation: *Karma Yoga* (disinterested action), *Bhakti Yoga* (devotion to a personal god), and *Jnana Yoga* (spiritual knowledge). This is summarized in Chapter 2 and amplified in detail in the subsequent chapters. I will not further consider Krishna's teachings and the content of the *Gita*, as that is not my intention nor the purpose of this chapter. What I focus on is the interaction between Krishna and Arjuna that constitutes the analytic process.

During Krishna's teaching, Arjuna asks many questions. The questions are reasonable enough, but from an analytic stance, they are resistances. In Chapter 3, Arjuna asks:

> "If to your mind understanding is superior to action, Krishna, then why, Krishna, do you enjoin me to the dreadful deed? You are bewildering my understanding with these apparently confused propositions. Therefore, tell me unequivocally the way by which I may gain what is good." [*Gita* 3:1–2]

Arjuna is not only asking a question but also seeking gratification from Krishna. He wants Krishna to tell him what to do and which path to take. Arjuna wants certainty, not ambivalence. While Krishna answers Arjuna's questions, he does not tell him which is the right path for him to take. That is Arjuna's decision. Krishna, as an analyst, is observing the analytic principle of abstinence, but only partially. I say only partially because he does gratify Arjuna's wishes to an extent by answering questions, but he does not say, "Do this." Krishna does say that Arjuna should fight. This prescription occurs in the beginning of the second chapter. Krishna's exhortations to Arjuna to fight in the battle become less and less frequent as the *Gita* progresses. In the first ten chapters, the discourse is heavily intellectual. Psychoanalytic techniques of abstinence and neutrality are partially observed. Anonymity is violated in the first ten chapters, but from an intellectual viewpoint. That is, Krishna tells Arjuna of his divinity as god but this is not revealed emotionally until the theophany in Chapter 11, where it is explicitly violated. The kind of violation of anonymity, in the first ten chapters, may be compared to an analyst telling a patient his personal theoretical stance but not what the analyst personally feels and does.

Chapter 10 is entitled the "Yoga of Manifestations." Arjuna asks Krishna: "Tell me at greater length of your self's power and manifestations, Krishna; For I am not *satiated listening to the nectar of your words*" (*Gita* 10:18, italics mine). Krishna says: "Come, I will tell you, Arjuna, my self's main glories. There is no end to the details" (*Gita* 10:19). Krishna proceeds to tell Arjuna how his self pervades all that exists. This is described in detail, and Arjuna delights in hearing Krishna's words. Once again, Arjuna is being gratified. In the last verse of the chapter, Krishna states: "But of what use is this detailed knowledge to you, Arjuna. I keep continually pervading this entire world with only one fraction of my self" (*Gita* 10:42). The point of this last stanza is that self-understanding is not coming to Arjuna, only voyeuristic (auditory) pleasure. It is significant that the discourse in the next chapter will not be through words and linguistic exchange, and the voyeurism is not pleasurable but frightening.

The Second Movement

The eleventh chapter is entitled "*Visvarupadarsanam*" ("Manifestation of the World Form") and is the pivotal chapter in the *Gita*. *Darsana* means view, vision, comprehension, and is derived from the root *drs*, which means to see, to contemplate, to comprehend. *Visva* means world and *rupa* means form; hence *Visvarupadarsanam*—comprehension of the world form. Arjuna, delighted by the words heard from Krishna in Chapter 10 and thinking he has comprehended Krishna's message, states:

"This delusion of mine has vanished, due to the words uttered, as a favor to me, speaking of the supreme secret called the self. For I have heard in detail from you, Krishna, of the arising and vanishing of beings, and also of your changeless greatness. As you say yourself to be, O Supreme Lord, so it is. I desire to see your form, O Supreme Vision. If you deem it capable of being seen by me, O Lord, then Krishna show to me your eternal self." [*Gita* 11:1–4]

Until now, the discourse has been in the realm of secondary process of words and linguistic exchange, which have aroused Arjuna's curiosity and gratified him. Self-understanding has been minimal. Krishna grants Arjuna's request:

"Behold, Arjuna, my forms, hundreds and thousands, divine, varied in color and shape. . . . Behold today the entire world of the moving and unmoving, standing in unity here in my body, Arjuna, and behold whatever else you want to see. But you cannot see me with this your own eye; I give you a divine eye: Behold my godly yoga." [*Gita* 11:5, 7, 8]

Krishna reveals his true divine self—the sensory modality is vision—and Arjuna's perception is no longer in the realm of the secondary process; it is primary process. Arjuna sees the entire universe in this vision. Frightened, he prostrates before Krishna and says:

"Tell me who you are with form so terrible; homage to you, Best of Gods, be merciful. I desire to understand you, the Primal One, for your manifestation is not intelligible to me. Krishna said: *Time am I, the world-destroyer, grown mature, engaged here in fetching back the worlds. Even without you, all the warriors standing over against you will cease to be. Therefore stand up, gain glory; having conquered enemies, enjoy a prosperous kingdom. By me they are already slain. Be you merely the occasion, Arjuna!*" [*Gita* 11:31–33, italics mine]

This is mystical and religious/spiritual experience. It is not the blissful experience of regression to narcissistic union with the primordial mother. One might argue that it is psychotic experience, but I think that misses the point. Arjuna now comprehends and, trembling, asks Krishna to return back to his human form. The manner in which he related to Krishna before the divine vision, his transference distortions, are made evident in verses 41-42:

"For whatever I said in rashness or negligence or affection, I have called you 'O Krishna,' 'O Yadava,' 'O Comrade,' having thought of you as my friend and being ignorant of this greatness of yours; For any disrespect done in jest while alone or with others, at meals or in bed or being seated or when at play, O Unshaken One, I beg forgiveness of you, O Boundless One." [*Gita* 11:41–42]

Arjuna's transformation/transmutation has occurred as a result of an interaction with Krishna in his divine form. A new object relationship (or a rediscovered one) has been formed between Krishna and Arjuna, and perhaps it is this new relationship, fashioned after prior object relations (that of Nara/Narayana or man/god), that leads to Arjuna's transformation. Loewald (1960), in "On the Therapeutic Action of Psychoanalysis," writes:

Beyond the issue of vested interest, I believe it to be necessary and timely to question the assumption, handed to us from the nineteenth century, that the scientific approach to the world and self represents a higher and more mature evolutionary stage of man than the religious way of life. But I cannot pursue this question here. I have said that the analyst, through the objective interpretation of transference distortions, increasingly becomes available to the patient as a new object. And this not primarily in the sense of an object not previously met, but the newness consists in the patient's rediscovery of the early paths of the development of object-relations leading to a new way of relating to objects and of being oneself. [p. 19–20]

Returning to the *Gita*:

"By my grace, and of my own self's power, this highest form was shown to you, Arjuna . . . do not tremble or be bewildered, having seen this so terrible form of mine. Free from fear and satisfied

mind, behold once again this other (human) form of mine." Having
spoken thus to Arjuna, Krishna revealed his own form again. The
great one, having become again the gracious form, comforted him
in his fear. [*Gita* 11:47, 49, 50]

The Third Movement

After Krishna's theophany in Chapter 11, the relation between
Arjuna and Krishna changes. Arjuna asks less questions, and when
he asks them, they are not "why" questions but "how" questions.
Arjuna has gained insight and wishes to understand more about
himself. Arjuna wishes to learn more about *bhakti* (devotion)
and the relation between *prakti* (the body/field) and *purusha*
(soul). Krishna has gone over these concepts in detail in the first
ten chapters, but they were intellectual abstractions to Arjuna at
that time. Now he wants emotional understanding. There are no
further exhortations to Krishna to reveal himself in one form
or another (i.e., transference gratifications). Arjuna's agenda has
changed after insight has been gained. He wants to consolidate this
insight, not question it. Antonio de Nicolás (1970) writes:

> In trying to understand the *Gita*, we have to bear in mind all the
> previous action the *Gita* has forced Arjuna to perform on his own
> view of the circumstance around him—and on himself. We have
> to bear in mind that Arjuna has touched his own emptiness
> (Chapter 11), the absolute bereavement of what he took to be the
> solid ground of his body-feelings, and that new lenses have been
> put before his eyes, new auditory devices have been put on his ears,
> and that for Arjuna, the world cannot be seen or heard in the same
> old way again. The very structure of Arjuna's meaning has changed
> forever. [p. 14]

Perhaps the most significant change for Arjuna is his new
relationship to Krishna—that between devotee and god. Chapter
12 is called "*Bhakti Yoga*" or "The Yoga of Devotion." *Bhakti*

means devotion or "love of god," not love of god in an abstract or intellectual sense but in a very personal, emotional manner. The emotional valence of *bhakti/bhakta* relation cannot be overstated; it is a very particular and uniquely Hindu form of emotional and religious sentiment. It is through *bhakti* that Arjuna's self-transformation has occurred. While Krishna argues that there are three paths to freedom and salvation (spiritual knowledge, selfless action and *bhakti*), he clearly suggests that *bhakti* is preferable to the other two methods.

> "Those, who fixing their minds on me, worship me with constant discipline and supreme faith, those I consider the most accomplished in yoga. But those who worship the imperishable and undefinable, the unmanifested, the omnipresent, and unthinkable, the immovable, the unchanging, the constant, who restrain their senses, are even-minded, who take delight in the welfare of every being, they also obtain me. The difficulty of those whose intellects are fixed on the unmanifested is much greater, for the goal of the unmanifested is painful for the embodied to attain. *But those who, intent on me, renounce all actions in me, worship me with complete discipline and meditate on me: Those whose thoughts are fixed on me, I become quickly their deliverer from the ocean of death and rebirth, Arjuna. Set your mind on me alone, make your understanding at home in me; you will dwell in me thereafter. Of this, there is no doubt.*" [*Gita* 12:2−8, italics mine]

Earlier, I commented on Krishna's facilitative role as an object that exacts Arjuna's transformation and suggested that Krishna takes on this role because of Arjuna's love and devotion to Krishna. Commenting on *bhakti*, Van Buitenen (1980) notes:

> Although as God he [Krishna] has all the lofty qualities that had already been ascribed to the supreme being, qualities that would have cut him off from all the consoling contact with the world, he has descended in the person of Krishna, a familiar hero in the *Mahabharata*, aloof from involvement in the war but nevertheless partisan, who has found a friend in Arjuna. In the narrative of the

epic this friendship antedates the revelation of Krishna's divine nature and his transfiguration, and this sequence is characteristic of *bhakti*. In *bhakti* there must be an extremely close, one-to-one relationship between god and each loyal follower, so that god can disclose his divinity gradually and to one at a time. [p. 27]

CONCLUSION

In the concluding chapter of the *Gita*, Krishna, with a true analytic attitude, states: "Thus the wisdom, more secret than any secret has been declared by me to you; having reflected fully on this, *do as you desire*" (*Gita* 18:63, italics mine). Arjuna says: "Destroyed is my delusion; by your grace, Krishna, I have gained remembrance. I take my stand firmly, with doubt dispelled; I will do your word" (*Gita* 18:73).

In the *Bhagavad Gita* something akin to a psychoanalytic situation and process occurs. Focusing on the process in the *Gita*, I have intentionally not explored the content or teachings of the *Gita*. This is because the *Gita*, as a religious text, contains assumptions that psychoanalysis does not admit—for instance, the existence of a soul that survives the body. The religious tenets of the *Gita* can certainly be approached in terms of man's need for an omnipotent father figure; Krishna's theophany can be viewed as a projection of narcissistic omnipotence, and the devotional mysticism of *bhakti* may be seen as a defense against infantile dependence and narcissistic regression to a primordial mother. While these are valid and useful ways to approach religion and religious sentiment, I think it would miss the point of the *Gita*.

NOTE

All the citations from the *Gita* have been taken from Antonio T. de Nicolás's translation of the *Gita*. They are in the form of the chapter followed by the verse. The reader may use this to refer to other translations of the *Gita*. I have taken some liberty to modify the citations by omitting the titles and names that are used to describe Krishna and Arjuna. Instead, I have used Krishna and Arjuna rather than the nicknames. These nicknames, while adding aesthetics to the text, can be confusing in translation and distract the reader from the meaning of the stanza.

REFERENCES

de Nicolás, A. T., trans. and ed. (1970). *Avatara*. New York: Nicolas-Hays.
———, trans. and intro. (1990). *The Bhagavad Gita*. York Beach, ME: Nicolas-Hays.
Etchegoyen, R.H. (1991). *The Fundamentals of Psychoanalytic Technique*. London: Karnac.
Freud, S. (1923). The ego and the id. *Standard Edition* 19:12–59.
——— (1940). An outline of psychoanalysis. *Standard Edition* 23:143–207.
Karve, I. (1991). *Yuganta: The End of an Epoch*. Hyderabad, India: Disha Books.
Katz, R. C. (1990). *Arjuna in the Mahabharata*. Delhi, India: Motilal Banarsidass.
Loewald, H. (1960). On the therapeutic action of psychoanalysis. *International Journal of Psycho-Analysis* 41:16–33.
——— (1970). Psychoanalytic theory and the psychoanalytic process. *Psychoanalytic Study of the Child* 25:45–68. New York: International Universities Press.
The Mahabharata. (1994). Trans. M. N. Dutt. Delhi, India: Parimal.
Van Buitenen, J. A. B. (1980). *The Bhagavad Gita in the Mahabharata*. Chicago: University of Chicago Press.
Winnicott, D. W. (1971). The use of an object and relating through identifications. In *Playing and Reality*, pp. 101–111. London: Routledge.
Zimmer, H. (1969). *The Philosophies of India*. Princeton, NJ: Princeton University Press.

7

GOD PLAYING PSYCHOANALYST: SOME LESSONS FROM THE *BHAGAVAD GITA:*

Discussion of Reddy's Chapter, "Psychoanalytic Reflections on the Sacred Hindu Text, the Bhagavad Gita"

Dwarkanath G. Rao, M. D.

Nothing in India is identifiable; the mere asking of a question
causes it to disappear or to merge into something else.

E. M. Forster, *A Passage to India*

When I was fresh from India, I once imagined what Indian
tradition might do with psychoanalytic insights. In my nostalgic
flight of fancy, every psychoanalytic idea was enshrined in a temple
of its own. The presiding deity of the temple of Oedipus was chief
among lesser shrines. The worshipful mingled with the scholarly, as
did the ascetic with the liberation seekers. Years passed into eons. In
some contemporaneous era, the temple of Oedipus became a house
of ritual. Prayers were chanted with exacting lilt and meter, magnificent austerities were performed, liturgy was set to deeply
intoned ragas, children played on the occasion of the Festival of
Oedipus which had become a government holiday, and gradually,
Oedipus the Sublime became Oedipus the Fabulous. The great
Indianization of Oedipus had been accomplished. No one any
longer remembered or dared to understand the fearful significance

of Oedipus. At this point my reverie ended. My irreverent feelings of that day disappeared and remained in a forgotten mind space. When I read Reddy's paper on the *Gita*, I felt similar trepidation. I readied myself for the tendency of Indian thought to resemble and seamlessly incorporate incompatible ideas.

What I found, at the outset, was a thoroughly readable account of the tragic battle of *The Mahabharata* and the protagonists of the *Gita*. Reddy had managed to write a concise yet fulsome and moving rendering of what is considered the living essence of Hindu imagination. His chapter allows a Westerner to grasp the essentials, and the psychoanalyst to grapple with the ideas contained within. It should be noted that Reddy's account is one of a few bearing on the psychological significance of Krishna's engagement with the Hamlet-like figure of Arjuna (see Neki [1973] for a wider discussion of the therapeutic goals of the guru–student relationship and the Krishna–Arjuna dialogue as paradigmatic).

I agree with the many parallels that Reddy draws between Krishna's efforts to help Arjuna and the psychoanalyst's striving to help an analysand. The idea of a dialogue with a knowledgeable friend when in crisis is in itself the archetypal psychoanalytic situation. Then we learn that there is a layered but not very obscure precipitant to the crisis in the *Gita*. It is the guilt- and grief-inducing deaths of father figures, who in turn represented the absent or failing father of Arjuna and his brothers. It also seems clear that were it not for divine intervention and assorted literary devices in *The Mahabharata*, fated acts would, to the trained eye, become unconscious intentions. Similarly, parricidal and fratricidal wishes, from an analytic point of view, would reveal themselves only too easily in this dense narrative with a cast of thousands. Reddy correctly emphasizes many other analytically plausible ideas, often by authors presumably unversed in psychoanalysis, as when he quotes Katz who writes of the two Krishnas representing mental conflict in one person. Krishna and Arjuna are working and struggling as one individual, as in real life an analyst and analysand often do in empathically attuned moments.

Consider next the role of Krishna as charioteer. By virtue of a felicitous choice of this story from the literally hundreds available within the story of *The Mahabharata*, and through a singular brilliance of psychological insight, the creators of the *Gita's* metaphoric dyad of charioteer and warrior appear to have had psychoanalysis in mind. The word "chariot" not only conveys the familiar concept of analysis as a journey or a vehicle, but captures the common transference view of the analyst as driver or captain; the idea of the analysand being the impatient or passive passenger, as Arjuna often is, is not far behind. As in an analysis, the relationship between the charioteer Krishna and the warrior Arjuna begins as a "real" relationship normal for a time of war. In time, as Arjuna's vulnerability and suffering become clear, Krishna the worldly charioteer becomes masterly expositor of the meaning of the universe. Paradoxes familiar to the analyst are highlighted in the complex relationship between Arjuna and Krishna. Is warrior the master and charioteer the servant? Yes, but on a battlefield the warrior is at the mercy of the charioteer's skills. On other levels, psychoanalytic imagination provides a range of possible meanings. For example, Freud compared instincts to mythical beasts, and the ego to a horseman. Krishna, in this sense, can be compared to the ego and Arjuna to the id.

Overall, Reddy's chapter convincingly portrays the dialogue of the *Gita* as providing ancient confirmation of our modern imagination. *The Mahabharata*, thought to be composed between 400 BC and AD 400, is the result of contributions by numerous writers and storytellers. The *Gita* is likely the result of efforts to include religious and cultural values extant around the first century AD (Miller 1986, p. 3). In this historical context, the *Gita* is as much a sociocultural document as it is a philosophical one. The Krishna-Arjuna relationship can then be assumed to be based on ancient human conflict, as universal then as it is now.

Reddy next suggests a reading of the *Gita* as three movements or phases and compares it to phases of an analysis. He likens the first ten chapters of the *Gita* to the questions and intellectual preoccu-

pations of the beginning of an analysis. When words fail to gratify
or be personally meaningful, Arjuna asks for more. In Chapter 11,
Reddy's phase two, Krishna in his reply reveals himself as primordial creator and destroyer, terrifying and phantasmagoric. He provides Arjuna existential understanding through a theophany. The
third phase follows in which Arjuna seeks to consolidate his
newfound insights about life and death. Krishna expounds on a
topic revered in India—the path of *bhakti*, or devotion, as superior
to other paths to transcendental insight. Krishna goes on to elaborate on how a life can be lived with discipline and duty, the twin
truths embedded in the concept of *dharma*. Nonattachment to one's
actions, he says, is the method by which one can take true action.

The reader and listener is challenged at this point to search for
meaning outside the parameters of ordinary reality. But life and
death are not rational. Grief and pain are not easily explained.
Disorder in the ordered world is perplexing. Manifest nature is
fantastical, with and without purpose, depending on whether one
has the short or the long view. Paradoxes abound, tantalizing and
confusing Arjuna. Rationality takes a back seat as the allure of a new
mind-set slowly seeps in. How can a person be dedicated and
nonattached? Arjuna asks. The stakes are fast becoming higher than
can be accommodated within the framework of psychoanalysis. In
the end, neurosis in the *Gita* is cured by revelatory insight into
man's relation with a creator, vast and unimaginable except through
a human manifestation. Krishna is not content with words; neither
is Arjuna. The model moment of transmuting interpretation,
according to the *Gita*, is achieved by conviction through transcendental insight.

I am persuaded that Reddy here is astute and original in his
efforts to bring together the transcendental and mundane realms. I
wonder, however, if his parallelism can be taken further from the
point of view of clinical analysis, especially phases two and three.
Phase one of the *Gita* seems to coincide with the opening phase of
a great many analyses. They are marked by intellectual preoccupations and defenses against the emergence of regressive desires.

Arjuna's naive questioning, for example, certainly dominates this phase. Phase two in the *Gita*, the *Visvarupadarshana* or vision of cosmic form, seems to represent, from a psychoanalytic perspective, a clear parallel to the power and tumult induced by transference awareness.

Here, the power of the *Gita*'s soaring words to uplift and give hope makes me pause as I revise its meaning into possible psychological reductionism. Thoreau, for example, said, "In the morning I bathe my intellect in the stupendous and cosmogonal philosophy of the *Bhagavad-gita*, in comparison with which our modern world and its literature seem puny and trivial." Emerson, similarly: "I owed a magnificent day to the *Bhagavad-gita*. It was the first of books; it was as if an empire spoke to us, nothing small or unworthy, but large, serene, consistent, the voice of an old intelligence which in another age and climate had pondered and thus disposed of the same questions which exercise us."

My main concern here is to attempt an understanding of the *Gita* as disguised psychological discourse, replete with its own points of reference, with correspondences in psychoanalysis. In verse after verse, Krishna is at once sublimely metaphysical, lovingly compassionate, or terrifyingly dangerous. The nearest mundane parallel is the child looking up at a parent. One wonders if the cosmic vision of Krishna can be understood as the terrifying, omnipotent, omniscient parent of vulnerable childhood:

Krishna describes his divine self (Miller 1986, p. 85), as limitless in power and knowledge and as the essence of all of life:

"I am the heat that withholds
and sends down the rains;
I am immortality and death;
both being and nonbeing am I . . .

I am the rite, the sacrifice,
the libation for the dead, the healing herb,
the sacred hymn, the clarified butter,
the fire, the oblation . . .

Dwelling compassionately
   deep in the self,
   I dispel darkness born of ignorance
   with the radiant light of knowledge." [p. 90]

Contrast this with the following passage, where parental images predominate. Note the loving and sheltering parental metaphors:

"I am the universal father,
mother, granter of all, grandfather,
object of knowledge, purifier,
holy syllable OM, threefold sacred lore.

I am the way, sustainer, lord,
witness, shelter, refuge, friend,
source, dissolution, stability,
treasure, and unchanging seed." [p. 85]

In the following stanzas, as Krishna speaks to a trembling Arjuna (p. 93), note the richness of phallic metaphor, accompanied by allusions to mastery of death:

"Among horses, know me as the immortal stallion
born from the sea of elixir;
among elephants, the divine king's mount;
among men, the king.

I am the thunderbolt among weapons,
among cattle, the magical wish-granting cow;
I am the procreative god of love,
the king of the snakes.

I am the endless cosmic serpent,
the lord of all sea creatures;
I am chief of the ancestral fathers;
of restraints, I am death. . . .

I am the beginning, the middle,
and the end of creations, Arjuna;
of sciences, I am the science of the self;
I am the dispute of orators.

I am the vowel *a* of the syllabary,
the pairing of words in a compound;
I am indestructible time,
the creator facing everywhere at once."

At the end of the chapter, Krishna shows with a return of parental concern:

"What use is so much knowledge
to you, Arjuna?
I stand sustaining this entire world
with a fragment of my being." [p. 95]

Even a cursory look at the selected stanzas reveals familiar psychoanalytic themes, of childhood awe of adults, of domination by the father through phallic display, of omniscience, and of sheltering parents.

Neki (1979) suggests that "awe" is a necessary garb for an Indian psychotherapist, suggesting that idealization of adults is so intrinsic to Indians that every therapist must begin with the proper kind of "awe-worthiness." Neki also believes in two kinds of autonomy, that of the "empirical ego" and that of the "transcendental ego" (p. 144). The empirical ego makes the person "more assertive" while the transcendental ego makes the person rise above its "small self." Following the tradition of the *Gita*, Neki feels that the autonomy of the transcendental ego is "objective" and leads to elimination of conflicts.

Kakar (1982), writing about the parental styles of gurus in India, describes a scene in which Mataji, a female "mother" guru, when criticized, admonishes and even threatens her audience with a curse of dire illness. She then follows this with sweet, calming words. "Oh, children," she says, "I am your mother. Give up all thought, only give me your faith and I'll take you across the waters. Who else will or can do that for you? Only I, your mother." At this point, "The eyes of the disciples in the audience shine with pleasure and excitement. They are a part of her, not vulnerable to feelings of helplessness but sharing the omnipotence of someone who appears fully capable of repulsing every threat. In identifying with Mataji, they have incorporated a part of someone who is supremely self-confident and self-contained, utterly free from the human needs and social restrictions that shackle the rest of us" (p. 212).

Mataji's imprecations and the loving reaction from her audience in modern-day India can be seen as vestiges of the *Gita* tradition, a view that will be decried or applauded, depending on how one sees the *Gita* and on how one sees Mataji. Kakar's own view is that there is a range of parenting "styles" in Indian gurus, all eliciting expectable reactions of regression in the audience. Gullible patrons, he implies, fall prey to the vice-like grip of the guru-parent.

What else might we include in our understanding of the display of the cosmic form of Krishna and the reactions of Arjuna? I favor the view that this "phase" of the *Gita* gloriously depicts the awe of the child before the adult. Terror, admiration, weakness, envy, and identification commingle in the regressed Arjuna. These moments in the *Gita* also appear as dream-like images filled with fear and significance. In this context, the second phase that Reddy describes is consonant with transferences, primarily of powerful and omniscient parents, with a surfeit of visual imagery, sensory overload, and barely functioning secondary process. As the one Krishna becomes the manifold, transference possibilities force themselves onto Arjuna with a hallucinatory intensity and clarity. In his anxiety, Arjuna swoons, nearly losing his own identity, until Krishna reverts to his ordinary form, a largely neutral figure from his everyday life. The analytic trajectory I see most clearly here is that of the analysand going from neutral or benign transference to a roiling, magical, and terrifying one, and ultimately back to an experience of transference that heals by insight.

In the third and final psychological phase, according to Reddy, Arjuna no longer needs or wants a pyrotechnic display of Krishna's powers. He craves emotional understanding. Gone are his metaphysical questions. He needs no proof by argument. He is a man seeking solace and finding hope in Krishna's teachings. Krishna describes the many ways of reaching God, or reaching resolution, from intellectual searching to moral action and finally to *bhakti*. The devotional mode of *bhakti* advocated so tenderly and emphatically by Krishna constitutes the thrilling conclusion of the *Gita*. *Bhakti* derives from the word for joy, and for even an unschooled Indian, instantly conjures up images of selfless and often desperate love. As in Sufi and other traditions, this devotional love is a transforming event that allows full democratic access to God. In the *bhakti* tradition, no barriers of knowledge, station, gender, or prior karma stand in the way of the transmuting power of *bhakti*. Krishna teaches Arjuna that this is the easiest way to transcendental peace, offering himself as the object of Arjuna's devotional love.

No analyst can be unmoved by or rest without inquiring into the nature of this love and its relation to the analytic process. The sort of love Krishna advocates in the name of clarity and knowledge, most analysts would fiercely analyze, for fear of fostering unethical and dangerous dependence. "Krishna-love," because it requires relinquishing the thinking mind on numerous metaphysical grounds, appears dangerous and misguided to the most skilled analyst. Loving surrender is the sine qua non of insight through the path of *bhakti*.

For the analyst looking for analytic meaning in loving surrender, however, the clue lies in the concept of therapeutic regression. A consciously motivated surrender to one's feelings of love, requited and denied, in the analysand is the beginning of healing and curative therapeutic experience. The trajectory from phase two, then, of ignited transferences and fantasy projections, can be said to lead to phase three, in which the analysand allows the emergence of deeply repressed affects. Only in this state of openness is transference love most easily traceable to a personal unresolved past. Tenderness and humility replace fear, rage, and dejection. Awareness increases of the preciousness of time and life itself. Libidinal investment of objects becomes easier, life becomes loving. Tolerance of imperfection and innocence is possible. Basic trust returns or is renewed. The crucible of change is sufficiently hot to melt resistances, one might say, in a *bhakti*-like openness to tolerating and experiencing affects, the result of everyday analytic work.

Reddy also raises the question of neutrality, anonymity, and enactment in Krishna's attitude toward Arjuna. He concludes that Krishna is inconsistent and unpredictable, but overall, like an enlightened contemporary analyst, puts the process of change and growth above rules and interdictions. I think Reddy touches here on matters of profound interest to the contemporary analyst. Krishna is neutral only until it becomes obvious that passionate and personal advocacy is necessary. He moves freely from the cosmic anonymity of an impersonal God to the secure fixity of a human friend, an attribute much adored by the Hindu reader. This is not unlike the relief experienced by analysands who understand the ordinariness of their analyst after a transference is resolved. As supervisors for years have taught the struggling student of analysis that neutrality refers to dispassion toward the conflict, not toward the analysand, so too does Krishna seem to move from the role of dispassionate seer to indefatigable booster.

With regard to enactment, there appear to be great philosophical and moral struggles in the *Gita*, to understand the related concept of action. Numerous attempts are made by both Krishna and Arjuna to understand the meaning of action, its role in human and moral life, its ties to Dharma or destined duty, and of course, the meaning of the celebrated concept of karmic reward or reaction, as inevitable as psychic determinism. Krishna takes on the burden of elucidating a teaching emblematic of the *Gita*, and of Hinduism in general—the concept of *nishkamakarma*, action without attachment to the rewards of action (literally, pleasureless action). To the analyst this appears to be an idealized, if not caricatured, view of dispassionate action. Such action is impossible from the analyst's pleasure principle point of view without serious accompanying psychopathology. Moreover, this attitude is asked of both guru and student.

These harsh and paradoxical demands of the *Gita* perhaps represent theoretical extremes of what is otherwise acceptable in analysis: for example, neutrality in *Gita* terms might mean action that does not hanker after pleasure; certainly it is not for pleasure alone. Our theory says pleasure is ubiquitous, however, and therefore neutrality can never be total. Moreover, neutrality, even if it were possible to take to extremes, would harm what is otherwise a useful distance from conflict. A conundrum confronts us here. The *Gita*, while advocating action without attachment to the results of the action, never proscribes pleasure. Indeed, it is implied that nonattachment somehow brings about a surfeit of pleasure. It is a view that is hard to reconcile without a fuller consideration of what is meant by pleasure in the *Gita*, and what is meant by nonattachment. While beyond the scope of this discussion, it can be said that nonattachment is not detachment. In the *Gita*, the concept of knowledge, discipline, and self-understanding are intimately related to the idea of mastery over the senses, the goal of which is to unshackle oneself from sense-borne reality and reach transcendental reality. This causes sense-borne pleasures to become unnecessary and be replaced by a transcendental pleasure principle. Thus the *Gita* posits two kinds of pleasure/joy.

Conversely, in analysis, where there exists one conceptual reservoir of pleasure, the concept of neutrality was intended to control unusually personalized responsiveness. Analytic discipline, in both analyst and analysand, while commonly practiced with great skill and patience, is usually taken for granted, and has not been studied deeply. Free association, for example, is commonly noted to be anything but free, but the idea of disciplined association is rarely studied; when it is, rarely is the concept of discipline taken up except as a superego demand. (See Kern [1995], however, for the clinical efficacy of the idea of "focused association.") Similarly ignored, for the most part, are related processes of attention and concentration. The conundrum in analysis is how full-tilt engagement with the analysand is possible while being objective, much less neutral. A last note of comparison between the *Gita* and analysis: both stress the idea of containing the work of war and the work of analysis, in a field demarcated by space, time, and housekeeping rules, a virtual *Dharmakshetra* (or theater of righteousness).

In the foregoing, I have often contrasted the psychoanalytic against the transcendental, giving the impression that the transcendental theory of cure is easily dismissible. On the contrary, I believe this discussion leads us to the borderland between cure through psychoanalysis and cure through transcendence. I mean by "transcendence" not mystical and religious transport to escape pain, but understanding of distal as opposed to proximal causes of suffering. Psychoanalysis deals with proximal causes, that is, cause and effect are linear and find bedrock in childhood experience. Existential questions to the analyst at work are rendered comprehensible only within the points of reference of clinical analysis. In fact, as clinicians, we might say that we are trained to turn every thought and act into psychoanalytic data. I believe it is theoretically possible, however, to alleviate anxiety through understanding of existential dilemmas. Obtaining a personal meaning of death for some people at a certain stage of life is key to achieving calmness, for example. However, as analysts, we are naturally disbelieving of understanding and wary of relief. But I do not think this cautiousness comes from fear of existential conundrums alone. I think it comes from our lack of knowledge of the connections between existential and other kinds of fears. There is no taxonomy of fear to distinguish a fear of oedipal annihilation from a fear of dying alone. We do not have as yet a psychobiology of existentialism, nor do we have a psychoanalysis of the quest for meaning.

It is time for a confession. Writing this, I discover that I have had to struggle to stay scientifically minded and objective. I find myself lapsing into my Indian past and finding surprising nourishment in the process. This experience leads me to offer comments on the special place the *Gita* holds in the cultural and personal space of many Indians. The specifics of the culture-bound experience of the *Gita* are an important way to understand its intellectual and poetic sway over millions. It is also a way to understand what may be its limited emotional applicability in other cultures.

As is well known, personal and cultural myth coincide in the personality of the hero (Arlow 1982). Each culture finds a hero capable of bearing and overcoming the special burdens of the culture. In Indian culture, Krishna is among many cultural heroes who do double duty. He is divine and mortal at the same time. The Indian, brought up on a steady, if not easily digestible, childhood diet of myths and stories lovingly told, usually arrives at the *Gita* feeling an old and affectionate kinship with Krishna.

This God of terrible mien, able to hold the universe in a strand of his hair, we know to be a lovable, wicked little child who tricked mothers, milkmaids, and friends, none of whom could bear to punish the adorable prankster. We know of grandmothers who shed tears as they spoke of Krishna's antics, or his mother's boundless love for him. We have thrilled to movie scenes of Krishna slaying Puthini, the demon-goddess, by sucking life out of her breast. We have seen Krishna worshiped as a crawling infant, and children wishing they could play with Krishna as with a doll. For the musically inclined, hymns of praise and wonder filled the air. The scholarly found much to preoccupy themselves. As we grew older, we enjoyed the divine dalliance of Krishna, the cowherd with his beloved Radha. We marveled at his sexual prowess as the dark and bewitching consort of thousands of ecstatic girls.

Imagine then, if you will, Krishna as an Indian Dennis the Menace rolled into John Lennon, joining with a rather meditative Hugh Hefner. By the time we came to the *Gita*, Krishna was immortalized and embedded in our souls, believers and nonbelievers alike. In fact, popular emendations to *The Mahabharata* even depicted Krishna as an unethical meddler who brought about a dishonorable death of Duryodhana, the evil king defeated by Arjuna and his brothers. Nandy (1995) writes: "In the Indian epics, as in most pagan worldviews, no one is perfect, not even the gods. Nor is any one evil either; everyone is both flawed and has redeeming features. If there is a touch of the amoral politician in Krishna, there is also a touch of the courageous but misguided warrior in Duryodhana" (pp. 53–54).

I read the *Gita* as a middle-class Indian youth in an English translation. I was transfixed by the power and audacity of its poetic imaginings. Against my better judgment, I felt elation and sublimity. Existential questions seemed to disappear in the flood of images of absolute certainty. I later heard the *Gita* chanted in Sanskrit, and marveled at the luminous intonation. The tone by itself bespoke and induced a resonant certainty in the listener. I went on to conclude that I was Westernized, impressionable, idealistic, and looking for indigenous examples of heroism. Whatever else I was looking for, I discovered how personal immersion in a shared communal fantasy is central to an understanding of the idea of Krishna.

O'Flaherty (1988), in speaking of the range of Western attitudes toward myth, applies the following classification: the "unmythologized" person is unequivocally disinclined to myth, the "mythologized" person is religious in a traditional way, the "demythologized" person is usually a professional rationalist, and last the "remythologized" person "reacts to secular humanism" and is hungering for a return to naïveté (p. 120). She believes the last group is most open and vulnerable to the communal experience of myth. She emphasizes, by contrast, that in Hindu literature, myth and life are self-consciously intertwined. She writes:

> The use of aesthetic experience in salvation was the subject of much discussion in classical Indian philosophy. By seeing, and therefore participating in, the enactment of the myth of Krishna, one was led

unconsciously into the proper stance of the devotee. Moreover, the viewer was not merely inspired to decide what role in the cosmic drama he or she wished to play (mother, lover, brother, or friend of Krishna); one was inspired to discover what role one *was* playing, had been playing all along, without knowing it. Alf Hiltebitel has beautifully described the way that the real world gradually absorbs the stage in Indian religious performances: "The nightlong dramas, acted out on a small patch of ground beneath the petromax lanterns, are finally unravelled at dawn on a stage that grows with the morning light to include first the surrounding outlines of village trees and buildings and then, in effect, the familiar world of the day." [p.122, italics in original]

There is a difference between a myth that is lived and a myth that is ossified. The lived myth (Arlow, personal communication, 1985) is replete with ritual and observance, alive with the power to exalt and share communal fantasies. Krishna in India is thus a living and lived myth. The closest such experience in the West would be the Hare Krishna movement. Hare Krishna writings were marked by fundamentalist Vaishnavism (Krishna is an Avatar of Vishnu, the Protector, one of the triumvirate of Hindu gods). Krishna's life and adventures were taken literally, and a life of devotion was prescribed by leaders. New Vrindavan, their shining temple in West Virginia, flourished until the defrocking of the leaders of the movement. It was perhaps the first time outside India that groups of middle- and upper-class Americans renounced their every possession and lived, dressed, and ate as Krishna Bhaktas of ancient days, spending their days in Krishna "consciousness."

In conclusion, Reddy's chapter provides convincing evidence that the *Gita* is a vast canvas that offers up layers of meaning for the interested analyst. Psychoanalysis can benefit from a closer study of the manifest and latent content of the text of the *Gita*. Studies from a psychoanalytic perspective on the historical Arjuna and Krishna are overdue, despite the usual caveats about psychobiography, especially about mythic figures. As analysts we will not be surprised at finding a range of omissions and commissions in the described life of these two. Even a cursory examination of Arjuna's described life of fatherlessness and his often tormented relationships with his warring cousins suggests that these are rich lodes for an analytic miner.

The *Gita*, while shedding light on the powerful effect of milieu on the expectations of the analysand and analyst, invites further study of this important dimension of analysis. While acceptance of cultural relativism has become mainstream, shared existential expectations remain shadowy in the consulting room. Termination is perhaps a time when such concerns consistently surface, and might allow us to more carefully examine bedrock values and beliefs in the analyst at work, and their effects on the effectiveness of analysis.

Additional subjects that Reddy's chapter suggest for future study include what may be called "guru" transferences, cults domestic and foreign, free association and its relation to meditation practices, and the psychology of Indian avatars. The *Gita* prevails as an exotic book of healing whose study is worthwhile, and likely to unearth psychoanalytic truths in unexpected places, and at the same time enliven our own clinical tradition by challenging the existential limits we set on our basic assumptions.

REFERENCES

Arlow, J. A. (1982). Scientific cosmogony, mythology, and immortality. *Psychoanalytic Quarterly* 51:177–195.

Kakar, S. (1982). *Shamans, Mystics and Doctors. A Psychological Inquiry into India and Its Healing Traditions*. Boston: Beacon.

Kern, J. W. (1995). On focused association and analytic surface: resolving stalemate. *Journal of the American Psychoanalytic Association* 43:393–422.

Miller, B. S. trans. (1986). *The Bhagavad-Gita. Krishna's Counsel in Time of War*. New York: Bantam.

Nandy, A. (1995). *The Savage Freud. and Other Essays on Possible and Retrievable Selves*. Princeton, NJ: Princeton University Press.

Neki, J. S. (1973). *Guru-chela* relationship: the possibility of a therapeutic paradigm. *American Journal of Orthopsychiatry* 43:755–766.

——— (1979). Panel discussion. In *Psychotherapeutic Processes* (Proceedings of seminar held at the National Institute of Mental Health and Neuro-Sciences, Bangalore, India), pp. 142–143. Bangalore: National Institute of Mental Health and Neuro Sciences.

O'Flaherty, W. D. (1988). *Other People's Myth*. New York: Macmillan.

8

THREE ARCHAIC CONTRIBUTIONS TO THE RELIGIOUS INSTINCT: AWE, MYSTICISM, AND APOCALYPSE

Mortimer Ostow, M. D.

Of course there is no religious instinct. I use the term as a metaphor for the almost universal readiness of individuals to cohere into social units in which all participate in cultic practices and shared beliefs in a supernatural entity with parent-like functions. The traditional psychoanalytic explanation of this tendency and the accompanying beliefs is based on the pattern of the Oedipus complex and has taken us only so far. The religious enterprise is clearly far more intricate than that, and the Oedipus complex is no more powerful an explanation of the complexities of religious thought and behavior than it is of the complexities of mental illness.

Religious behavior and thought seem to possess both primary and universal components and secondary and more diverse components. The primary components should be sought in the psychobiology of the human organism. The secondary components can best be understood in terms of local cultural, environmental, and historical differences.

This chapter discusses three of the many primary universals or perhaps determinants of the religious "instinct," and describes their psychodynamics, their neuroscience background, and how they develop. I address these determinants from within the Jewish religious tradition since that is the only one in which I have any competence, as an informed amateur, but I believe that with respect to these archaic mechanisms, the various religions resemble each other more closely than they do with respect to more derivative issues.

I place awe, mysticism, and apocalypse in a specific sequence—the sequence in which they appear at the inception of the prophecies of the three major prophets of Israel, and at least in some truncated form in the biographical writings of many of those individuals who claim religious authority on the basis of divine inspiration. The most complete statement comes in the first three chapters of the book of Ezekiel. These three elements are given different emphases in each of the variant accounts. In a paper that I consider inspired though widely unappreciated, Jacob A. Arlow (1951) called attention to the similarity among the opening chapters of each of the three major prophets. He spoke of the experience as the consecration of the prophet and pointed out in each case that the procedure involved is identification with the superego by incorporation of the divinity through one of the body orifices. Arlow also spoke of awe and apocalypse.

[handwritten margin note: i.e., ident. ⸺ an aspect of the self]

AWE

The *Oxford English Dictionary* (OED) defines awe: I. As a subjective emotion;

1. Immediate and active fear; terror, dread (obsolete).

2. From its use in reference to the Divine Being this passes gradually into: Dread mingled with veneration, reverential or respectful fear; the attitude of a mind subdued to profound

reverence in the presence of supreme authority, moral greatness or sublimity, or mysterious sacredness.

3. The feeling of solemn and reverential wonder, tinged with latent fear, inspired by what is terribly sublime and majestic in nature, e.g., thunder, a storm at sea. [pp. 593–594]

Note here the elements of fear, wonder, and the almost implicit association with a religious feeling. The word *Numen* is defined as "a presiding deity or spirit" and numinous as "indicating the presence of a divinity, spiritual, and awe inspiring." Rudolf Otto spoke of a *mysterium tremendum*, the shivering mystery.

Awe is not an experience that is frequently encountered in clinical practice, although almost everyone can recall experiences of awe. These experiences are favored by exposure to structures whose size is almost incommensurate with human dimensions, so large perhaps that they cannot be included within a normal visual field at a reasonable distance. These are usually natural formations such as mountains, bodies of water, or, on a smaller scale, buildings such as great cathedrals. The cathedrals seem to have been built in such a way as to inspire awe. Sometimes one experiences awe in the presence of a person of prodigious accomplishment, and in the presence of enormous masses of people.

Phyllis Greenacre (1956) wrote three essays on awe based upon literary accounts and upon clinical experience. It was her impression that the experience of awe is not reported before age 4 or 5. However, in her accounts she does not clearly distinguish between awe and mysticism, our next subject. She suggests that the child experiences awe first when exposed to the sight of the naked body of the parent, especially the father's erect penis.

Can we relate awe to physiologic function? Although the temporal lobe is not a homogeneous structure, and the specific functions of its individual structural components are only now being discovered, nevertheless clinical experience permits us to make some guesses about the relation of some clinical phenomena to the anatomy of the brain.

Temporal lobe seizures may include experiences of illusion. Among these, illusions of size, distance, and loudness are fairly common. Since awe is generally associated with preternaturally strong perceptual experiences, we may wonder whether the evocation of awe involves the mechanisms of perceptual regulation. Presumably in the presence of extreme dimensional variance, the discrepancy in size or intensity or loudness between a percept and normal human dimensions may be sufficient to create the affect state that we call awe.

Wilder Penfield and Herbert Jasper, in their magisterial work, *Epilepsy and the Functional Anatomy of the Human Brain* (1954), record the mental productions of epileptic patients whose brains were stimulated during surgery. One patient, during such stimulation of the right temporal region, stated that he was dead, that he was in the House of the Lord, and that he saw saints who were both violet and blue. He repeated a prayer over and over and subsequently recalled having had this impression and interpreted it as a dream that he was in heaven. He had been said by his father to be given to religious and mystical thinking. Another patient during her seizures would dream that she was in church or in a convent and hearing a song. These scattered observations hardly constitute proof that the sensation of awe is generated within the temporal lobe, but they do encourage us to look further.

Gloor and associates (1982) report responses to stimulation of several points of the right temporal lobe of a patient with temporal lobe epilepsy. Among the responses were expressions of fear associated with water, mostly a fear of being pushed into or falling into water. One could wonder whether the allusion is to what has been called the "oceanic feeling."

On the other hand, Bear and Fedio (1977) have described interictal behavior in temporal lobe epilepsy. From reports of a number of investigators, they have put together a list of eighteen qualities that were said to have been observed more often as personality characteristics of patients with temporal lobe epilepsy. Among these eighteen, one finds: "*religiosity*, which is defined as holding deep religious beliefs, often idiosyncratic, multiple conversions, mystical states; *philosophical interests*, defined as nascent metaphysical or moral speculations, cosmological theories; and *dependence*, positively defined as cosmic helplessness, at the hands of fate, protestations of helplessness" (p. 458). I associate awe with religious feeling in general and I take these reports to suggest that awe might be associated with temporal lobe function.

Let me add another neuroscientific consideration, actually a hypothesis rather than an established fact. It does seem to be true that memories are laid down categorically. That means that memory images that fall into the same category are stored in close proximity to each other, and distant from memories that fall into other categories. For example, Squire and Kandel (1999) cite work to the effect that images of living creatures are stored in locations other than those that hold the images of inanimate instruments. Also George and colleagues (1999) have established that images of faces that are familiar are recognized as such at a point in the fusiform gyrus, while faces that are unfamiliar are recognized as faces in locations slightly posterior to that.

I suggest that when categorical boundaries are crossed, the crossing is regularly accompanied by the appearance of a specific affect. Consider for example Freud's description of his feelings when he visited the Acropolis for the first time. Let us assume that images that are conveyed to us indirectly, that is by verbal accounts, written or heard, or even by photographs or drawings, are stored in a place other than where the images created by immediate perception are stored. Then when one actually perceives the Acropolis directly and recognizes it as something that was hitherto known indirectly, the boundary crossing creates the special affective sensation that Freud described.

I had a similar experience only recently. Someone gave me a gift, a slim volume for which he had had a special slipcase prepared. He had known of my interest in Freud's thoughts about religion, and so I was not surprised when it turned out that the book was *Moses and Monotheism*. Since I already had several copies, I was grateful for the gift but not impressed. However, as I removed the book from its case, I came upon a flyer advertising this particular edition and pointing out that it was printed as the first edition of *Moses and Monotheism* published in any language. I realized for the first time that the book had initially been published in English rather than German, because Freud was living in London at the time. That was a little more impressive. When I opened the cover and looked at the flyleaf, before I was able to appreciate cognitively what I found there, I felt a sudden brief thrill. Only a fraction of a second later did I realize the reason for the thrill, namely, that I saw an inscription to Wilfred Trotter penned by Sigmund Freud himself. Now if that inscription had been printed rather than written, I would not have reacted as intensely or in the same way. But here again, there was a direct personal experience of something that had hitherto remained in my mind as historical, almost legendary. It was the crossing of the boundary between the immediate and the historical that created the momentary thrill.

To get back to the subject of awe, Squire and Kandel (1999) report that memories are categorized by size. Specifically, they distinguish memories of inanimate and small objects from images of large objects and living creatures. Category-specific knowledge of the former is impaired by damage to the left frontal or temporal parietal region, and of the latter, by damage to the ventral and anterior temporal lobes If size discriminates between categories, then the application to the experience of awe is immediate. Many awesome experiences depend upon size, specifically large size, in fact scale rather than size.

If that is so, then we may imagine that when the individual who is aware of his human limitations confronts structures of an entirely different scale, such as huge mountains, endless spaces, even deep chasms, he may experience a special affect, namely the sense of awe.

As the quotation from the OED illustrates, the association of awe with religion is almost implicit. In both the Jewish and the Christian Bibles, references to awe appear on almost every page. To start with our paradigm, the opening of the book of Ezekiel, the first chapter describing Ezekiel's chariot contains many and repeated awesome features: the storm, the fire, the radiance, the preternatural creatures, the lightning, penetrating flashes, wheels, "tall and frightening" and "covered all over with eyes," the "awe inspiring gleam as of a crystal," the loud sounds suggesting "mighty waters," and the "din of an army," the sapphire throne, the radiant genital, the rainbow.

The biblical word for awe is *yirah* from the word *yarei*, to fear, to respect or stand in awe of; *nora* means awe inspiring.

Direct allusions to awe constitute a large part of the formal prayer service. The centerpiece of each of the three or four daily prayer services in the Jewish liturgy begins by characterizing God as great, powerful, and awesome. During the congregational repetition of this liturgical piece, the congregation reenacts antiphonally with the reader the angelic devotion to God as given in the awesome description of God in his Temple in Chapter 6 of Isaiah. There God is described as sitting on his great throne, surrounded by countless numbers of angels worshiping him with antiphonal singing. The Kaddish, the best-known liturgical piece, known primarily as the mourners' prayer, is also the most frequently recited element of Jewish worship. It is recited in full at the end of each of the three or four daily services and in part at the end of each unitary portion of the service. It does not speak directly of awe, but alludes to boundlessness in time, the universality of God's kingdom in space, and of his virtually inconceivably extravagant qualities. I believe that it is a prayer for the reign of order in the infinite and timeless universe, under the kingship of the inconceivably superlative God. In most religions, places and conditions of worship seem designed to inspire awe. I include here magnificent temples and cathedrals, compelling music, unison singing, pageantry, and the assembly of large numbers of worshipers in one place.

Since exposure to extremes of size is important in generating the feeling of awe, one will not find it surprising that the historic mythology of many religions includes giants as predecessors of the group or community. Places of worship are located on high ground or within sacred buildings or temples. We are familiar with the high places in the temples of Western religion. The universality of this phenomenon is suggested by similar observations in the case of the Mayan religion. According to Brady and Ashmore (1999), mountains, caves, and water, originally sacred places, combined to constitute the "ideational landscapes" of the ancient Maya. (I am indebted to Larry Coben for this observation.) We find these three elements combined also in Ezekiel, Chapter 47 (see Ostow 1995).

In the light of these several considerations, I propose some hypothetical inferences. Since awe seems to be a response to major discrepancies of scale, it would seem reasonable to attribute its origin to the earliest experiences of the infant who must be impressed by, and responds to, the large sizes, loud sounds, and bright lights that he first encounters at the hands of his parents and the world in which they live. It is inconceivable that there is no affective response to the enormous scale of these perceptions, though it would seem impossible to retrieve them. We psychoanalysts infer from dreams, associations, screen memories, and symptoms that many early events are recorded even though they are not consciously remembered; they leave traces that can be recaptured in these clinically observable phenomena and can label related derivative events with their own specific affect.

Addressing this issue of nonretrievable but yet influential memories, neuroscientists have created the category of nondeclarative or "implicit" memory. Squire and Kandel (1999) describe a number of varieties of nondeclarative memory. One variety attaches affective labels to current perceptions that relate instinctual imperatives to previous experience. Hence, I suggest that the affect of awe appears when an individual is exposed to the major discrepancies of scale that we have mentioned, even though the early perceptual experience itself is not retrieved. I do not know that the awe that we experience reproduces literally the affect of the early experience; it may be that the activation of the nondeclarative residues of the early experience now yields an affective experience different from that which it originally elicited, but I would suspect that it resembles it in some way.

We recognize two varieties of awe: fearful awe and pleasant awe. As the OED definition indicates, awe is mostly associated with fear or at least reverence, which I suppose may be considered to be fear modified by submissiveness. However, one often encounters awesome experiences that arouse feelings of comfort and even active pleasure. Such awe encourages the wish to remain in the presence of the awesome stimuli.

To understand the relation between these two aspects of awe, we must recall that, perhaps with some exceptions, most types of affect arise in the context of instinctual function. Ethologists have taught us to distinguish between appetitive and consummatory behavior (Ostow 1957, 1958). And Jaak Panksepp (1998) reminds us that each of these phases is associated with its own characteristic affect. For example, if we examine the instinctual response to danger, then we must label the alertness to it and scan for evidence of it as appetitive behavior and flight or fight as consummatory behavior. The appetitive affect then is apprehension and the con-summatory affects are fear and determination. When the danger has been successfully evaded or overcome, the fear gives way to relief or to a feeling of triumph.

If we return now to the image of the tiny infant in the hands of the gigantic parent, when circumstances are not propitious, the infant will scream in terror. When the screams bring relief in the form of cuddling and feeding, the terror and screaming will both subside. The feeding will be enjoyed and give way to a pleasant sense of satiety. The giant can threaten and can also protect and give pleasure. The child's fulsome smile will reward the giant for its beneficence; the fearful smile will seem intended to propitiate it. I conclude that the fearful awe corresponds to the fear in the presence of danger, and that comforting awe corresponds to the sense of relief from danger and the comfort that follows.

I will illustrate these two types of awe and their associated affects with the following dream, which was reported by a woman in psychotherapy: "I was in a redwood forest. I hate redwood forests. I very much enjoy large open spaces but I am very uncomfortable in redwood forests. I did something wrong to my mother's car. She was enraged at me. She was empress of the kingdom. She had a huge bellowing voice, condemning me. It turned into a huge thing."

This was a timid woman, always fearful of her mother's anger, which was exhibited, however, not by scolding or shouting, but by silence and coldness. The text of the dream, as presented, describes two awesome situations: the open vistas, which she had always sought out and enjoyed, and the tall, thick redwood forest, which made her uncomfortable. The latter was associated in the dream with the image of a loud, bellowing, punitive mother, who made "a huge thing" of it. Note the dimensions of the percepts: tall, large, loud, empress, huge.

Although my argument is more suggestive then compelling, I interpret the foregoing collection of observations to imply the following propositions. The original awe-generating experience creates a complex of feelings. Living in the presence of a gigantic, parent-like figure, this figure can at times seem dangerous, at other times comforting. The behavior of this figure cannot always be anticipated or controlled, but it can be propitiated and it can be aroused to anger. The influence of this constructed universe persists into adult life as a readiness to experience awe under off-scale and unusual circumstances, and to associate it with the complex of feelings that I have just noted. The situations that inspire awe change as we mature and acquire more diverse experiences and memories. Neither the original experience nor its derivatives in later childhood and adult life are religion in the full sense of our understanding of that complex entity. Yet awe can generate feelings that those who experience it consider religious. (Note that the experience of awe implicit in the foregoing dream is associated with a proto-religious scenario, "the empress of the kingdom.") I

propose therefore that a complex generated by the infantile pre-
cursor of awe, represented by awe itself, contributes a way to
understand the world, a set of expectations of the course of destiny
and how it may be influenced, and an affective orientation to the
perceived universe.

MYSTICISM

I observed above that the initial chapters of the Book of Ezekiel
could serve as a paradigm for my discussion—awe, mysticism, and
apocalypse presented serially in that order. Following the description of the remarkable, awesome spectacle, the *merkavah* or chariot,
we read that Ezekiel recognizes the presence of the Lord and flings
himself on his face. He experiences the entrance of a spirit into his
body and hears God's message. God feeds him a scroll in which
were written "lamentations, dirges, and woes." He is then carried
away by a spirit, presumably accompanied by the awesome creatures that he has seen.

Students of mysticism define it, in general, as the personal
experience of contact with a deity or with a universal secular entity.
In the brief section from Ezekiel that I have summarized, God
stands Ezekiel on his feet, enters his body, speaks directly to him,
feeds him the information that he needs, carries him aloft to land in
a place prepared for him to perform his assignment. He commands
him to perform certain symbolic acts. By any definition, this is an
intense mystical experience.

There are many varieties of mystical experience including
theosophic mysticism, theurgic mysticism, and ecstatic mysticism.
(This is Idel's [1988] classification.) To avoid getting too far afield,
we shall confine ourselves here to unitive experience, such as that
described by Ezekiel.

I quote here a letter sent to me by a patient who had suffered
a long course of bipolar illness, with many episodes of mania and
depression alternating, which had created great difficulties in his

object relations and business judgment. The episode that he describes occurred during a period of depression associated with frightening visual impairment, during the course of which he wrestled with the problem of how to provide material security for his wife if he should predecease her, without significantly depleting his valuable collection of Middle Eastern antiquities:

My worries increased regarding the financial situation, and I began to look for even more drastic ways to solve it. This was undoubtedly due to the blow of the virtual loss of my sight, to the increasing pessimism about my health in the near term, and therefore, the need for procuring additional security for my wife. I was lost in juggling all of the possibilities of how to keep the essence of my collection, the integrity of my commitments, and the security of my wife.

For several days of intense thinking, I struggled with these conflicting needs until I happened to see an old story that I knew well, of David and Bathsheba, which was rather well done with Gregory Peck as David, in one of the better biblical movies, most of which have been pretty horrible. Far be it from me to compare myself to David, but if you remember, he beat Goliath and became king at a young age. He was a young shepherd who beat Goliath, and for the early part of his life, fought sincerely for the Lord of Israel. As he grew in power, and prestige, and adoration of the people, his life turned to materialism, greed, lust, and he committed, for that period, one of the most heinous crimes in Jewish history.

Now, I was never a little shepherd with the characteristics described, nor did I commit any heinous crime. So, it's hard for me to understand why, when David realized or was told by a prophet what a dreadful sinner he had been, he went to the altar of the temple still existing, and made one of the most noble repentance speeches I have ever heard, and pled not for himself, but for his wife Bathsheba, who was about to be stoned as an adulteress. What is amazing to me is that indirectly the Lord signified to David either (a) that he was forgiven for his repentance or (b) that he was to be punished for his very repentance because as David asked God to forgive him and kill him, God said, "I am not finished with you.

You will restart your life as the little shepherd of old and think not of yourself or of the goods of this world, but think of your people and of Israel. Furthermore, I make you an elect, and from the house of David will one day come the Messiah, but you will suffer for all your life and this very temple where you are will be destroyed by the enemies of Israel."

What amazed me about this story was how God was able to look into his heart and to know that not only was his repentance true, but he was a man of such genius, in spite of his crime, that he made him his choice as the elected antecedent of the Messiah.

What all this has to do with me, I still can't figure out, except that suddenly—and never before have I had such an experience— some power told me how to solve my present problem and not knowing exactly what to do, I went to the synagogue on the following Friday and made an anonymous offering of $1,000 with a note saying, "I thank the Lord of Israel who showed me what my tasks and solutions should be." The solution, of course, was that I could not have my cake and eat it too, and that while I did not regret the collection I had amassed, it was time now to give it up, even with pain, for the sake of assuring a greater security to my wife, which would permit me to sleep and die in a much happier frame of mind. And furthermore, if I did not die, it would relieve some financial strains in order to have a more joyful ending.

As God had predicted for David, for me it was not only painful, but also very difficult, more than I expected, and remember I insisted on protecting my reputation and the integrity of my commitments. I was really not surprised that for whatever reasons and especially as my sight goes down, my spirits go up and down day by day, but on the whole, I am happy with the route I have taken, though I do not really know why I took it. All I know is that hard as it may be, it is the right thing to do.

This letter was written to his sister. From that fact and from the fact that he is eager to do something important for his wife and to please "the Lord of Israel," I infer that the Lord represents his father whom he venerates. He was inspired also by a particular rabbinic authority whom he respects.

Classical mystical experiences reported to me have invariably been associated with longing for reunion with a lost object, usually an object of childhood, the mother or the father. The earliest post-biblical recorded Jewish mysticism, *merkavah* mysticism, focuses on the image of Ezekiel's chariot with its divine passenger. The mystic visualizes and hopes to encounter God there. A somewhat later variant, *hekhaloth* mysticism, based on the images of Chapter 6 of Isaiah, sees God presiding from a large throne in a huge temple. In both cases God is to be encountered within an enclosure. I interpret the enclosure as a symbol of the mother. Similarly, mystical dreams often present images of the maternal claustrum, a chair, a room, a garden, an enclosure. I infer that the mystical experience represents a fantasy of reuniting with mother, undoing the experience of separation-individuation.

Scheidlinger (1999), discussing the Japanese concept of *Amae* and the mother-group, quotes Guntrip (1961, referenced in Scheidlinger 1999), who relates the child's unconflicted tie to the mother, to the mystic experience of persons seeking merger with the deity, to Plato's myth about the melted-together lovers, as well as to Freud's notion of an oceanic feeling.

Mysticism, in fact, encompasses more than unity with God; it includes the notion that the entire universe is integrally related, one part to the other. The "oceanic feeling," the term for such unity that Freud (1930) attributes to Romain Rolland, signifies the feeling that the individual is materially immersed in and part of the universe. This is a sensation of "eternity," a feeling of something limitless and unbounded. This feeling is a purely subjective fact, not an article of faith; it brings with it no assurance of personal immortality, but it is a source of religious energy which is seized upon by the various churches and religious systems, directed by them into particular channels, and doubtless also exhausted by them. One may, he thinks, rightly call oneself religious on the ground of this oceanic feeling alone, even if one rejects every belief and every illusion.

A man, who was asked whether he had ever had a mystical

experience, told the following story: When his second child was born, he bought a goldfish and the family playfully spoke of the goldfish as almost a twin of the new baby. As the baby developed it seemed to them that the fish too was developing in a parallel way. When the baby was almost a year old, the fish inexplicably and suddenly died. The father then said, "This stops the parallel between the baby and the fish. This event has no relevance to us." In fact, though, the next day the baby died, too, a victim of sudden infant death syndrome. It seemed to him that he had witnessed a mystical connection between the two. He had the strong feeling that a common force destroyed them both. This feeling is mystical because it affirms that there are invisible forces in the universe that unite not only all lives in the universe, but unite living creatures with material objects too.

In a state of mystical union (*unio mystica*) the individual regresses to the pre–separation-individuation state. He sees the universe in a regressive way, as though distinctions and differentiations of the first chapter of Genesis had been reversed, and the universe, in his imagination, had reverted to an undifferentiated whole: everything influences and is part of everything else. The mystic loses his ego boundaries in waking life.

The object with whom the mystic unites is a symbol of and derived from sometimes mother, sometimes father, and often an undifferentiated parental object, not gender specific.

Do we know enough about neuropsychoanalysis to suggest a structural or functional locus for these mystical operations? The mystical process is driven by a hypertrophied attachment drive, the expression of the tie attaching the infant and child to its mother; and subsequently attaching all of us to those we love. Panksepp (1998) demonstrates that the anterior cingulate cortex must be intact if attachment forces are to prevail. Visual images such as occur in mystical speculations, hallucinations, and trances probably require the activity of the occipito-parieto-temporal regions (see Solms 1997). Penfield was able to elicit visual hallucinations by stimulating the lateral aspect of the diseased temporal lobe (Penfield and Jasper 1954, Penfield and Kristiansen 1951).

However, a more direct clue comes from the patient whose mystical illumination I described above. Within a few weeks after his wonderful illumination, he developed, for the first time in his life, déjà-vu experiences, at first frequent, then virtually continual. They acquired delusional intensity. He came to believe that he could anticipate the future because he had already experienced everything that he had encountered. He knew what was going to happen next.

Déjà-vu phenomena almost always result from disorder of the temporal lobe (Penfield and Kristiansen 1951). This man had a full neurologic workup including imaging. Nothing of significance was found, and his neurologist dismissed him without diagnosis or treatment. (He had complained of painfully dry eyes, and Sjögren's syndrome was suspected though never confirmed. Sjögren's syndrome is a diffuse systemic disease involving tissues of many organ systems including, at times, the brain.) It may be that the déjà-vu was caused by an associated brain lesion.

We are then led to the proposition that the déjà-vu phenomena and the newly acquired susceptibility to mystical experience are to be attributed to the same brain lesion or to a disorder at a different but closely approximated location. Indeed, thereafter both the déjà-vu and the mystical tendency continued concurrently. There was at least one subsequent experience of mystical illumination and the tendency to venerate religious authority and to seek religious guidance.

If we try to assemble these several components of the mystical experience, we can attribute the tendency to reunite to the attachment mechanisms of the anterior cingulate gyrus (as well as other scattered sites; see Panksepp [1998]); the capacity to express the longed for, usually divine object and union with it, in visual form, to the parieto-temporal occipital region; and the ability to create the gratifying illusion to a structure or system in the temporal lobe. There too one finds loci that govern reality testing and the sense of familiarity. If our speculations about the locus for the feeling of awe are correct, the mystical experience may require the participation of structures close by.

Since the reunion with the parent images is meant to be comforting, and to provide surcease from stress, anxiety, and depression, it seems to me comparable to the various antistress efforts that individuals pursue with a determination that seems almost instinctual, similar to recreational eating, recreational sexual activity, and the recourse to intoxicating substances. If this hypothesis is correct, the opioid-endorphin mechanism might be involved. In addition, there is reason to suspect that it is related to the oxytocin attachment mechanism.

Let us try again to imagine the development of the phenomena of our interest. As the infant becomes aware of his caregivers and himself, or even before explicit awareness, he reacts to the differences in size and power, as well as to his own automatic, instinctual responses to them as being comforting or frightening. Memories of these experiences—probably nondeclarative—are laid down and the affects associated with them are recaptured when the child or adult again encounters major discrepancies of scale in size, power, and voice.

As development proceeds, the sequence of separation-individuation unfolds, and with it both the novelty and gratifications that it brings, but also the separation anxieties with which they alternate. When anxiety supervenes, it elicits a tendency to reverse the process, to restore the original union. Freud suggested that infants' attempt to fulfill their wishes by hallucinating them as fulfilled, and the possibility of achieving hallucinatory fulfillment, become available even later in dreaming. Dream hallucination may provide whatever gratifications it does, by elaborating the same neurotransmitters that the actual experience would—qualitatively similar though much attenuated.

I am proposing that the attempt to restore unity with the parent gives rise to the mystical experience. In adults the experience may consist of a sense of being united with the image of the parent figure—now displaced onto a deity—or, in a trance, conviction of the literal experience of visual, auditory, or touch contact, or in a dream the image of being transported to the deity in a vehicle or encountering him in a chamber. As in the case with dreams, the mystical experience probably affords gratification by elaborating appropriate neurochemicals. The dream makes it possible to imagine a perceived contact without loss of ego boundaries. As I see it, the adult experience of awe recapitulates the earliest experience of the infant that is remembered, and the mystical experience attempts to revisit the archaic sense of union with the parent. The two experiences are often associated.

The following vignette should perhaps be classified under the rubric of ecstatic mysticism. The speaker is a middle-aged Jewish woman.

The first time that I was in Israel was in September 1961. The last time was last year (1998) on Yom Ha'atzmaut (Israel Independence Day), except I was here in Riverdale. I generally do not consider myself a "mystical" person. I was taught from an early age to analyze and weigh in an intellectual fashion. There have been many wonderful emotional experiences in my life—the birth of my children, a wonderful moment at the top of a mountain after a hike, and some indescribable emotional high points here and there. But last year something happened that was very different from anything that I had experienced before.

The Riverdale Jewish community had organized a parade and celebration. I went partly because I wanted to and partly because I figured I should. Well, am I glad! The parade, about a mile long, started from our shul and wound through the streets of the neighborhood, passed Riverdale Temple, ending up at the Hebrew Institute. The parade was okay, led by the Cathedral High School Marching Band (yes, from a Catholic school), and at the end there was the Manhattan College bagpipe band. (Only in New York!) At the final location there was a bandstand and an orchestra. They played a medley of music, people started to dance, and after a short time the program started.

First was a moment of silence with a siren blaring in memory of all of the fallen of *Tzahal* [Israel army]. The cantor sang a special "*El maley rachamim*" for the army dead. And then was one of the most unusual moments of my life. It is hard to describe. The cantor from Riverdale Temple sang Hatikvah [Israeli national anthem]. She has an incredible operatic voice. But while she was singing I was someplace else and not standing on a street corner of Riverdale. Suddenly I really was in Israel, seeing again some special places. It was as if I were in the taxi in 1961, when I first visited Israel, going up the old road to Jerusalem just as the sun was coming up, and in the Emek looking out over the fields, and in Haifa somewhere and visiting the Kotel [Western Wall] for the first time. I was in one place and in all of the places, seemingly at the same time. It was absolutely unbelievable. I don't think that I have ever had an experience just like this before. Even now an hour or so later, if I close my eyes, I can continue to see places where I have been, and some not for many, many years, so vividly. It is as if I were there right now. I left at 9 P.M. not quite waiting for the end because I didn't want it to just fade out. I needed to come home and to try to capture a little of this experience in words. Hard to believe that when I began this evening I was feeling discouraged, and not excited about the holiday at all.

I have thought about this experience a few times in the year since it happened. And I still don't understand it at all. Is that what a mystical experience means?

I have actually never studied mysticism, Jewish or otherwise, preferring the safer ground of intellectual pursuit. But such an experience makes one wonder.

a longing

The last sentence of the account of the experience, which seemed like a postscript, tells us something important about mysticism, namely that the mystical experience may be encouraged by a feeling of discontent, a depressive unhappiness. It is that that induces the wish to reunite with the parents. Also, the mystical transport was encouraged by the several acts of union that she witnessed, members of the local Jewish community with differing

good? familiar?

loyalties, Orthodox, Conservative, and Reform; Catholics and Jews; the assembly of large numbers of people. She was affected also by the music, by the moving liturgical tribute to the fallen soldiers of the Israeli army, the singing of the Israeli national anthem. The physical and emotional assembly of many individuals creates a feeling of unity that is a source of mystical experience. As to her memory of her Israeli taxi ride, vehicular travel is a consistent component of *merkavah* mysticism.

A somewhat similar experience of high emotional transport was described by another woman. She was an American, studying at the Hebrew University during her third year abroad college program in June 1967. She remained in Jerusalem during the Six-Day War. Israel took possession of the Old City of Jerusalem on June 7. The festival of Shavuot began on the evening of June 13. The following incident occurred on the following morning.

> I am 21 years old. It is *erev* [the eve of] Shavuot. I am staying with my first cousin, and his family. His parents are also here. At four in the morning he interrupts his studying to awaken us so that we can prepare for our journey, the *aliyah beregel* [festival pilgrimage] to the Kotel [Western Wall]. First we go through the winding streets of Rehavia. Then Rehov Jabotinsky and Mamilla. Now we are joining the multitudes of *Am Yisrael* [the people of Israel] in a curving unbroken *shalshelet* [chain] as we climb the pathway up to Sha'ar Zion and then onward to Sha'ar Ha Ashpatot [gates of the Old City]. I looked in all directions and viewed this orderly sea of humanity. I am here with family and my people. We all recite a *Shehecheyanu* [a liturgical expression of gratitude upon attaining a goal] as we get our glimpse of the Kotel.

This is a simple description of what happened, but she told me that she had been overwhelmed with a feeling that, though she is otherwise quite articulate, she could not express in words. She felt herself almost dissolved in the mass of her people, *Am Yisrael*, and, at the same time, one with historical Israel, a grand unitive experience. Here too the mystical experience was elicited by the experience of being a part of a mass of people with a single interest and a single feeling, moving eastward into the sunrise toward reunion with a holy place, and the feeling was mingled with awe.

Like religion itself, mysticism is a complex, many-sided, variegated phenomenon. It is far too complex to be dealt with in any complete way within the compass of a book chapter. (I discuss aspects of psychodynamics in my book on the subject [Ostow 1995], including such subjects as curiosity, sexuality, and group psychology—all important aspects of mysticism.)

How are awe and mysticism related to religion? If we are to try to answer that question, we need a reasonable definition of religion. Dictionary definitions speak of belief, worship, adoration, reverence, and rites; and *religious*, defined as an adjective, expresses commitment to such beliefs or forms of worship. That may do as a working definition in the world of affairs, but as psychoanalysts we know that such a definition fails to tap the psychological essence of what I have called the "religious instinct," that is, the psychologic readiness and need to engage with others in common submission to a divine entity recognized by the community of others. I do not propose that as a satisfactory definition; religion is a multifaceted enterprise, so that the religious have many things in common but also hold many things related to religion individually. I have not undertaken to discuss religion in all of its many aspects and manifestations, only those aspects that relate to the three issues that I have chosen to discuss here.

If we revert to the question of the relation between awe and mysticism on the one hand, and religion on the other, we find that we don't have a proper description of religion to use for comparison. If we refer back to the dictionary definitions of the three terms, we discover that they are circular, that is, that they each use the same terms, or refer back to one another. To be sure, they are not identical, but they do form an almost closed circle. I infer that awe and mysticism are not *related* to religion, *they are essential components* of religion. Awe and mysticism can occur outside a religious

context, but they seldom do. I doubt that anything that is called a
religious experience can fail to include elements of awe or mysticism or both. As an example, a woman had gone to a resort on the
Gulf Coast of Florida for a professional meeting:

> That summer's meeting was at the South Seas Plantation on Captiva
> Island. I had never been on the Gulf Coast and was totally swept
> away. I was used to the Atlantic Ocean—cold water and waves.
> The Gulf was unexpected—the water was warm and "bouncy." I
> could stand for an hour, with my sunglasses on, up to my neck in
> water and never get pulled off my feet. It was totally relaxing.
>
> In the evening, people would go down to the beach and go
> swimming. It was hot outside and going in the water cooled us off
> and it never got so cold that you couldn't stay in the water. The
> third evening we were there we learned that there is a kind of
> plankton that is phosphorescent and that there was a large area of the
> water around the resort where these creatures were swimming. You
> couldn't see them, but they made the water glow. None of us really
> knew what that meant, but it was an interesting fact.
>
> That night when we went down to the water, I was blown
> away. The effect of these creatures' being in the water is phenom-
> enal. When I would bring my hands out of the water over my head
> the water dripping off my hands and arms looked like it had silver
> glitter in it. People were jumping up and down making splashes of
> glitter. Each night more and more people came down to swim and
> that night there must have been about fifty people in the water. The
> moon was full, beautiful, and really bright. When I looked out over
> the water, I saw all of these jumping, bouncing people, silhouetted
> against the horizon, throwing up splashes of glittery water.
>
> I had never experienced such a combination of things. I stood
> in the water, up to my neck, and felt like I stepped back and saw it
> all spread before me—the people (all of whom were having a blast),
> the glittery water, the moon, the temperature. It came to me so
> clearly that such a combination of wonder and beauty could only
> happen because of the existence of a God, of a higher being. Never
> had I so surely felt that presence as I did at that moment.

This was literally an "oceanic feeling" of which Romain Roland spoke, and which he, properly I think, associated with "religious energy."

Compare the following statement by Einstein associating awe, mysticism, and religion:

> The most beautiful emotion we can experience is the mystical. It is the power of all true art and science. He to whom this emotion is a stranger, who can no longer wonder and stand rapt in awe, is as good as dead. To know that what is impenetrable to us really exists, manifesting itself as the highest wisdom and the most radiant beauty, which our dull faculties can comprehend only in their most primitive forms—this knowledge, this feeling, is at the center of true religiousness. In this sense, and in this sense only, I belong to the rank of devoutly religious men.

APOCALYPSE

Apocalypse is a literary, religious type of prophecy that began to appear in Israel about two centuries before the Common Era, though perhaps earlier in Persia. It purports to foretell the future on the basis of a divine revelation (the word *apocalypse* means revelation) to a divinely inspired sage or prophet. The prophecy usually consists of a series of dire implications directed at a specific population—sometimes the prophet's own people, sometimes their enemies—warning of punishment of the utmost severity. However, in the end there is reconciliation and rebirth. All of this will happen at the "end of days"—the *eschaton*. The genre includes certain other stylistic characteristics, such as the use of numbers, symbols, symbolic animals, calculations of the amount of time that will transpire before the "end," and often a messianic deliverer. The classical biblical apocalypses are the Book of Daniel and the Revelation of John.

From the name given to the phenomenon, apocalypse, it is

evident that theologians and scholars of scripture consider the phenomenon of revelation to be the essence. As a psychoanalyst, however, I find the succession of expectations of death and destruction followed by the expectation of rebirth to be the essential center of the issue. Such alternating expressions of doom and rebirth constitute major portions of the text of the prophetic books of the Jewish Bible.

Apocalypse is ordinarily thought of in connection with religion because the well-known classical apocalypses are found in scriptural and apocryphal literature. The secular apocalypses are relatively few and far between. However, there is an even more significant link, namely, that the destruction that is threatened is seen as punishment for immoral and irreligious cultic behavior. The prophets denounce Israel and her neighbors for their corruption and villainy, and threaten severe consequences, sometimes using the word *kez* (doom). True classical and other apocalyptic types of thinking that we encounter in the Prophets and the other books of the Bible have seized on a complex of fantasies and their associated affects that seem to grasp the imagination of the people, which are then used to enforce religious discipline and conformity.

But why is the apocalyptic mode of thought so congenial? I believe that it gives expression to a basic psychophysiologic function. Patients with borderline or cyclothymic personality often exhibit recognizable and sometimes intense mood swings in daily life, manifest during a psychotherapeutic sessions and certainly in their dreams. Unless we listen attentively, we may miss mood swings in depressed or manic patients, but we can still see them easily in their dreams. Among patients without affect disease, close attention will detect much more subtle yet definite mood swings during the session, but not always in their dreams. I infer that mood swings occur constantly among all of us, subtle, controlled, and limited in range among most of us, and frequent and striking in the presence of affect disease. What we see, I believe, is the operation of a normal mechanism for mood regulation that strives toward but does not achieve homeostasis. As our mood rises toward euphoria, sooner or later a corrective downward swing begins, which arrests the movement and then proceeds to reverse it. Conversely, as mood declines to depression, the corrective tendency reverses it toward euphoria. Most of us are not aware of these subtle oscillations, but we do acknowledge occasionally waking up in a bad mood or being moody during the day. I believe that normally mood oscillates with a period of about 45 to 90 minutes, corresponding to the REM cycle. Panksepp (1998) speaks of a 90-minute basic rest–activation cycle. When the moods are sufficiently pronounced, we become aware of them though seldom of the oscillations that bring them about. Though most often we see them as internally generated, when they are pronounced—or even when not so pronounced—many who are so disposed will attribute them to some external source. Enmities will be generated, and social disruption.

Strong moods often violate ego boundaries and color perceptions of the world about us. It is not that we are depressed; the sky is falling. When an individual recovers from depression the world seems new and fresh and promising.

It becomes evident then that the anticipation of apocalyptic catastrophe is frequently no more than the anticipation of a depressive crash, and the anticipation of rebirth and salvation is an outward projection of our inner rebirth tendencies—the internal homeostatic correction. The alternation of destruction and rebirth that we see at least one time in each apocalyptic episode, and sometimes repeatedly, reflects the internal mood oscillations that I have described.

In fact we may distinguish among at least three types of apocalypse, each corresponding to a phase of the depression-mania cycle. These variations are more readily recognized if we do not restrict our study to true, fully developed apocalypses, but include also examples of what I call the "apocalyptic complex," that is, the sequences of death and rebirth that are not necessarily associated with revelation to a divinely appointed agent, nor with other peripheral features such as numerology, symbolism, messianism, and calculation of an eschaton. These apocalyptic complex variants are found in great abundance in the writing of the prophets and in the psalms. For example, the Book of Lamentations consists primarily of dirges and, as indicated, lamentations, but also includes elements of hope for, and anticipation of, recovery. It includes material (Chapter 3) in which one individual speaks for himself as an individual, rather than the community. This sounds very much like the anguish of a depressed individual, scarcely hoping for salvation, a hope expressed only in the penultimate verse.

The classical apocalypses speak of the coming destruction of the wicked kingdoms that persecute the prophets' people—the Jews in Daniel and the Christians in Revelation. In each case the victim will be rehabilitated. These voices of doom resemble what must be the internal fears of the manic, often expressed in delusions of persecution.

One must include in the category of apocalypse those persecutory campaigns attacking a designated enemy who is seen as a source of danger (e.g., representing the anti-Christ), and thereby inviting the messianic redemption. Such persecuting sects from the Middle Ages are described in Norman Cohn's definitive work on *The Pursuit of the Millennium* (1970). These apocalyptic persecutions mirror the acute rages of the borderline and of the affectively psychotic patient who believes that his violent, apocalyptic attacks on others will achieve his own personal redemption from persecution.

In both the personal and community apocalypses, guilt is owned by the victim; that is, he feels guilty (see Lamentations). But guilt is also applied to the persecutor. This subjective guilt and the divine inspiration attributed to the prophet establish the link to religion. This is the guilt that is ordinarily found in most cases of depression and that usually invokes moral condemnation to explain it.

We know something more about the brain's participation in apocalypse than we do in the case of awe and mysticism. Mood can be influenced by the activation or deactivation of a number of loci in the brain. One system that I find especially interesting is that which Panksepp (1998) calls the seeking system. It serves to sustain the activity of the principal instincts, holding them in a state of readiness to be triggered. It consists of a neural tract that arises in the periaqueductal gray of the brainstem, courses through the medial forebrain bundle of the lateral hypothalamus, and reaches the orbital medial region of the frontal lobe; it operates by means of the dopamine neurotransmitter system. These circuits, Panksepp says, contribute heavily to feelings of engagement and excitement. Under the influence of electrical stimulation of the system, subjects report "invigorated feelings that are difficult to describe. They commonly report a feeling that something very interesting and exciting is going on" (p. 149). The system is activated by dopamine stimulants such as cocaine and amphetamine, which create "an energized psychic state," while a "sluggish depressive state" (p. 149) accompanies blockade of the system with antipsychosis drugs. If the system is damaged, a generalized behavioral inertia results.

We know of no corresponding single source of depressive sentiment. Simply arresting the activity of the seeking system causes not only inertia but also depression. Corticotropin-releasing factor secretion is elicited by stress but also creates negative moods. Panksepp (1998) describes a fear system, which originates in the central and lateral areas of the amygdala and projects downward into the brainstem. Stimulation of this system creates subjective feelings of foreboding such as one experiences in apocalyptic dreams. Clinical-anatomical imaging studies suggest that the right brain exerts a generally depressive affect so that gross lesions affecting the right cerebral hemisphere leave the patient not appropriately depressed by his disability, whereas lesions on the left, which seems to exert an antidepression tonus, leave the patient depressed. Which of these several depression mechanisms participate in the spontaneous depressive process and whether others may be involved as well is not evident at the present time. I suspect that those structures of the right brain that exert a depressive influence oppose the seeking system in effecting mood alternation and regulation.

It is my impression too that the several psychopharmacologic agents exert their influence at different points in the mood regulating system. Unfortunately, the psychopharmacology itself is fairly obscure. Dopamine and norepinephrine seem to be associated with primary antidepression activity. Whether serotonin has a direct antidepression effect or whether it merely alleviates psychic pain or facilitates norepinephrine release is not clear. Since serotonin exerts an essentially inhibiting influence in the brain, I would guess that the serotonin-sparing antidepression drugs (e.g., the serotonin specific reuptake inhibitors) act to suppress the activity of the right brain depressive mechanism, whereas the dopamine agents reinforce the energizing activity of the seeking system.

The interplay of apocalyptic mood and dreams with psychopharmacology is nicely demonstrated in a patient's dream (Ostow 1995):

> "My wife and I were somewhere in the mountains in some small village. There were four people coming on horseback. They were knights like the Four Horsemen of the Apocalypse. They had stopped to tell us that there was going to be an earthquake and some of the area will be flooded. We were on a small island. They told us to move to a larger island, which we did. While we were there, the earth began to quake, fire began to flow and the small island where we had been was inundated with water. We were clinging close to the ground while the earth was shaking." [p. 54]

The four knights in the dream were identified by the patient with the Four Horsemen of the Apocalypse. He could not, however, remember their names or exactly what they stood for, but he knew that they represented portents of great danger and ultimate destruction. In the dream, however, he was struck by the fact that the four horsemen were actually saviors and helpers.

This case illustrates the prospect of destruction as punishment for sin. The patient, however, is not punished with the wicked, but escapes with the aid of the Four Horsemen, who, in the dream, abandon their classic role of portents of death and destruction and became helpers and rescuers. The reason that the threat fails is that, in view of the patient's lifelong masochism and depressive character, at the suggestion of Jacob Arlow, who had been treating him, the patient had begun a program of antidepression drug therapy with me a year earlier. His response to all medication had been positive but only temporary. On June 22, 20 milligrams of fluoxetine (Prozac) had been prescribed, in addition to the 60 milligrams of methylphenidate (Ritalin) per day and the 0.5 milligrams of lorazepam (Ativan) three times a day that he had been taking. He had responded to the fluoxetine with pronounced improvement of mood and remission of masochistic behavior. The dream, which occurred on July 6, reflects the remedial effects of the latter in the patient's seeing himself as one of the saved rather than one of the doomed, and the Horsemen as friends rather than demons. This case illustrates the influence of mood on the outcome of the mythic drama as it is played out.

We see here not only the congruence between the affect correction homeostatic mechanism and the prototypical apocalypse, but also how antidepression medication modifies the outcome of the dream apocalypse.

From the point of view of the practicing psychiatrist and psychoanalyst, it is important to observe that just as prevailing mood determines the content of dreams, so it determines also the content of waking thought. For us it seems counterintuitive to attribute the determination of current fantasies, beliefs, and intentions to anything but the influence of one's surroundings, the people who surround us, and the circumstances that influence us. Careful studies of transcripts of sessions will reveal that shifts of mood often arise internally and are reflected in the free associations, which is not to deny the influence of the reality that impinges upon us all. But reality is not the only determinant of our moods. Moods are generated internally, in a regular and often predictable succession, and determine how we see reality.

Perhaps to an even greater extent, the social organism, the group, adopts common moods and attitudes and interprets current experience in this light. Groups can be in belligerent moods, pacific moods, generous moods, or defensive moods. We see alternating group enthusiasm and group despair in market behavior. Group apocalyptic thinking and behavior, persecutions, pogroms, and religious enthusiasms are usually entrained by the prophets of apocalypse.

What can we say about the development of mood regulation and the apocalyptic thinking that accompanies it? I have proposed that we locate the origins of awe and mysticism in the earliest experiences of the infant, which are not retrievable in declarative memory. I do not know how soon after birth the attempts at early mood regulation start. Of course moods are powerfully affected by the mother, her attentions, and her moods. But at some point an internal mood-regulating mechanism begins to function.

I think that we can obtain some idea of how apocalypse, awe, and mysticism are linked psychologically by going back to the prophetic books to which I have been referring. It is in each case immediately after the vocation and initiation experience of the Prophet and the direct communication with and commissioning by God that the Prophet begins his apocalyptic prophesies.

Jeremiah (1:9): "The Lord extended his hand and touched my mouth and the Lord said to me: Here I have placed my words in your mouth. See, I have appointed you today over nations and kingdoms to uproot and pull down, to destroy and eradicate, to build and to plant." The clinical mystical experiences or dream is immediately followed by a strong affect, elevated when the approach to God has succeeded, depressed when it fails. The examples of mystical experience that I have given above have each been followed by a strong alteration of mood, all positive.

Here is a dream of a man who had been depressed for years, but was in partial remission.

> I was in Brooklyn on Eastern Parkway, driving past the headquarters of the Lubavitch Rebbe. I was sitting in a room with Hasidim. They said, "This time it really happened." "No, it couldn't." What were they talking about? I walked out. They were all talking. It turned out that the Rebbe had died and these people believed that he was directly related to God. A number of times he'd been sick, but hadn't died. Now he had died. If he had had divine protection, he should not have died. They paraded him around on a chair. He would ascend to heaven in a fire. They put me in a chair, which I thought was strange. They were rocking me back and forth. I fell off the chair. There was a fire. I fell into it.

There is a room in a headquarters. The Lubavitch Rebbe is presented as a charismatic, religious figure. We find a *merkavah*, the chair in which the Rebbe would be translated into heaven. The patient associates to the Jewish wedding custom of elevating bride and groom on chairs carried by the more vigorous guests. Occupying the chair represents an oedipal (or perhaps Promethean) violation of the father's privilege. The dreamer specifies a host of ministering subordinates, the Hasidim, who, like the hostile angels of the *hekhaloth*—a form of mysticism based upon the imagery of Isaiah 6—throw the dreamer down to his fiery death. Fire both accompanies the ascent to heaven and awaits the traveler who is ejected. Clearly, the intent of the dream is Promethean, to ascend to divine heights and to displace the father god. For that, the dreamer is punished.

The successful mystical experience in general terminates with a positive mood. The attempt to ascend to see God in classical *merkavah* mysticism and similarly in fantasies and dreams permits of either success or failure. When the patient is in a good mood, he succeeds in the dreams; when he is depressed, he fails. In the latter case the attempt reveals the effort to overcome a depression, and its success or failure depends upon the patient's readiness, which in turn, is determined by neurochemistry, endocrine contributions, and current enviromental influence.

The reason that the *merkavah* paradigm is so cogent as well as common is that it is based upon the general principle that prevails in I believe almost all religions, namely that God is to be found above and his opponents below. The designated holy places of most religions are elevated places, hills and mountains, or else caves reproduced in temples. Classically we need to think only of the hills of Rome, Athens, and Jerusalem.

My interpretation of the association of holiness with elevation is that the very small child finds ultimate salvation in his mother's arms, lifted to her shoulder. "Up, up, up!" is the usual cry when the child needs to be comforted. It is this elevation to mother's breast, face, and shoulders that is the original source—and subsequently the paradigm of all mood elevation. In fact, I suggest that the very terms *high* and *low* and *elevation* and *depression*, as applied to mood, serve now as metaphors for euthymia and dysthymia, respectively, but may indeed unconsciously recall the original experience of closeness and remoteness with respect to mother's head and breasts.

The *hekhaloth* paradigm sees God located inside a chamber and that is where the mystical worshiper encounters him. However, mother's body is here reproduced only symbolically. Center stage is taken by the father's imago. The shift is the consequence of the fact that the earliest images of the parents are probably gender neutral and the earliest impressions might be of a chimerical combination. The point I wish to make here is that the fantasy chamber, the *hekhal*, is duplicated in religious worship by the temple, the church, or even the cave. Both represent the cavity of the mother's body, the ultimate claustrum.

In fact the small child will alternately bury his head in mother's lap, which he can do with little assistance, or demand to be elevated to her breasts, shoulder, or head.

Since developmentally the *fons et origo* of comfort and benefi-cence is attachment to the mother's body, it is not surprising that attempts to regain good feeling in the presence of distress lie in the effort to return to that ur-experience, symbolically if not veridically. It is this principle that lies at the heart of the mystical experience. *Merkavah* and *hekhaloth* mysticism create the illusion of transport back to mother's body.

From this point of view, mood regulation may be regarded as the continuing effort to return to the situation of satisfying closeness or attachment to the image of the archaic parent—resisting the stresses of negative reality experience and of depressive inner pulls.

In this way the mystical endeavor can be employed in the service of apocalyptic mood regulation.

But it is not only the mystical endeavor—it is the entire religious enterprise that takes us back to the effort to reexperience the earliest parental comfort. Therefore, mood oscillation and the apocalyptic complex in which it is projected out onto the outside world form one of the major archaic components of the religious instinct.

CONCLUSION

The sense of awe derives from the newborn's nondeclarative memory of his impression of his adult, giant parents. The tendency to mysticism derives from the infant's wish to undo the process of separation-individuation, that is, to merge back into the mother. Apocalyptic thinking is created by the externalization of early mood swings, before, and to the extent that it fails to achieve, perfect homeostasis. Together awe and mysticism create an affect that is generally described as religious. I adduce some evidence for the proposition that they are associated with temporal lobe function.

It will, no doubt, have occurred to the reader that some but not all of those individuals who have reported experiences of awe, mysticism, and apocalyptic thinking, usually and obviously in a religious context, are religious in the conventional sense of attending religious services and complying with ritual, cultic rules. What then can be the relation between these archaic proto-religious experiences and conventional religion?

First let me note that the persisting affects associated with nondeclarative memories leave a gap in the continuity of the conscious experience of the world. This gap is commonly filled by the image of a deity, usually given by the surrounding society, though sometimes created idiosyncratically.

Many people, though, reject this image of the gods of their fathers and are left with their naked emotions and the sense that something is missing. It is the feeling that Romain Rolland described: "One may, he thinks, rightly call oneself religious on the ground of this oceanic feeling alone, even if one rejects every belief and illusion" (Freud 1930, p. 65). The rejection may be based upon the need to emphasize one's independence from parental influence, or a hypertrophied need to reject any beliefs but those unequivocally established by scientific observation.

These affects all subserve the attachment instincts, creating the urge to reinstate the earliest state of affairs. In fact it is fulfilled initially by the obvious anaclitic clinging to parents in childhood, then by integrating oneself into a social group, finding a marital partner, and ultimately coming to depend, in one way or other, upon children and the wider family. To the extent that the community is a religious community, it is held together, as if a group of siblings, by a common belief system that includes the nature and name of the common deity, and a mythology that attempts to satisfy childhood curiosity.

This is a possible framework for a religious system within which the archaic components to which I have drawn attention serve as primary motivation and earliest affective expression of the need for attachment. Individuals may accede to, or dissent from, any aspect of the frame, while retaining the central affects and being moved by them. One may have religious feelings without being formally observant.

REFERENCES

Arlow, J. A. (1951). The consecration of the prophet. *Psychoanalytic Quarterly* 23:324–397; reproduced in: Ostow, M., ed. (1982). *Judaism and Psychoanalysis*, pp. 45–72. New York: Ktav; reprinted by Karnac, London, 1997.

Bear, D. M., and Fedio. (1977). Quantitative analysis of interictal behavior in temporal lobe epilepsy. *Archives of Neurology* 34:454–467.

Brady, J. E., and Ashmore, W. (1999). Mountains, caves, water: ideational landscapes of the ancient Maya. In *Archaeologies of Landscape*, ed. W. Ashmore and A. B. Knapp. pp. 124–145. Malden, MA: Blackwell.

Cohn, N. (1970). *The Pursuit of the Millennium*. New York: Oxford University Press.

Compact Edition of the Oxford English Dictionary, The (1971). Oxford, England: Oxford University Press.

Freud, S. (1911). Formulations on the two principles of mental functioning. *Standard Edition* 12:215–226.

——— (1930). Civilization and its discontents. *Standard Edition* 21:59–143.

George, N., Dolan, R. J., Fink, G. R., et al. (1999). Contrast polarity and face recognition in the human fusiform gyrus. *Nature Neuroscience* 2(6):574–580.

Gloor, P., Olivier, A., Quesney, L.F., et al. (1982). The role of the limbic system in experiential phenomena of temporal lobe epilepsy. *Annals of Neurology* 12:129–144.

Greenacre, P. (1956). Experiences of awe in childhood. *Psychoanalytic Study of the Child* 11:9–30. New York: International Universities Press.

Idel, M. (1988). *Kabbalah, New Perspectives*. New Haven: CT: Yale University Press.

Ostow, M. (1957). The erotic instinct: a contribution to the study of instincts. *International Journal of Psycho-Analysis* 38:1–20.

——— (1958). The death instinct: a contribution to the study of instincts. *International Journal of Psycho-Analysis* 39:1–12.

——— (1995). *Ultimate Intimacy: The Psychodynamics of Jewish Mysticism*. Madison, CT: International Universities Press.

Panksepp, J. (1998). *Affective Neuroscience: The Foundations of Human and Animal Emotions*. New York: Oxford University Press.

Penfield, W., and Jasper, H. (1954). *Epilepsy and the Functional Anatomy of the Human Brain*. Boston: Little, Brown.

Penfield W., and Kristiansen, K. (1951). *Epileptic Seizure Patterns*. Springfield, IL: Charles C Thomas.

Scheidlinger, S. (1974). On the concept of the mother-group. *International Journal of Group Psychotherapy* 19:417–428.

Solms, M. (1997). *The Neuropsychology of Dreams: A Clinico-Anatomical Study*. Mahwah, NJ: Lawrence Erlbaum.

Squire, L. R., and Kandel, E. R. (1999). *Memory: From Mind to Molecules*. New York: Scientific American Library, Freeman.

9

A TO Z: AWE, CABALISM, AND ZOHAR:

Discussion of Ostow's Chapter, "Three Archaic Components of the Religious Instinct: Awe, Mysticism, and Apocalypse"

Philip J. Escoll, M. D.

The most beautiful and deepest experience a [person] can have is the sense of the mysterious. It is the underlying principle of religion, as well as of all serious endeavor in art and science. . . . He who never had this experience seems to me, if not dead, then at least blind. The sense that behind anything that can be experienced there is a something that our mind cannot grasp and whose beauty and sublimity reaches us only indirectly and as feeble reflection, *this is religiousness*. . . . To me, it suffices to wonder at these secrets and to attempt to humbly grasp with my mind a mere image of the lofty structure of all that there is.

Albert Einstein

Ostow (1982) states in his abstract that religious feelings and behavior are derived from the infant's earliest experiences of his parents. Affects relating to persistent nondeclarative memory invite the content and the image of the deity. The three precursors—awe, mysticism, and apocalypse—then succeed each other. Ostow has had a long-standing interest in Judaism, in which he is very knowledgeable, as he is in psychobiology, psychopharmacology, neuroscience, and mood disorders. He is a skilled clinician, which is evident in the very interesting experiences and clinical cases that he presented. I will begin my comments by addressing the three aspects of religious feeling outlined by him.

OSTOW'S TRIAD

Ostow and Scharfstein (1954) discuss the primary universal religious "instinct." They focus on the Jewish religious tradition. Ostow feels that the core features of various religions resemble each other more closely than do their derivative issues. Now to turn to the three archaic contributions placed by Ostow in a specific sequence. I think it would be helpful to begin by defining the terms.

Awe is defined in the *Oxford English Dictionary* (OED) (1999) as follows: A subjective emotion that relates to immediate and active fear, terror, dread; from its use in reference to the Divine Being, this passes gradually into: dread, mingled with veneration, reverential or respectful fear; the attitude of a mind subdued to profound reverence in the presence of supreme authority, moral greatness, sublimity, or mysterious sacredness; the feeling of solemn and reverential wonder, tinged with latent fear, inspired by what is terribly sublime and majestic in nature, for example, thunder, a storm at sea.

Mysticism may be defined as a personal experience with a deity or with a secular entity, often universal, and this before the days of psychedelic drugs (Ostow 1962). *Apocalypse* is a religious type of prophecy. It foretells the future on the basis of divine revelation to an inspired sage or prophet. The prophecy usually consists of dire implications. For example, Ostow and Scharfstein (1954) write about the succession of expectation of death and destruction followed by the expectation of rebirth, which is central. Doom and rebirth are important along with threat and conciliation.

Awe, mysticism, and apocalypse (Ostow 1995) are presented in a sequence because they relate to the three major prophets of Israel, who are found in the Book of Ezekiel. I am going to focus first on awe, then mysticism, and subsequently apocalypse. Awe engenders a belief in supernatural forces or a supreme being (Ostow and Scharfstein 1954). Awe of nature's spectacular manifestations is a primary root of what eventually may become religion. We know that the primitive gods were nature gods that could appear through prayer, dance, sacrifice, and so on, to fulfill the basic needs for survival, survival in a world that could be terrifying or magnificent—in other words awesome.

Greenacre's (1956) essay on awe states that this experience is not reported before age 4 or 5. She suggests that the child experiences awe first when exposed to the sight of the naked body of the parent. I question some of Greenacre's points, because I think young children may experience awe earlier than described. Also, Ostow writes of the infant's experiences of his parents, but we need to remember the subsequent significance of child development and the intrinsic parental role.

In the *Random House Dictionary* (1966), the archaic characteristic of earlier or primitive time is suggested. The definitions of awe (from the OED) include latent and respectful fear and mysterious sacredness. Note that the word *archaic* is used. However, I believe there are other seemingly somewhat ordinary experiences that are not *archaic*, but nevertheless engender significant awe. Spirituality, for example, reflects the awe of nature in all of its majesty with the almost implicit associations with a religious feeling.

Ostow (1982) emphases size. He points to many awesome experiences that depend upon size and are large in scale, but there are other dimensions that also stimulate awe. Awe relates to thrills, to highs, to being uplifted to a higher plane in the exhilaration of the moment. Balint (1959) writes about risk taking; in today's world it could be hang-gliding and parachuting. There are transcendent experiences ranging from the first sight of the Taj Mahal to hearing a magnificent performance of Beethoven's violin concerto. For my 2-year-old grandson Dylan, who is enamored of trucks, the sight of a large backhoe in action causes excited awe.

On the other side of awe there may be great expectations for awe-inspiring experiences that may lead to frustration and disappointment. While size, such as that of enormous bodies of water and soaring cathedrals, inspires awe, there are many other situations that stimulate spiritual feelings in many of us. We all have the capacity to experience awe, and what is awe for one person may not be awe for another. Awe is enhanced by the child's own observations and experiences so that size is not the only significant aspect, in my view.

I tend to see nature's mysterious and awesome behavior. There are the aurora borealis, volcanic eruptions, earthquakes, solar eclipses, and the ancient experiences of humankind. Tribes such as the Incas and Aztecs were in awe of the sun god idols.

As a personal anecdote about awe, many years ago I developed a urinary infection for which I needed to take two different medications that would cause the urine to be blue or orange. My 2½-year-old son, who liked to keep company with his Daddy in the bathroom, after noting this phenomenon inquired, "What color you going to do today, Daddy?" My son was clearly awed by the powers of his God-like Daddy. In analytic terms, transference and projection were involved.

In other situations of awe that are adversative or involved with death, the comfort of a God or a God-like person could be very helpful.

While awe can represent reverential fear, wonder, or inspiration, mysticism entails a person seeking by contemplation and self-surrender to obtain unity with or absorption into the deity or the ultimate reality, or a person who believes in the spiritual apprehension of truths that are beyond understanding. This involves the occult, the esoteric, the hidden meaning of serious and awe-inspiring situations.

As for mysticism, there are many variations (Ostow 1995) that relate to personal experiences of contact with a deity, a unitive experience such as described by Ezekiel and his chariot. Mysticism encompasses more than unity with God; the entire universe is intricately related. There is also the "oceanic feeling," a term whose origin Freud (1930, p. 64) attributes to Romain Rolland. The individual is immersed in and is part of the universe. Rolland describes a feeling of something limitless, unbounded, as it were, "oceanic." There can be a mystical union and the individual may regress to the pre–separation-individuation state. There is intent to restore the oneness, the unity with the parent, and it may give rise to the mystical experience. Mysticism is directly involved in the Jewish tradition with cabalism, which I will discuss subsequently.

In Jewish or early Christian texts there is symbolic writing about a final cataclysm destroying the powers of evil and ushering in the kingdom of God. There is also the biblical Book of Revelation and the prophetic revelation.

CLINICAL MATERIAL

An accountant, a single man in his fifties, had a very, very close relationship with his now-deceased mother. She was someone whom he admired and revered from his early childhood. He endeavored to exclude his siblings and also in many ways ignored his father. In her early forties, his mother became ill and died of colon cancer. When the patient came to see me because of anxiety, loss, and depression, he expressed much guilt about his mother's death and also rage at his doctor-father for not saving his mother. Over time he began to talk about his mother in greater detail and with a powerful affect of emotion. At first he expressed understandable grief, but as he became more deeply involved in his treatment he began to speak of his mother as though she were alive. This was much more than the usual grieving because he then spoke of his mother being lonely in her grief in her tomb. It was cold there, he said, and he thought of bringing a heater to warm her. He spoke of her in the present tense with the virtual conviction that she was alive in her tomb. He berated himself for not putting her in a more comfortable, larger tomb, and he was on the verge of removing her from this one. At times he pictured her as a tremendously and awesomely powerful person who could see him during our sessions. He was comforted by her presence and companionship.

I regard this case as a possible example of mysticism. One could certainly see this case as an expression of mystical experience, in the patient's continuing union with his departed, yet not departed, mother. This is an afterlife experience, yet my patient did not express any religious beliefs. He did not bring spirituality directly into play in our sessions. Could we conjecture that his supernatural experiences reflected these spiritual beliefs even if he was not directly discussing them?

In another case, the patient spent most of his life gambling. In effect, it was his occupation. He used all kinds of charms and incantations. He rubbed lucky coins in his hands. There were particular numbers to avoid such as 13, and he had special dates on coins related to various quarters and pennies. This behavior involved mysticism, and when he won big at the table, or lost a lot of money, people looked at him with some awe. He worked at gambling with the intensity of the most harried businessman, yet he called on some supreme being, some mystical power, or force. But belief in God or a higher force did not help his cause most of the time.

HISTORICAL ANTECEDENTS

The definition of the three categories I have been discussing can be broadened. For example, a newspaper article entitled "Mystic Surfing" (1999) stated:

A mystic is one who is absorbed in spiritual experiences. Any experienced surfer comes to the realization that surfing is definitely a spiritual experience. To the ardent devotee, surfing becomes a natural religious ritual—an unorganized group of like-minded individuals seeking a "link-back" [religion] to powerful, inner and outer forces. Mystic surfing is nature worship. The definition of "worship" is to respect and to revere. Any wave rider quickly learns to do both. One learns to respect and to revere the elements. Every surfer tunes into the energy of wind, sun, and water, worshipping its power, spontaneity and ability to transform. The fountainheads of this spiritual exercise, the Kahunas, priests and Hawaiian royalty, fully realized this natural mystical connection.

Ostow talks about death and destruction followed by rebirth (Ostow and Scharfstein 1954). Eastern religions vary in apocalyptic ideas. For Hindus the goal is to escape an endless cycle of death and rebirth and to become one, outside of time, with the "eternal absolute," called God in Judeo-Christian belief. Note that Devi-Hindu Goddesses have enormous powers to both destroy and protect. Men are not the only powerful deities!

In regard to the religious "instinct," it has been said there is a psychological readiness to engage others in a common submission to a divine entity, recognized by the community of others. Awe and mysticism are essential components of religion. There is a response of wonder and beauty that can influence one to infer the existence of a higher being. Many of us say, "Thank God" when a seemingly miraculous happening occurs, such as winning the lottery, a battle in war, or recovery from a serious illness. It is something that we all respond to automatically.

Now to turn to the ancient Jewish cabala. The power of Jewish mysticism and apocalyptic ideas run like a thread through Jewish history. The word *cabala* comes from the Hebrew root verb, "to receive," and it alludes to the ancient traditions passed down from generation to generation of the multilayered dimensions of everyday reality—from the most manifest and evident to those hidden and occult features. The vital processes of study, prayer, and good deeds are mixed with gigantic cycles of revisitation that are analogous to the Buddhist concept of karma. The word *cabala*, which also literally means tradition, is used by cabalists to contend with their mystical messages, which were transmitted directly to Moses by God, regarding the divine revelations of Exodus, Chapters 19 and 20. Cabalism is implied ambiguously to involve the totality of Jewish esoteric mystical lore, and also the systems of philosophy of theurgy (Ostow 1955). Jewish mysticism involves images of God and enthroned mysticism. The chariot and the mystical seat of God and the Diety during the Middle Ages are represented by a number of different entities.

Cabala in the final two centuries of the Jewish presence in Spain became the major philosophical current of the time. Cabala is an esoteric and mystic doctrine. It was directed to a limited rather than a mass group. Cabala is a part of rabbinical Judaism, for it possibly was influenced by Eastern religion. The way was opened from Babylon into India, and cabala developed possibly under the influence of Buddhism.

Late in the thirteenth century, the Zohar was written and compiled in Spain (Dimont 1962). This was considered to be the masterpiece of cabalistic literature. The Zohar, meaning radiance, can best be described as an encyclopedia of occultism and metaphysical speculations on God, universe, and science. The Zohar looks to Divine redemption as a miracle, unrelated to earthly conditions. Its title translates as "Splendor," which can be understood as a halo or Divine radiance. Undercurrents of mysticism appeared with the publication of the Book of Formation, which was concerned mainly with ecstatic experience of God. Two books combined constitute the cabala, which deals with mysticism and occult thought—a metaphysical philosophy distinctly Jewish.

The cabalists introduced symbolic thinking and language. They abandoned the ordinary meanings of words, and gave mystical properties to both letters and numbers. The cabalists described thrity-two avenues to wisdom. They developed a fantastic metaphysical world where one element was transferred into another, where numbers stood for properties possessed by objects, and where the world revolved around its own axis. The cabala has many symbols and numerical values, Messianic deliverers, and three types of apocalypses, each corresponding to different phases. There is death and rebirth and destruction of the wicked kingdom.

The cabalists were seen as scientists. Early Jewish scientists (twelfth century) translated Greek and Arabic scientific works into Latin, but also wrote about astronomy, mathematics, and scientific methodology. Since the eighth century, mystics had attempted to use secret formulas as a means of hastening the coming of the Jewish Messiah. Earlier prophets, Elijah, for example, announced the coming of the Messiah.

In 1502, a young cabala student in Venice woke up with the realization that he was the prophet Elijah who had been returned to canonize the coming of the Messiah that very year, and Jews flocked to this cause. In the seventeenth century, after the Thirty Years War, Shabbatai Zvi proclaimed his messiahship. A million Jews from Turkey to England followed him as the long-awaited deliverer. At this time, there were scenes of paranoia, and voices were heard. He then went to Egypt and subsequently to Palestine, with the masses who hysterically adored him as the Messiah.

In 1665, there was a widespread Messianic movement with major Jewish mystical involvement. More recently, Hasidic doctrines based on cabala were modified by time and circumstance. Cabala was concerned with sexuality, with birth and rebirth, and with the dialogue between the human mystic and the Divine. Mysticism had begun with Judaism itself, and existed before the giving of the Torah at Mount Sinai in twelfth century B.C. Cabala was revealed only to a few select saints, and handed down to a small group of mystics. Mysticism grew up with the Torah, but in its shadow were the back alleys of Jewish occult philosophy. It fed on prophecy, numerology, gnostic heresies, and the written book describing the ecstatic experiences of God. Cabalists had an ear for language and a flair for style. They wrote significant poetry, which survives in Hebrew liturgy and literature.

In his book, *Eros and the Jews*, Biale (1997) wrote about sexuality and spirituality in the cabalist movement. In the early part of the thirteenth century, an anonymous Spanish cabalist wrote a treatise on marital relations. This became a standard work in which there was a very positive attitude toward sexuality in traditional Judaism.

The Jewish mystics, the cabalists, sought to restore the integrated relationships of body and soul that have prevailed in biblical and rabbinic culture. The mystics celebrated human sexuality as a requirement for Divine harmony, portrayed in sexual terms. The cabalists, holding opposite views to medieval Christian writers, favored intercourse between man and wife, bringing the Divine presence into the conjugal bed (Biale 1997).

Aspects of cabalism and mysticism are developed in Isaac Bashevis Singer's book, *The Slave* (1962). The chief characters are the biblical Sarah and Jacob.

> Every now and then Jacob had a murmur in his ear, as if some unseen being was whispering to him. He was surrounded by powers, some good, some evil, some cruel, some merciful . . . Sarah . . . made ready for childbirth. Jacob had placed the *Book of Creation* and a knife under her pillow to discourage those she-devils who hover around women in labor . . . Jacob had also acquired a talisman from a scribe to keep off Ygereth, the queen of the demons, Machlath, her attendant, as well as the Lillies who resembled humans but had bat wings, ate fire, and lived in shadows of the moon and tree trunks. As for Sarah, she secretly practiced the magic native to her village . . . she wore on her throat a piece of meteorite, and she took the shell of a newly hatched chick, mixed it with dry horse manure and frogs' ashes and drank the concoction in milk . . . He would not have left a woman about to go into labor alone if there had not been charms and inscriptions on the wall to protect her . . . . [pp. 163, 176, 179]

There is now a renaissance of interest in cabala. Students are studying it, especially in the city of Safed in Israel, ranging from pious, committed, orthodox Jews to alienated secularists who suddenly feel a need to satisfy spiritual longings. Celebrities such as Madonna and Roseanne are also studying it.

It is interesting to see the swings from the mysticism of cabalism to the cabalists who provide a spiritual rationale for ethical behavior even in the present day. Cabalism evoked horrible punishment and fearful warnings, but cabalists have also used mystery and magic in an endeavor to protect themselves from harm. The cabalists were taught through devotion to God and love of fellow man. They saw every human action as a spiritual repercussion somewhere else in the universe, and when people directed their energy with good intention, God would reveal himself and the universe would be repaired, so that humankind was made not just in God's image but was, in a vital way, his partner in creation.

I now turn to some interesting present-day issues. When the Lubavitcher Rebbe died, *The Jerusalem Report*'s (1999) article was titled "Chabad's Messiah Complex." Five years after his death there continues to be a flourishing movement. Many of his Hasidic followers insisted he was the Messiah: "It is nearly midnight in a basement synagogue. As powerful music blasts, two dozen bearded, frenzied men dance in a circle, chanting in Hebrew, long live our master, teacher and rabbi, the King Messiah forever and ever." The about-to-be-revealed Messiah was the Rebbe himself. No one is considering a replacement because "we believe this is the hiatus succeeded by the Hasidism of today." This particular Hasidic group believes that their rabbi will return to the earth as their Messiah.

A recent book about cabala, *Dreams of Being Eaten Alive: The Literary Core of the Cabala* (Rosenberg 2000), was reviewed in *The New York Times* by Richard Bernstein (2000). Rosenberg writes of the Zohar attributed to Moses deLeon, a thirteenth-century Spanish cabalist. Rosenberg states that the Zohar "is purposefully in disguise," adding to its mystical nature, DeLeon having "presented

a long-lost manuscript composed a millennium earlier by a legendary rabbi," (p. 15). For Rosenberg, the Cabalists were "our first
post modern writers" (p. 16). He offers, according to Bernstein, a
medley of fashionable concepts—the importance of the body in
literary criticism, the Freudian interpretation of dreams, and so on.
Rosenberg also deals with cabala and sex; he says that "sex is
Messianic, future-oriented, and that it is yearning for unity and for
the body of the mother" (p. 16). Bernstein reports that the book
expresses "the sexual imagery in the Cabala, as well as stories of
selection of the patriarchs by sexual demons," a reminder of
Singer's book, *The Slave* (1962), and an erotic symbolism connected with the Tree of Life.

Another intriguing recent matter relates to Rabbi Abraham
Twerski (2000), who is an Orthodox Jewish psychiatrist and
self-help author. Rabbi Twerski is a direct descendent of the Baal
Shem Tov, the eighteenth-century founder of Jewish Hasidism.
Rabbi Twerski locates himself in the mystical tradition, which
combines intense individual religious experience with charismatic
leadership. The Hasidic tradition is known for its parables and
stories. Twerski became a friend of the cartoonist Charles Schultz.
Twerski says that he learned important lessons from "Peanuts."

Rabbi Nilton Bonder (1996, 1997) was born in Brazil, where
he lives and works (Simon 1997). He was ordained at the Jewish
Theological Seminary in New York and he is the author of eight
books, several of them best sellers in Brazil, where, because of his
activism in environmental causes, he is known as "the green
Rabbi." According to a Jewish aphorism, a man reveals his character in three ways: By his cup (his appetite), his pocket (his
relationship to his money), and his rage. *The Kabbalah of Money*
(1996) deals with the "pocket," while *The Kabbalah of Envy* (1997)
published a year later, deals with the ramifications of rage, which
envy engenders. In both volumes, Bonder alludes to "the Rabbis,"
the keepers of the cabalist method, and cites their stories from the
Talmud, and from legendary figures in the Hasidic world.

RELEVANCE TO THE CLINICAL SITUATION

Now, we can address the question, "Does God help?" as discussed by Rizzuto and Meissner in earlier chapters. What is the role of God here? What is the role of pastors, ministers, religious concerts, and so forth? It depends a good deal on the individual and his childhood upbringing. For example, a patient of mine, a young man, went to see his priest. As the patient related, this priest was commanding, overly directive, and harshly critical, and the young man experienced the priest as being very hostile to him. In time, he stopped seeing this priest and then consulted with a different priest. This priest expressed caring for the patient, was willing to listen to him, and was responsive to his needs. Whether it be a priest, a teacher, or a rabbi, so much may be influenced by the individual seeking help and by the clergy. We also need to consider the patient's other beliefs and customs, and the attitudes within the family structure. There are many different views, opinions, and reactions in the spectrum of religion, ranging from people who are "born again" to atheists. There are also many different beliefs and customs related to one's background and feelings and ideas about religious experiences.

To raise other questions, how much does the therapist disclose of his or her own views about the culture, the upbringing, and the religious beliefs of the patient? How does one deal with the patient's questions and the choices the patient makes based on his religion, upbringing, needs, and beliefs? It is not infrequent for patients to ask the therapist: "What is your religion?" I think the therapist has to discuss these issues frankly with the patient. If the patient expresses the wish to see a psychoanalyst or therapist of a particular faith, we need to respect that. Of course, this can be discussed, but it is up to the patient to come to the final decision.

I think that faith in God certainly can and does help, as in my example, cited above, of the second priest, who was so different from the first priest, a punitive, strict person, that the patient developed not only a need for him, but also a feeling of love for him. This tells us that the individual teacher, minister, psychiatrist, or psychoanalyst plays an important role in terms of personality and in terms of acceptance of those who disavow religion. The psychoanalyst needs to understand the role of transference and the significance of separation-individuation, which Ostow (1955) has noted.

CONCLUSION

Early religions reflect primitive ways of viewing nature, as in ancient Egypt. In the United States, Hopi Indians have their ritual dances; Judaism can be traced back to archaic forms of primitive religions. Buddha has been deified by his followers, and Hindus revere gods who assume many forms, such as Shiva who is the creator, as well as the destroyer, of the universe.

Some mystic cults promote dangerous behavior and mass deaths, as have occurred recently in Uganda, and with the Millennium Group in the United States, who poisoned themselves and died in their beds; they had fantasies about getting on a space ship and going to heaven.

REFERENCES:

Balint, M. (1959). *Thrills and Regression*. London: Hogarth.
Bernstein, R. (2000). Review of *Dreams of Being Eaten Alive: The Literary Core of the Kabbalah*, by D. Rosenberg. *The New York Times*.
Biale, D. (1997). *Eros and the Jews*. Berkeley and Los Angeles, CA: University of California Press.
Bonder, N. (1996). *The Kabbalah of Money*. Boston: Shambhala.
——— (1997). *The Kabbalah of Envy*. Boston: Shambhala.
Chabad's messiah complex (1999). *The Jerusalem Report*, June 21.
Dimont, M. (1962). *Jews, God and History*. New York: New American Library.
Freud, S. (1930). Civilization and its discontents. *Standard Edition* 21:64–145.
Greenacre, P. (1956). Experiences of awe in childhood. *Psychoanalytic Study of the Child* 11:9–30. New York: International Universities Press.
Mystic surfing. (1999). *Sandpaper*, July.

Ostow, M. (1962). *Drugs in Psychoanalysis and Psychotherapy*. New York: Basic Books.

———— (1982). *Judaism and Psychoanalysis*. New York: Ktav.

———— (1995). *Ultimate Intimacy: The Psychodynamics of Jewish Mysticism*. Madison, CT: International Universities Press.

Ostow, M., and Scharfstein, B-A. (1954). *The Need To Believe: The Psychology of Religion*. New York: International Universities Press.

Rosenberg, D. (2000). *Dreams of Being Eaten Alive: The Literary Core of the Cabala*. New York: Random House.

Simon, J. (1997). Editorial. *Academy Forum* 41(3):2–3.

Singer, I. B. (1962). *The Slave*. New York: Avon.

Twerski, A. (2000). Lessons learned from "Peanuts." *Philadelphia Inquirer*, May 28.

10

THE MEDIAN: ISLAMIC FAITH AND MENTAL HEALTH

Yasser Ad-Dab'bagh, M.D., D.P.M.

Those who believe, their hearts being at rest in God's remembrance. Indeed, in God's remembrance are at rest the hearts of
those who believe and do righteous deeds; theirs is blessedness
and an excellent resort.

Holy Qur'ān 13:28–29

Does God help? The answer to this question may be elusive, yet a
simple one. The answer may be an outgrowth of a certain belief
system; if religious it may be called faith, if otherwise it may be
called science. The challenge to human intellect posed by this
question is whether the gap between these two sources of belief can
somehow be bridged by reason, and a new perspective can be
gained from viewing the dilemma of the answer from the center of
that bridge. This chapter discusses this question from the perspective of the Islamic faith.

AN INTRODUCTION TO ISLAM

"To submit to God's will and law" is probably the literal meaning
of the word *Islam*. Islam is the monotheistic religion preached by

Muhammad in Makkah, in the sixth century A.D. *Prophet* and *Messenger* are terms frequently used to refer to Muhammad, who was the chosen *human* to receive the *Holy Qur'ān* despite his illiteracy. *Qur'ān*, which literally means "the gathered readings," was conveyed to the Prophet in numerous installments over a period of twenty-three years, and delivered to him from God by the angel Gabriel. The *Qur'ān* is believed by Muslims to be God's spoken, rather than created, words. It is the whole expression of revelation. Its highly sophisticated text is, in fact, the miracle of the *Qur'ān*: a unique form of Arabic literature and linguistic style that not only mesmerized readers and listeners throughout the centuries, but also challenged the intellect of theologians and scientists alike.

The *Qur'ān* has been the source of many principles, laws, and institutions in the life and culture of Muslims throughout history. The second source of Islamic doctrine, knowledge, law, and way of life is the *Sunnah* of Prophet Muhammad. The *Sunnah*, a word meaning the way or the example, is the collected traditions, sayings, and actions of the Messenger that were narrated by his followers in reports called Hadiths.

Over a billion people worldwide are believed to be Muslims. They belong to a number of divisions. The Sunni Muslims are by far the majority division, with approximately 85 percent following various Sunni schools of religious law, or *Shari'ah*. The Shi'a, commonly known as Shiite, is the second large group of Muslims and comprise roughly 10 percent of all Muslims. Whereas the Hadiths of Sunni Muslims are essentially traditions of the Prophet, the Shi'a Hadiths are dominated by traditions of the twelve Imams, or religious leaders, that substantially contribute to the Shi'a religion. Many other Islamic religions have branched off from these two major divisions, and are commonly more prevalent outside of the Islamic world—countries that recognize Islam to be a majority or large minority religion. The Ismaelians are an example of a comparatively rare sect that exists largely in North America made famous by their leader, Aga Khan, and by their revolutionary abrogation of all the religious laws of the orthodox Twelver Shi'ism they arose from. Sufism is a phenomenon of spirituality, commonly called "Islamic mysticism," that exists across all sects of Islam and originally was a manifestation of ascetic piety.

The Islamic fundamentalism, erroneously equated in Western media with extremism and terrorism, and more accurately called "orthodoxy," started as an eighteenth-century awakening from a state of theological and spiritual stagnation that the Muslim world lived in at the time. It aimed to bring Muslims back to the *Qur'ān* and the *Sunnah*, and reestablish the pure ideals of pristine Islam. Most groups of extremists have actually deviated from the mainstream revivalists of fundamentalism and have adopted political and military goals. Islamic modernism is, in fact, revivalist in nature. Many of its leaders are intellectuals who aimed to introduce elements of flexibility and reform they thought were increasingly needed to allow the fundamentalist revival to maintain its progressive recapture of the hearts of Muslims. A new resurgence of fundamentalism took place in the twentieth century in the aftermath of the fall of European colonialism of much of the Islamic world.

This chapter highlights some major aspects of Islamic faith and methods of worship. God, whose supreme name is Allah, is almighty, all merciful, omnipotent, omniscient, omnipresent, the creator of all things from no matter, and the source of sustenance, guidance, and the integrity of all existents. God is infinite and original, while all else is finite. He is indescribable by mental efforts of creatures, and man is *not* made in his image. He cannot be grasped by minds, conceived by intellect, or comprehended by thought.

Allah orders Prophet Muhammad: "Proclaim: He is Allah, the Single; Allah, the Self-Existing and besought of all. He begets not, nor is He begotten; and there is none equal to Him in His attributes." [*Holy Qur'ān* 112: 1–4]

Muslims are to believe that the purpose of human creation is first to worship and serve God, and second to cultivate, protect, and healthily utilize Earth and nature while creating a generative and just community on its lands.

The *Qur'ān* accepts the earlier religions and biblical prophets as coming from God. For example, Moses was God's messenger to the Israelites of Egypt and recipient of the message of the Torah. Jesus, son of Mary, is described by the *Qur'ān* to be a human prophet of Allah, created by him with no father, described as the Messiah, and given by him the message of the Evangel. According to the *Qur'ān*, Jesus (*Isa* in Arabic) was not crucified. He was raised to the heavens alive and will remain so until his eventual return to fight the anti-Christ and bring justice and faith in Allah back to the world.

Muhammad is the final Messenger of God to the world, and the prophecy of his emmergence was mentioned in all previous messages, including both the original Torah and the original Evangel. The *Qur'ān* not only succeeds these messages, but also supersedes and replaces them for Muslims.

To become a Muslim, a person must both believe and verbally profess the *Shahādah* (testimony) of faith: "I bear witness that there is no God but Allah, and I bear witness that Muhammad is the messenger of Allah." The *Shahādah* is the first of five pillars of Islam. The others are the *Salāt*, the rituals and acts of Islamic prayer (not just supplication); *Zakāt*, obligatory charity; fasting the month of *Ramadan* (Arabic lunar calendar); and performing the *hajj*, pilgrimage to Makkah during the month of Thul-Hij'jah (Arabic lunar calendar), at least once in one's lifetime. All postpubescent Muslims are required with few exceptions to perform the five daily prayers. *Zakāt* is conditional on defined thresholds of plentifulness, fasting on ability and health, and hajj on both physical and financial capacity to travel and perform the rituals of pilgrimage. During prayer, Muslims everywhere face the direction of the *Ka'abah*, an ancient structure at the center of the Holy Shrine of Makkah that was first rebuilt by Prophet Abraham and his son Ishmael. The

Ka'abah serves little purpose other than being a geographic land-
mark that symbolizes the unity of all Muslims around the world.
The Holy Mosque of the Prophet in Medinah and the Aqsa
Mosque of Jerusalem complete the three sites of the highest regard
to Muslims.

The above account summarizes the central terms frequently
encountered whenever Islam is discussed. It is far beyond the scope
of this chapter to detail the history, evolution, law, structure, and
way of life of Islam. Also, I possess neither the knowledge nor the
expertise required to explain with confidence and facility the basics
of Islamic theology, *Shari'ah*, or Hadith. Indeed, my attempts at
translating texts from both the *Qur'ān* and the *Sunnah* are fallible
and can hardly claim to capture the miraculous richness of the
meanings of the *Qur'ān* in its original Arabic form, nor the
Prophet's remarkable command of the language. Wherever a
translation of the *Qur'ān* is presented, the interpretation of the
Qur'ān rendered by Muhammad Zafrulla Khan was largely utilized.

In the following sections, aspects of Islamic thought are
formulated to shed light on how Islam influences the psyche and
mental life of its followers. The concepts explained pertain more to
the orthodox Sunni tradition than to other sects, but are probably
generalizable without inordinate difficulty or need for radical
changes. It should be noted that the Islamic ideals addressed below
are often far from the reality of any Muslim's life or the state of
affairs in any Muslim community. The impact of local customs and
unique social, political, and cultural factors warrant much study but
would require volumes to elaborate. It cannot be understated that
intrapsychic organizations and behavioral patterns among Muslims
might be dependent not only upon the religious dictates and issues
of faith, but also upon the specific cultural traditions, which vary
from country to country. Thus, Muslims from India or Bangladesh
are both similar to and quite dissimilar from Muslims from Iran,
Morocco, or Saudi Arabia. It was felt, however, that identifying
ideals that most Muslims can easily subscribe to would be of great
utility when approaching the issue of mental health. A comment on

the applicability of the elaborated concepts in the psychotherapy of Muslims is made at the end of this chapter. To give credit where it is due, it is essential to note that my readings of Fazlur Rahman's writings (1979, 1980, 1987) have had much contribution to the formation of the thought process that preceded the writing of this chapter.

MORALITY, REASON, AND FAITH

Islam proclaims that it is impossible for humankind to either agree on what constitutes morality or reach conclusions that would be applicable in all situations at all times. This claim may be shocking, or even revolting, to some intellectuals. However, no great effort in the examination of human history is needed to reach such a conclusion. The point of departure here is the presumption that it will never be possible for increasingly enlightened minds to create a universal ethical and moral code. Rather than debate this point, the rationale and subsequent impact are presented.

In Islam, God has dictated what is good and what is evil through a series of revelations from Adam to Muhammad. This is what religious law is. Moral values, on the other hand, are present even when an individual is ignorant of these laws. Did these moral values develop along the pathways of human mental development as products of the human psyche without divine influence? The Islamic answer is no. It results from the gift of reason as ordained by God. Natural reason of people is clearly described in Islam to be under the influence of various forces, chief among which is one's desires and self-interest. As a source of moral values, the individual's perspective or reason is seen as extremely restricted in its scope, unique and ultimately inapplicable to the masses. God is the creator of all, including the natural reason through which such moral decisions are made, and is knowing of the outcome of all human behavior and thought until the end of time. In other words, he is the expert on what is human. Not only that, but he also has a plan for humanity that we seamlessly follow. If one held these beliefs, it would be virtually automatic to accept that God's revelation should be the source of our moral and ethical codes. Accordingly, if one had the instinctual desire to indulge in a helpful deed, even if it was classified as righteous by God, satisfying such desire is only considered a moral act and a deed deserving of reward if God's revelation of its righteousness contributed to contemplation of the act and the seeking of such reward was included in the aim of such deed. Because of this assertion, a good deed could be righteous, and could be "just an inconsequential act," one that would not lead to reward.

It may be thought that following a divine moral code requires faith in God and, hence, resignation of one's reason in favor of revelation. However, it is not quite the case, and reason is never truly abdicated. Fazlur Rahman (1987) has eloquently explained why:

> Faith in God is an absolute necessity, for without this faith human values become distorted; the entire human conduct, both individual and collective, becomes mechanical and is thrown out of perspective. But faith is not something irrational; it is indeed, in a sense generative of its own reason although in itself it is not reason but a commitment. Still, it is not generated by any *formal* or theological reasoning: it arises, rather, out of observing a certain empirical evidence in a certain way. The evidence is the *empirical fact of being*, and faith is the awareness that this universe, this plentitude of being, points to a certain ground upon which it must rest. [pp. 14–15]

It is reason that leads a Muslim to believe that only God is capable of producing a universal moral code, but it's the kind of reason generated by faith in God. The value of human reason has been particularly emphasized in the *Qur'ān*. It is, in fact, reason that makes humans noble compared to other creatures and the only ones accountable to God. The use of such reason is one aspect of judgment most people are unaware of: God will judge how one used his or her reason and intellect, and the rational and intellectual processes preceding their actions. This includes an emphasis on understanding, as opposed to just accepting, as part of resignation and faith. People are expected to attempt an understanding of religious obligations in addition to performing them, and of God's moral code in addition to following it.

> Thus does Allah expound to you His commandments that, it is hoped, you may understand. [*Holy Qur'ān* 24:61]

Thus becomes manifest a tension between the poles of human reason in its pure form, uninformed by religion, and unconditional faith, uninformed by understanding. Islam posits a moderate position that finds it free of contradiction to concurrently understand and believe. This moderate position is the median. The *median* is the term used in this chapter to describe the balancing act that Muslims carry out mentally when negotiating such tensions and attempting to remain "in the middle."

> Allah addresses Prophet Muhammad: "If thy Lord had enforced His will, surely all those on the earth would have believed, without exception. Will thou, then, take it upon thyself to force people to become believers? Except by Allah's leave no one can believe; and He will afflict with wrath those who will not use their understanding." [*Holy Qur'ān* 10:99–100]

The above verses lead the way to the next section, as they allude to another area of tension: the polarity between free will and determinism.

DESTINY, FREE WILL, AND ACCOUNTABILITY

According to the *Qur'ān*, God produces all "natural" laws. Creatures fit into a pattern they were predestined to find and obey physical, chemical, and biological rules set by their creator, to result in a seamless, autonomous "Nature." This also applies to humans.

Although possessing of free will and capable of moral choice, divine will and activity is operative through both natural causation and human activity and volition, whether physical or mental. The *Qur'ān* finds no contradiction between the determinism of God's plan predating creation on the one hand, and free will on the other. This is seen rather as tension between two opposing poles, one of many such tensions in Islamic ideology.

> Allah orders Prophet Muhammad: "Tell them: Allah lets go astray those whom He wills and guides to Himself those who turn to Him." [*Holy Qur'ān* 13:27]

Divine omnipotence and predetermined destiny are always the source of the entirety of causation. They cause humans to cause events. However, each individual perceives his or her actions to be autocratic. This perception is the basis upon which God's judgment of one's actions takes place. A unique set of preoccupations with these facts may unconsciously lie behind a Muslim's thought: "Does what I intend to do fit in God's plan? If so, why was I chosen to do it? What is it about me that brought this choice upon me?"

Muslims are expected to believe their actions to be of fundamental importance to the outcomes, and are as such accountable for them. Concurrently, a sense of reliance on God, and knowledge that His will is what ultimately gets fulfilled, creates a middle-of-the-road position where the anxiety and anticipation related to outcome of one's actions are tempered. This median is the rationale behind the commonly used phrase "*Insha'Allah*," or "If God wills," that Muslims say when they predict a future action on their part. It merely asserts one's faith in destiny, and therefore reduces the preoccupation with apprehensions that may serve as impediments, if not sources of mental pain. Often misunderstood, the reliance on God's will is not an excuse for one's actions or lack of them, nor is it justification for complacency in Islam. This was illustrated by Al-Dhahabi in the fourteenth-century book *At-Tibb An-Nabawi* (*Prophetic Medicine*): "*Tawakkul* is to trust God by one's heart.

However, this does not contradict natural causes or their use. Indeed, *tawakkul* itself presupposes acceptance of causation—for an expert doctor first tries his best by way of treatment and then puts his trust in God for his success" (p. 103).

It is the inexcusable nature of complacency and the emphasis the *Qur'ān* puts on people's responsibility for their fate through their efforts to change their status quo that the following verse describes:

> Surely, Allah would not change the matters of a people until they change their own. [*Holy Qur'ān* 13:11]

The accountability of people to God takes as a central premise that human action is not only unique to each individual, but is also always new, original, and unrelated to past deeds. There is no original sin in Islam. The time of birth of a person is a time when there are no deeds or sins on their record, which is described as a white sheet. The *Qur'ān*'s stress on the purity of the original state of humans cannot be underestimated. The fall of Adam and Eve from the blissful state they lived into temporal life on Earth when Satan misled them into testing the tree of life was described in the *Qur'ān*. According to the *Qur'ān*, they then repented and reconciled to God, and were forgiven. Since repentance, when absolutely genuine and associated with reconstructive remorse, is actually an "eraser" of sin, it was as if they never committed the sin. As such, the *Qur'ān* suggests no preexisting or phylogenetic deviation from morality that humanity is forever stigmatized by. Humans have the ideal equality of potential for deviation toward evil or ascendance toward righteousness. In other words, the human condition lies on the median at the inception of life.

The *Qur'ān* has described the weighing of deeds, which determines the future of every individual insofar as the Last Judgment is concerned. Accountability is conditional on the presence of the mental capacity of reason. As will be explained later, the weighing of deeds is an appraisal of both the individual and the collective, or societal, human performance. The performance that is weighed is judged based on two basic principles. The first, and arguably the most important, is *will*.

> Al-Bukhari narrated: "That the Messenger of Allah, peace be upon him, said: Deeds are, in fact, [judged] by wills, and it is each person's will that they have." [*Holy Qur'ān* 50:16]

A righteous deed has been already performed in Islam once it has been willed. Therefore, an individual will start earning credit for a good action he or she intends to perform prior to its inception. However, the same does not apply to sins. Unless the ill-favored action is carried out, no debit is made from the person's balance of deeds. What this implies is of profound impact on the way the Muslim's mental apparatus induces guilt or pride. If one has planned and actually started to take mental action on one's way to one's neighbors, intending to greet them, but was impeded from doing so, one would have already committed a righteous deed. Feeling content with this fact, rather than being discouraged, imparts peace of mind but doesn't prevent a subsequent attempt. This is due to the second measure of deeds presented below. On the other hand, if one had the impulse to harm one's neighbor but was impeded from doing so, one would not have sinned. In other words, the same individual would more likely feel guilty once physical action has taken place than when he or she contemplated the act. A polarization between good and bad deeds is easy to grasp, but the Muslim mind needs to be aware of a mental polarization: the continuum that lies between good and bad intentions.

An internal observing agency, whether preexisting or introduced, is at the forefront of Islamic theology. *Taqwa*, or piety in Arabic, literally means "protection from peril"; in this case peril is moral and behavioral corruption and disintegration. *Taqwa* is a quality in the Muslim that is only developed through constant self-examination to the extent of truthful appraisal of one's thoughts, impulses, emotions, moral values, and beliefs. It utilizes a disciplined and informed observing ego that attempts to see beyond self-deception arising from personal desires, family interest, or group demands. Arguably, people will always have intentions that may result in sin. As it is essential to faith to realize that God is fully aware of these thoughts, one can imagine the endless source of guilt that lies within our mind. If the ego psychological paradigm were to be our magnifying lens, the superego would never run out of reason to punish an individual, as long as the id actually exists.

> Assuredly, We have created man and We know well what kind of doubt his self whispers to his mind. We are closer to him than his jugular vein. [*Holy Qur'ān* 50:16]

The merciful stance of counting only sinful acts moderates the power of the guilt-inducing agency of the mind in a way that makes it more just but not in any way less powerful. Along the same line, a constant mental awareness, conscious or otherwise, of the fact of God's observance of what transpires in one's mind, as well as one's person and life, is a source of a quality of shame probably unique to Muslims. For there is more than our ego-ideal that expects and observes, more than our internalized paternal figures who feel pleasure or displeasure in our action, and more than human and societal visual observation of what we do that determine the pride–shame continuum. God is not only observing, but has also employed angels to follow each individual and record his or her actions in order to present written proof to individuals on the Day of Judgment.

> There are two, one sitting on his right and the other on his left, who learn everything concerning him and preserve it. He utters not a word, but there is by him an alert watcher who takes care to preserve it. [*Holy Qur'ān* 50:17–18]

The presence of such an external observing "agency" in the mind of a Muslim is also a contributor to *taqwa*, and adds a dimension of priority: shame in front of God is not in the same league as shame in front of peers. The mind of the Muslim, hence, is situated at equal distance from each of these observing agencies, the external and the internal. Volition, thought, impulses, and behavior are negotiated along this median.

The second parameter used to judge one's performance is its *real worth*. For it is the ultimate value of an act when evaluated longitudinally, including all of its future consequences, that constitutes its real worth. This is why a completed deed is logically better than one that was merely intended or willed. In addition, the appearance of greatness of performance at the point in time it took place is of little consequence on the Day of Judgment. The ultimate impact of the deed is only evaluated then, at the end of time.

> Muslim narrated: "Then the Messenger of Allah, peace be upon him, said: Whoever in Islam sets a good example will receive its reward and the rewards of whomever followed his example after him without discount from their rewards; and whoever in Islam sets a bad example will carry its burden and the burdens of whomever followed his example after him without discount from their burdens." [An-Nisabury 1978, pp. 704–705]

It is part of the Islamic view of the individual's position in society to include vigilance with regard to the impact of one's actions on others. This, as is illustrated in the above quoted Hadith, goes beyond contemporaries of the individual and includes subsequent generations. It is, however, an equal emphasis, although in opposing directions, on the entirety of impact of both righteous and ill-favored deeds. The social awareness and conscience imparted is in contradistinction to the present widespread ideology: the microscopic perspectives of individualized accountability. Such a narrow field of vision contributes a degree of dehiscence of an individual from his or her society, and possibly leads to reduced respect for the existence of others.

THE INDIVIDUAL, PARENTS, AND SOCIETY

Individualism and socialism are concepts that lie at opposing poles of a continuum. Islam attempts to situate Muslims at the midpoint of this continuum. The selflessness Islam calls for is an essential component of its socioeconomic and sociopolitical ideals. According to the *Qur'ān*, the noblest of all creatures, humans, can also be "the lowest of the low" if they did not redeem themselves from their fundamental deficits of pettiness, narrow-mindedness, and selfishness.

> We have created man in the best mould; then, if he works iniquity We cast him down as the lowest of the low, except those who believe and work righteousness, for them is an unending reward. [*Holy Qur'ān* 95:4–6]

The value of being human and the value of life are extraordinarily emphasized in Islam, but almost consistently described within a social dimension. Individually, a person's life is, in fact, a property of God and a responsibility for which the individual was entrusted for safekeeping until the time of his destined death. This is one of the central principles behind the prohibition of suicide, and the command to preserve one's health. In a similar vein, other people's lives are properties of God, cannot be violated, are irreplaceable, and are to be protected.

> On account of this we prescribed for the children of Israel that whosoever kills a person, except for killing another or for creating corruption in the land, it shall be as if he had killed all people; and whosoever helps one to live, it shall be as if he had given life to all people. [*Holy Qur'ān* 5:32]

It is both a respect for personhood and an obligation to protect it that Islam calls for. Race, color, gender, ethnicity, language, heritage, culture, and ancestral lineage are explicitly described to make no difference to the value of an individual in God's view. The only difference in God's judgment between people is the extent of their *taqwa*. This conceptualization is essential to Islam's egalitarianism of humankind. Further, freedom of religion and conscience is at the foundation of Islam. It is this freedom that justifies Jihad, commonly called "holy war," as it is pronounced whenever persecution on the grounds of religious beliefs is threatened. In Islamic jurisprudence, the five basic human rights that the state must protect are life, property, faith, private honor, and reason (mental faculties).

Interpersonally, Islam presents opportunities to collect credits of good deeds in almost every aspect of human interaction. A smile is a righteous deed, and so is the expression of love and affection to one's family. The Islamic greeting, *"As-Salamu-Alaikum,"* "May peace be upon you," is encouraged and rewarded, and aims to spread actual peace in the community. Once the community enjoys peace, the entire community is rewarded. Islam, in essence, produces in the mind a motivation to add to all other motivations when embarking on any interpersonal discourse: the motivation to please God, or *ikhlas*. This is just as important intrapsychically as it is interpersonally. For if *ikhlas* was even partially included as a motive to the individual's volition, contentment will invariably result no matter what the outcome is. On the social front, contentment and even joy in positive and prosocial deeds is a common experience for Muslims.

In Islam parents have a central position that is heavily emphasized in both the *Qur'ān* and the *Sunnah*. Numerous verses in the *Qur'ān* command benevolence toward one's parents, and often make the command immediately following the command to worship none but God.

Thy Lord has commanded that ye worship none but Him and has enjoined benevolence towards parents. Should either or both of them attain old age in thy lifetime, never say: Ugh; to them nor chide them, but always speak gently to them. Be humbly tender with them and pray: Lord have mercy on them, even as they nurtured me when I was little. [*Holy Qur'ān* 17:23–24]

The significantly exalted position parents hold in the mental life of a Muslim deters not from the natural development of internalized parental imagos. It may actually enhance it in such a way that emphasizes the inequity of the parental roles of mothers when compared to fathers. If parents are of central significance collectively, mothers are situated on a proverbial pedestal in the minds of Muslims, in spite of the patriarchal structure of the family. The following Hadith illustrates this point eloquently:

> Ahmad Ibn Hanbal narrated: "I said: O Messenger of Allah, who should I revere? He said: Your mother. I said: Who next? He said: Your mother. I said: Who next? He said: Your mother then your father." [Ibn Hanbal 1978, p. 3]

It is therefore evident that such powerful ties of childhood remain so in adulthood. Separation from parents in Islam is neither encouraged nor seen as essential for the development of autonomy. A total relinquishment of the real maternal figure, in favor of the internal mother, arguably never takes place in the mind of a Muslim reared in an Islamic society. Although presently considered unusual in a Western society, such a situation creates in the mind a continuous balance between the demands of the internalized and the real mother. It is perhaps another median in Islamic thought that this presents, one that possesses a great deal of influence on the intrapsychic functioning of Muslims. It also continues to play a role in the interpersonal and social spheres. A married man's parents are never totally excluded from the heart or the mind, and the man's obligations to his parents never cease until the man and his parents are parted by death. Similarly, a woman's relationship to her mother is possibly strengthened, rather than weakened, by her marriage and child bearing. Although autonomy increases, total separation is often never achieved.

If one examined the Islamic emphasis on family values and neighborliness, the position of an individual in relation to parents, spouses, children, extended family, and neighbors will be found to be bound by obligations and by individual rights. The interwoven structure that develops is that of cohesion, at the center of which stands human well-being. One way of describing this would be a state of incomplete individuation, an "in-the-middle" position between total enmeshment and complete isolation from others. At this level, groups based on family ties and groups based on being neighbors intertwine to form larger communities that are characterized by interpersonal relationships as the "adhesive substance" holding these different "blocks" together. The Prophet has described this "collective" as having a "life-like quality" to it.

Al-Bukhari narrated: "The Messenger of Allah, peace be upon him, said: You see the faithful in their mercy of one another, their loving of one another and their fondness with one another, as the example of the body; if an organ complained, the rest of the body is summoned with watchfulness and fever." [Al-Asqalani 1989, p. 537]

The outcome, the solidarity that Islam brings about in the Muslim community, is a result of a collective identity formed by more than just the sharing of religion. This collective identity is one that has priority over all other sources of identity, and in most cases supersedes them completely. This is again achieved through devaluation of other major sources of identity, such as race, gender, nationality, tribal affiliation, and so on. Importantly, Islam includes in the repertoire of obligations and rights of individuals a dimension of Islamic society. Integrity of the Muslim community is as much the responsibility of the subject as it is the ruler's. When conflicts of interest arise, priority is afforded to the community over the individual. Accordingly, a continuum between conformity and self-realization exists, the center of which is the aim of a Muslim's behavior. It also follows that self-service and selflessness should be in balance, and so should the dyads of humility and assertiveness, and self-effacing modesty and vainness.

In the ideal Muslim community, personal *taqwa* is assumed in each individual, and *taqwa* is expected to express itself in the social dimension. In the *Qur'ān*, the responsibility that humanity carries is that of reforming the earth and removing corruption, while following God's divine commands, and "ruling" a just and faithful community. Such a community enjoys God's rewards for both its individuals' and collective deeds, as well as suffers the consequences of both sources of ill-favored acts. In Islam, the community works on behalf of God, is expected to command good and forbid evil, and is accountable, as a community, to God. The community is not assured of salvation if it only claims to be a Muslim community. It needs to come up to its tasks.

The tension arising from this polarization between the individual as the center of the universe, and individual as a nonconsequential particle of a large mass called society, is tension that the Muslim is at ease with if he or she walked along the median.

HOPE AND FEAR

The hope that God will have mercy on the individual on the Day of Judgment, that he will reward one with an eternity in one of the Gardens (e.g., the Garden of Paradise and the Garden of Eden), that he will accept one's deeds and answer one's supplications to him, that he would guide one to the straight path of righteousness, that he will forgive one's sins, and that he will provide contentment in both the *Dunya* (the present life) and the *Akhirah* (the later life or Hereafter) are what Muslims hope and pray for everyday. Fear of punishment and agony on the Day of Judgment, the consequence of an eternity in the Hellfire, rejection of one's deeds and prayers, retribution from one's sins, and misery in both the present and the later lives are the other side of the coin. God in the *Qur'ān* describes himself to possess all the qualities required to maximize this polarization of hope and fear. At times the *Qur'ān* presents only the hope-inducing side, at other times only the fear-producing side, and yet at others the two opposing poles intertwine.

Despite variations in the practice of different schools of Sunni thought, the *Qur'ān* actually emphasizes the need to maintain a balance between hope and fear, that is, to lie in the middle of the continuum. This median is one that inspires and cultivates *taqwa*. It moderates foolhardy hope and extinguishes the paralyzing horror aspect of fear, where hopelessness leads to utter despair. If proactive forces springing from unlimited hope are about to run amok with one's mental processes, thus removing inhibition and allowing chaos, the prohibitive forces function as the reality censor that prevents anarchy. Should fear-induced prohibition attempt to tyrannize the mental functions of an individual, or inculcate hopelessness and despair, hope takes the role of the reality censor, antagonizes unjust inhibition, and combats despair. A battle between the two may not, in the real world, exist in the mind; the example provided is for illustration only. The reality is that the source and subject of both the fear and the hope is the same one God. Whatever it is that is contemplated in the mind will have to situate itself along the continuum of fear and hope as the moral apparatus of the mind evaluates it.

Examine the following passage in the *Qur'ān*, wherein the contrasts between God's mercy and his punishment are made along with a most stark contrast between righteousness and sin in a way that illustrates the extreme polarization of hope and fear in the minds of Muslims:

Allah is the Light of the heavens and of the earth. The example of His light is a lustrous niche, wherein is a lamp contained in a crystal globe, the globe as bright as a glittering star. The lamp is lit with the oil of a blessed tree, an olive, neither of the east nor of the west. The oil would well nigh glow forth even if no fire were to touch it. Light upon light! Allah guides to His light whomsoever He wills. Allah sets forth all that is needful for humankind. Allah knows all things

well. This light now illumines houses that Allah has ordained that
they be exalted and in which His name is commemorated. Therein
is He glorified morn and eve by men whom neither trade nor traffic
beguiles from the remembrance of Allah and the observance of
Prayer and the payment of Zakāt. They fear a day on which hearts
and eyes will be agitated, so that Allah may bestow upon them the
best reward for their deeds, and give them more out of His bounty.
Allah provides for whomsoever He wills without measure. The
works of those who disbelieve are like a mirage in a wide plain. A
thirsty one imagines it to be water until, when he comes up to it, he
finds it to be nothing, and finds Allah near him, Who then pays him
his account in full. Allah is Swift at reckoning. Or, their works are
like thick darkness spread over a vast and deep sea, the surface of
which is agitated by waves rolling upon waves, above which are
clouds; layers of darkness one upon another so thick that when a
person holds out his hand he can hardly see it. For him whom Allah
grants not light, there is no light at all. [*Holy Qur'ān* 24:35–40]

This continuum of hope in opposition to fear and the median
along its center is one that invades the contemplation of all thought
and the assessment of all action. It may appear to be exclusively
applicable to acts seen as either righteous or sinful, but it is, in fact,
a general attitude toward life that Islam inspires. It is arguably
possible to examine an individual's emotional state and cognitive
appraisal of his or her past, present, and future, and situate this
appraisal along the hope–fear continuum. The more proximate
the appraisal to the median, the more appropriate, and the more
distant from the median, the more pathological.

ILLNESS AND HEALTH

A narrow definition of health will restrict it to the optimum
performance and integrity of known physiological and psychological functions. A wider definition would include the wholesomeness
of the entire person, including spiritual, psychological, social, and

physiological dimensions. Spiritual health in Islam would also include a bipartite dimension or bipolar continuum of contentment in both the present life and the Hereafter.

A human being in the *Qur'ān* is a single organism, united and possessing personhood. Although faith in the presence of the soul is part of Islam, no elaboration, definition, or description of the soul is provided. This is in contradistinction to the word *self*, which is used to mean personhood. One's mind is a component of one's person, which is contained in the outer body. Although the distinction between the self and the body exists, the radical doctrine of mind–body dualism does not. Therefore, in approaching illness, a holistic appraisal and, if possible, a holistic treatment are called for by Islam, both for the patient and for the treating professional.

As for the patient, Islam presents illness in the framework of God's plan for the person. Illness is a state that puts the person's mind to the test. Coping strategies are enlisted, the meaning of illness is contemplated at the psychic level, the appraisal of what the future holds changes, and the social role of the person may be modified. Of chief importance to all these is Islamic faith. Take the following Hadith, for example:

> Al-Bukhari narrated: "The Prophet, peace be upon him, said: Whatever strikes the Muslim, whether fatigue [or hardship], illness, anxiety, sadness, harm, or grief [or distress], even a thorn sting, but is countered by Allah's forgiving some of his sins." [Al-Asqalani 1989, p. 126]

With facility, it is possible to understand how the misfortune of illness is tempered by the fortune of pardon from sin. The punitive interpretation of illness does not exist in Islam. Illness is seen as a test of faith, whereby patience during such trial and reliance on God (*tawakkul*) are called upon to help cope with the distress. Both patience and *tawakkul* are virtues subject to being rewarded by God. One not only reduces the debit, but also increases the credit. Since *tawakkul* is enlisted, the necessity of seeking causes of cure is preventive of turning illness into a celebrated occurrence that is allowed to flourish without opposition, and enables the person to resign his or her future to Allah as long as what has to be done to get over the disability incurred is carried out. It also means the person will be more likely to accept with contentment, rather than contempt or despair, any chronic or permanent consequences of illness. In addition, the hope–fear continuum exists in dealing with illness, and keeping close to the median would be the healthiest position to take.

In the social sphere, the patient is often excused from many religious obligations, and is expected to be the recipient of empathy and support from the family, the community, and even the state. The faithful are encouraged, and rewarded, for visiting the sick, praying for them, and providing them with both comfort and hope. This deed is often equated in its "weight" to the selfless, charitable giving to others that sustains life. Does Islam encourage a passive, helpless stance toward illness? Ideally it does not. For if the internal agency of *taqwa* was operative, willful exaggeration of illness or delay of cure can only make the person subject to God's wrath. Imagine the internal voice of reason saying, "Am I genuinely excused from my religious duties? Am I utilizing the causes of cure conscientiously enough to regain my health? Am I adequately responding to God's command of preserving my life and health?" Clearly, Islam attempts to position the ill person at the center of the continuum connecting two poles: the passive reception of empathy and care, and the extreme proactive and self-asserting rejection of it.

The above-described median is of immense relevance to the nature of the doctor–patient relationship. Leading physicians in the history of Islam set examples of professional conduct vis-à-vis the patient, one of which is worth mentioning here. Ar-Rāzi (tenth century A.D.) advised physicians to have patience with all patients, and to generously give time to them; the physician should listen more and talk less. This sensitivity to the psyche of the patient is a sine qua non to the Islamic practice of medicine. *Tawakkul* applies to the doctor in that he needs to do what is necessary and depend on God for the outcome of his actions. For the physician, Islam instills hope in finding a cure by asserting that God has created illness and created a cure for each one. No effort should be spared in finding a diagnosis or a cure. When no cure is known, scientific inquiry in the form of research and experimentation is strongly encouraged.

These principles apply equally to physical and mental illness. In addition, Islam deals in depth with the issues of competence, obligation, and accountability of the mentally ill or deficient. Suffice it to say, the integrity of reason has the most central role in the determination of these states.

In spite of the absence of any unequivocal evidence in the *Qur'ān* and the *Sunnah* to support relegation of the etiology of all mental illness to supernatural forces, a great many Muslims do so, and some believe that only certain forms of spiritual healing can be hoped to meet with any success in the management of these conditions. A full analysis of this state of affairs is beyond the scope of this chapter. It is important to note, though, that Islam introduces another median to the treatment of all illnesses in general, and to mental illness in particular. This is the moderate position situated between complete reliance on spiritual healing mechanisms without resorting to known and tested medical approaches, and the exclusion of spirituality in pure forms of medical treatment. Islam suggests the combination of the two, the concurrent utilization of experimental medicine and religious sources of healing. The depressed person, who has retained enough reason and reality testing to be able to perform prayer and supplications, is expected to pray for relief as well as receive psychosocial and biological intervention provided by the mental health professional. The helping professions, often devoid of great influence from religious ideology and claiming objective empiricism as their sources, are expected to respect the religious beliefs of this depressed person; not only that, but also to investigate the reality of these beliefs, the degree to which the person can and does utilize them, and to encourage integration of the forms of spiritual healing that are supported by the *Qur'ān* and the *Sunnah* with medical interventions. Exclusion of spirituality may, in fact, be injurious to the Muslim who strongly holds the faith and practices Islam in his or her life. This moderate position is yet another of those medians influencing the mental life of Muslims.

THE SELF IN ISLAM

The *Qur'ān* and the *Sunnah* have described the human *nafs* (an Arabic word meaning "self," "psyche," or "person") to have many characteristics or types. At the base of mental functioning is the driven or urging *nafs*. This is a driving, motivating, and demanding element of the human mind that aims at satisfying the needs, desires, and frustrations of the person. These needs and desires have been elaborated by many to include sexual, aggressive, material (greed, possession, desires), social position, and life-preserving urges. In Islam, the urging self is the impatient, impulsive part of the person that requires monitoring and control in order for the person to be able to fulfill his or her duties to God. Although it includes instinctual, nonconscious elements of mental functioning, the urging self can also be conscious. The impulses that one is aware of, or is made aware of, are included in this realm of the mind according to the Islamic tradition. Some have referred to the forces of this component of the self as the "present life forces" or "urgent passions," as opposed to the "later life forces" or "deferred passions," which would propel the person to "moderate" the impact of these impulsive urges on the mental life of the person. Humans were described in the *Qur'ān* to be driven and hasty to gratify their needs. Shafii (1985), who has elaborated the structure of the mind and personality in his book *Freedom from the Self* from the Sufi perspective, described this urging component of the self:

> These forces drive animals and human beings to action without pause, inhibition, or thinking. Human beings, like animals, can be

impulsively driven by this *nafs* to perform acts which they generally would not do. Indulgence in sexual wishes, immediate need gratification, and loss of control in the form of rage, destruction, homicide, or suicide, are extreme forms of expression of driven *nafs*. [p. 121]

As is the case in Christianity and Judaism, Islam accepts the presence of the Devil as a fact. The Muslim's vulnerability to the Devil's "whispering" or suggestions stems from the urging self, which also is the recipient of these suggestions. However, Islam attributes the motivating forces of this urging part of the mind ultimately to the person, rather than to the Devil. Islam recognizes that this part of the person's mind or self is a component of the God-created human being, and cannot be disavowed, rejected, or stigmatized as being evil. Islam, however, favors employment of the other components of the self to keep the urging self from dominating the life of the person. Shafii (1985) has pointed out the similarities that the concept of the urging self shares with the Freudian id. Compared with the urging self, however, the id is a more restricted concept that focuses primarily on unconscious libidinal and aggressive drives. Nevertheless, the presence of this type of *nafs* in Islamic thought is a clear indication of an understanding that unconscious processes are important components of the mind and that a task of awareness is to moderate their rule and tame their passions.

The *Qur'ān* has described another type of *nafs*: the blaming or accusing *nafs*. This component of the person is what contains the moral censorship, conscience, sense of guilt, and possibly shame. Although Shafii (1985) has likened the blaming self to the superego of ego psychology's structural theory, Islam does not clearly espouse it with punitive, unmerciful strengths that are capable of tormenting the individual. Nonetheless, it is a major component of the inhibiting agent in the mind, and it does so in the Muslim's psyche by contrasting the individual's intentions to the rules of morality. It is a component of the internal observing agency, and is essential to the development of *taqwa*. Although it functions primarily in the realm of awareness, the blaming self acts in part unconsciously, or at least automatically, and may be motivational to the individual's behavior.

Muslims have always been aware of a component of the mind that perceives and reasons, the *aql*, Arabic for "reason," or the faculty that perceives, knows, or understands. The two components of *aql* are perception and reason. Reason is in Islam the prime attribute of humankind. It is the seed of the intellect and the source of rationality, logic, conceptualization, and abstraction. Reason is, at least in part, another component of the internal observing agency. The "heart" in Arabic, *qalb*, is the equivalent to the affect perceiving and experiencing, and faith-holding component of the mind. The heart possesses some of the more creative and emotionally laden attributes of the human psyche. It also is the place where knowledge is transformed into conviction, and reality into ultimate reality. Essentially, the heart adds emotional investment to thought—cathexis. The heart is the part of the mind that may experience knowing that was not preceded by a logico-mathematic stream of thought, but that just happened. This is a kind of knowing that is more intuitive and less rehearsed than that which is produced by reason, and may have origins in, or be influenced by, the unconscious. The intuitive function of the mind is encouraged and supported in Islam. However, it is clearly attributed to the person's mind, and he or she is equally accountable to acts out of intuition and to acts based on results of logical calculations.

> Have they not traveled in the earth that they may have hearts wherewith to understand or ears wherewith to hear? The truth is that it is not the eyes that become blind, but blinded are the hearts that are in the breasts. [*Holy Qur'ān* 22:46]

Although reason can influence the heart and vice versa, both reason and heart have equal potential to lead the mental functioning of the individual.

These different and often opposing components of the mind are held by the principle of moderation in Islam. The interplay of these various mental functions seeks to find a median that would lead to and usher in the stability and contentment that the mind aims for. The urging self can be seen as one end of a continuum, the opposing end being the blaming self. Similarly, urgent passions and deferred ones are opposing ends of a continuum. The stance of Islam along a metaphorical median here can be illustrated by an ancient Arabic traditional saying of wisdom: "Work for the Later Life as if you know that you die tomorrow; and work for the Present Life as if you know that you will live forever."

Reason and heart are another continuum of mental functioning. Moderation in this area is implied in Islam by its move to incorporate the heart in decision making, its respect for human emotions, and its endorsement of the heart as the seat of faith, while concurrently honoring reason and making it the precondition for accountability and an essential attribute of humanity that must be preserved.

THE MEDIAN OF ISLAMIC FAITH AND PSYCHOTHERAPY

By that We have made you a median people. [*Holy Qur'ān* 2:143]

Thus far, the medians explored were along the continua of divine morality and reason; irreligious reasoning and unconditional faith; determinism and free will; potential gravitation toward righteousness and evil of the human's original state; the polarization between good and bad intentions and impulses; internal versus external observing agencies; guilt and shame; individualism and socialism; intrapsychic and interpersonal motives; relinquishment of parental figures and enmeshment; individual and community accountability; hope and fear; wholeness and duality of personhood; positive and negative appraisals of illness; passivity and proactivity; authoritative and empathic stance of physicians; spiritual and medical healing; urging and blaming *nafses*; and reason and heart.

There are innumerable areas of life where such a median of moderation is the Islamic stance. This mediation can be between any two perceived extremes. Extremes are probably always more restrictive and ultimately enslaving than the moderate stance. If one's mental activities are regularly moderated by the individual's attempt to walk along the median, it would take little imagination to perceive his or her psyche to be more creative, less burdened, and mostly content. When each area of one's life has been pervaded by this attitude in the ideal Islamic life, the clarity of aims, the justice of interpersonal discourse, and the balance and equilibration of all the naturally occurring tensions pulling on humanity will invariably create a generative yet safe state of tranquillity and satisfaction. Fazlur Rahman (1987) put forth this argument:

> *Taqwa*, or sense of responsibility, in fact, cannot be maintained unless one synthesizes these contradictory poles in one's conduct. This is what the Qur'an calls the "straight path," the "upright religion," and this is also why it characterizes the Muslim community as the "median community" which was expected to synthesize extremes rather than negate them. For by negating the polarities, human conduct becomes abstract and loses its grip on concrete life. [p. 22]

To what extent can this understanding be utilized in the psychotherapy of Muslims? The possibilities abound to use this paradigm in a number of therapeutic approaches. Without doubt, any individual's psyche has developed along unique pathways that are influenced by genetic endowment, intrapsychic organizations, interpersonal and environmental interactions, and cultural values that are only distantly, if at all, related to the Islamic ideals. All have very important contributions to therapeutic interaction, as does the course this therapeutic interaction follows. Nevertheless, to maintain the theme of this chapter, only the study of the impact and utility of elaborated concepts will be the focus of the following section. Both psychodynamic and cognitive-behavioral therapies are addressed. Applicability to most other forms of therapy may require the use of similar conceptualizations and approaches to the unique issues of treating Muslim clients.

PSYCHOANALYTIC
AND DYNAMIC APPROACHES

In the case of psychoanalysis, adhering to the antireligious doctrines that may still be in practice would probably be disenchanting to the average Muslim analysand. Therefore, such doctrines pose a threat to the formation of therapeutic alliance or create a source of bias that preferentially brings out mechanisms of resistance otherwise not utilized by the analysand in his or her daily life among other Muslims. Arguably, this may be systematically overcome by careful analysis, but will probably introduce an aim to the psychoanalysis other than simply "analysis." Alternatively, if the analyst were to adopt a middle-of-the-road stance that allows integration between religious teachings and psychoanalytic understanding, it is conceivable that a productive endeavor will result. Rigidity, after all, is an extreme, and past rigid stances of psychoanalysis have made it unpopular in the Muslim world as a form of psychological treatment.

To make this integration possible, an understanding of the sources of morality in Muslims should concurrently inform the analyst along with material related to identifications with parents and authority figures early in the development of the Muslim analysand. The analyst should be sensitive to the degree of relinquishment of "real" parental figures, or lack of it, as they examine the internalized identifications, part-objects, and imagos. A respect for the social and interpersonal motivations and drive for interdependence, as opposed to independence, should co-occur with analysis of intrapsychic motives. The need for conformity should temper the psychoanalytic tendency to maximize self-realization. Awareness of the uniqueness Islam brings to the emotions of shame and guilt is essential. Moreover, the analyst must have an understanding of the principles of *tawakkul*, lest they may be falsely invoked as excuses for certain behaviors, if not resistance.

Although sexuality was not extensively dealt with in the previous sections, suffice it to say that the non-Muslim analysand presenting with extreme inhibition is probably similar to the unduly inhibited Muslim. The difference is stark, however, when a moderate Muslim is encountered. This is because present Western values with regard to sexuality will be appraised by the religious Muslim to be permissive to the extreme, even when they constitute normality in the West. It is therefore a matter of relativity, and requires a careful consideration of the degree of adherence to religion by the analysand. This evaluation of adherence should take in consideration both the norm in the analysand's background as well as the fit with the analysand's present life circumstances. Hence, the analyst takes a more moderate view by walking along the median. In general, one could assume that emotional expression of all forms would be more inhibited in the average Muslim, as there is also a median for such expression. This would be somewhere between the encouraged total expression of Western culture, and the total inhibition or restriction of expression seen in some individuals. Finding this median should take into account the degree of emotional expression or restriction that is socially advantageous for each client.

Although dynamic psychotherapy and psychoanalysis are different, they have much in common both theoretically and in relation to technique of intervention. It will, therefore, follow that the same considerations need to be carefully negotiated during the course of psychotherapy.

The analyst or the dynamic psychotherapist may be faced with the task of negotiating a parent–child dyad that will almost inevitably dominate much of the therapeutic relationship (see Al-Issa 2000). Its origins are in the exalted value of parents and both the patriarchal culture and the incomplete separation from parental figures. If the analyst or therapist conforms to this dyad, a more active and directive stance that allows for less exploration and reflection may develop. It can be argued that such a stance is less therapeutic, or that the drive to create such an interaction in the dyad is subject to analysis. Alternatively, one could possibly create a more lasting therapeutic relationship by permitting this interaction initially and slowly analyzing it. There is probably no strong evidence to support either of these attitudes, and this situation may unfold in therapy and analysis in various other ways. Therefore, a median approach may be useful. Such a median will have to be tailored to each client's particular needs and circumstances.

Another commonly encountered difficulty in the therapy or analysis of Muslims is the higher expectation for self-disclosure. Although not unique to the Muslim client, it probably is a more prevalent attitude among Muslims. Consider the communal, interdependent, incompletely separate, and family-like social sphere of the Muslim. The norm is for people to share, and this may be the expectation of a Muslim client in therapy or analysis.

Many Muslim psychotherapists and psychiatrists claim that the psychoanalytic and dynamic forms of therapy are at much disadvantage when applied to Muslim clients. In addition to the issues discussed above, it has been argued that the Muslim client is more likely to be intolerant to exploratory and insight-oriented therapy (Al-Issa 2000). They have, perhaps, reached a premature closure on this issue. Even if one presupposes that Muslim clients are more anaclitic, as opposed to being predominantly introjective, certain of the mechanisms of change attributable to dynamic and analytic therapies will continue to apply (Gabbard 2000). The quality of the therapeutic relationship may therefore be of greater importance than interpretations. In Wallerstein's (1986) analysis of the Menninger Foundation Psychotherapy Research Project, such factors as the transference cure connected to unanalyzed positive dependent transference, transfer of the transference to another important object in the client's present life, antitransference cure, corrective emotional experience, and supportive treatment were examples of mechanisms of change.

COGNITIVE-BEHAVIORAL THERAPY

Michael Mahoney (1995) lists among the recent developments in the field of cognitive-behavioral therapy that issues of value, including aspects of religion and spirituality, have come to be recognized as inevitable in psychology and psychotherapy. He reports that there is a softening of the mainstream aversion to the relevance of religious and spiritual issues in human development and in psychological interventions. With the increasing influence of the constructivist movement, and the rapid growth of the schema-focused type of cognitive-behavioral psychotherapy, which attempts to form a developmental understanding of the client, this softening should not come as a surprise. Interestingly, the utilization of cognitive-behavioral therapies in the Muslim world has not met with resistance, and was found to easily fit the bill for Muslims. It is usually assumed that the active, directive, educational, and nonreflective nature of the therapy is the explanation of this spread. Although certainly probable, these explanations fall short of recognizing two major issues. The first is the scarcity of other forms of therapy for which experienced therapists exist in the Muslim world. The second, and arguably the most relevant, is the ease with which a Muslim therapist could evaluate the extent of deviation from rational Islamic thinking that a troubling belief, thought, or obsession is characterized by.

The emphasis in cognitive-behavioral therapy on the appraisal of thoughts has everything to do with the concept of the median when treating a Muslim client. If the client presents with hopelessness based on the committal of a sinful deed, the median of the hope–fear continuum may be utilized to aid the client to come closer to a more rational appraisal of the situation. The client who complains of social anxiety may be aided by an appraisal of the distance from the median, and the location of his feelings on the continuum of humility and assertiveness. Similarly, the median would be helpful in the evaluation of the somatizing client's appraisal of the meaning of illness. Accordingly, it would be advantageous for the therapist to gain some understanding of the areas of Islamic thought that are pertinent to the client's symptoms, and, in most cases, assume the presence of a continuum between extremes. Subsequently, the median paradigm becomes easily applicable.

Finally, the role of spiritual support and reassurance in the psychotherapy of Muslim clients cannot be underestimated. Utilizing the understanding of the medians of Islam may be helpful in this form of supportive therapy. Al-Abdul-Jabbar and Al-Issa (Al-Issa 2000) have elaborated on the use of four basic religious ideals in spiritual support: faith, particularly emphasizing issues of predetermined fate and reward on the Day of Judgment in the course of therapy; prayer and hope, utilizing the injection of hope that prayer can give to the faithful; patience, a concept in Islam that includes endurance without protest, acceptance of God's will, and expecting reward for withstanding God's tests; and the role and limitations of responsibility, with emphasis on separating guilt from the intention sphere and linking it to the action sphere, and on the human limitations that relieve individuals from accountability. Stressing the limitless and unconditional mercy that God endows upon humanity is integral to this approach:

Allah addresses the Prophet: "Convey to them: O My servants who have committed excesses against your own selves, despair not of the mercy of Allah, surely Allah forgives all sins; He is Most Forgiving, Ever Merciful." [*Holy Qur'ān* 39:53]

CONCLUSION

The devout Muslim who holds a healthy and correct faith will undoubtedly believe that "God helps." The conclusion is unequivocally affirmative. The reasoning behind this is evident to that individual even if revelation did not proclaim that attribute as one of God's, which it actually did. If God has gracefully endowed upon one the gift of life, has permitted the individual to fit into and follow his predetermined plan, and has the omnipotence to "run the show," it follows that should help occur, it would be with God's leave. The ideal Muslim will also recognize all the tensions that he or she negotiates, and will consciously attempt to remain close to the median. That way, prevention of much anguish will be in place. Should mental illness strike, he or she will know the tools for help furnished by God, unless touch with reality is lost. These tools include the spiritual, the mental (e.g., the median conceptualization), and the medical, among others.

The opposing argument is one that could be made without subscription to Islamic faith. What empirical evidence is there for this affirmative conclusion? The answer is, unfortunately, elusive. To avoid what might be considered circular reasoning, faith-induced reason cannot be utilized. Is there research evidence to support a positive relationship between Islamic faith and mental health or pathology? To date, little research has attempted to tackle that question. In essence, and in spite of some promising early efforts and reports, there is neither adequate experimental evidence for nor evidence against these affirmations. Whenever evidence is lacking for a phenomenon, a faulty syllogism could lead one to believe that a positive link does not exist. In order not to use faulty logic, the following should be remembered: Evidence against a theory will indicate faultiness of the theory, whereas evidence for a theory could not prove that theory according to the rules of logic. Since there is no evidence to disprove the theory that God helps, and none to disprove the helpful impact of Islamic faith, then we should keep our minds open to the possibilities and be ready to take up the challenges they impose.

REFERENCES

Ahmad, K. (1994). *Family Life In Islam*. Leicester, UK: Islamic Foundation.

Al-Asqalani, A. (1989). *Fat'h-ul-Bari: Sharh-u-Sahih-il-Bukhari (Al-Bukhari's Authentic Narrations*. Beirut: Dar El-Kutub El-Ilmiyah.

Al-Dhahabi, M. (1963). *At-Tibb An-Nabawi (Prophetic Medicine)*. Cairo: Dar-ul-Maaraif.

Al-Faruqi, L. (1994). *Women, Muslim Society and Islam*. Plainfield, IN: American Trust Publications.

Al-Issa, I., ed. (2000). *Al-Junun: Mental Illness in the Islamic World*. Madison, CT: International Universities Press.

Ar-Razi, A. B. (1955). *Al-Hawi fit-Tibb (The Admirer of Medicine)*. Hyderabad, India: Oriental Publication Bureau.

Beck, A. T. (1967). *Depression: Clinical, Experimental and Theoretical Aspects*. New York: Harper & Row.

Dols, M. W. (1992). *Majnun: The Madman in Medieval Islamic Society*. New York: Oxford University Press.

Freud, S. (1927). The future of an illusion. *Standard Edition* 21:1–56.

Gabbard, G. O. (2000). *Psychodynamic Psychiatry in Clinical Practice*, 3rd ed. Washington, DC: American Psychiatric Press.

Ibn Hanbal, A. (1978). *Al-Musnad (The Collection of Tradition)*, 2nd ed. Beirut: Dar El-Fikr.

Izetbegovic, A. A. (1994). *Islam Between East and West*. Indianapolis, IN: American Trust Publications.

Mahoney, M. J., ed. (1995). *Cognitive and Constructive Psychotherapies: Theory, Research, and Practice*. New York: Springer.

Rahman, F. (1979). *Islam*. Chicago: University of Chicago Press.

——— (1980). *Major Themes of the Qur'ān*. Minneapolis: Bibliotheca Islamica.

——— (1987). *Health and Medicine in the Islamic Tradition*. New York: Crossroad.

Ricoeur, P. (1970). *Freud and Philosophy: An Essay on Interpretation*. New Haven, CT: Yale University Press.

Shafii, M. (1985). *Freedom from the Self: Sufism, Meditation and Psychotherapy*. New York: Human Sciences.

Wallerstein, R. S. (1986). *Forty-Two Lives in Treatment: A Study of Psychoanalysis and Psychotherapy*. New York: Guilford.

Zafrulla Khan, M. (1997). *The Qur'ān*. Brooklyn, NY: Olive Branch.

11

A MATTER OF FAITH:

Discussion of Ad-Dab'bagh's Chapter,
"The Median: Islamic Faith
and Mental Health"

M. Hossein Etezady, M.D.

discuss / understand / make sense of / seek to

P sychoanalysis can deal with spiritual and religious faith only from the perspective of the individual's emotional and subjective state. Objective validity and the veracity of faith-related assertions, which are the province of theology and of a philosophical nature, are not matters that psychoanalysis can address. Since the dimensions of the object of faith are beyond the reach of cognitive and emotional grasp, neither science nor the scientific tradition of psychoanalysis can do more than pose questions and remain, at best, quizzically attentive.

Clinical accounts of religious experience frequently find their manifestations in the form of defenses or regressive modes of expression, as this is the state in which we usually find our patients. Additionally, we have tended to regard matters of dogma and authoritarian sanctions with skepticism and doubt.

Whatever faith or religion of the patient, psychoanalysis can be successfully applied to restore health and enhance quality of life. Divergent or opposing value systems on the two sides of the couch need not be a hindrance to the therapeutic process if the analytic principles of technique are consistently applied.

This chapter discusses the problems inherent in psychoanalytic considerations regarding faith and spirituality and their attendant technical concerns during the couse of treatment. In addition, I propose an object relations and developmental perspective on faith that places the focus of our attention and locus of intervention on the intrapsychic dynamics and the psychic reality regardless of the environmental variations of cultural traditions, social and religious sanctons, or value systems.

KEEPING AN OPEN MIND

"Does God help?" is the question posed to us, perhaps playfully, yet earnestly. As a psychoanalyst, I am not in a position to elaborate in a theological vein on such a question. Ad-Dab'bagh has done our field a valuable service by providing a well-founded and soundly reasoned response to this question from an Islamic perspective. I can only remark that from the point of view of a religious individual, such a question sounds at once absurd, naive, and sacrilegious. Religions leave no room for doubt in the belief that the will of God permeates, regulates, and sustains all events and the whole of the universe, the known and the unknowable, the content of all levels of existence, across the continua of time and space. Perhaps a more legitimate question for a person of faith might be, Under what circumstances and how might we expect divine intervention on a personal level in a moment of need? Philosophy or theology could expectably provide answers here, but as a psychoanalyst I do not see how we might be able to use the principles of our discipline to arrive at the answers. When an individual tells us in total sincerity and complete conviction that he or she has experienced such an intervention, do we have at our disposal more than our observation that our subject reports this as a true event? The subjective reality may not be the whole of reality, but it is an aspect of a sort of reality, not always amenable to objective verification.

As psychoanalysts in Freud's tradition, we strive to maintain a scientific and objective frame of mind. Ideally we are open-minded, ready to be surprised, skeptical and capable of reformulating our understanding based on the validity of the evidence at hand. The evidence unfolds before us as we participate in an intersubjective process that can be unpredictable, irreducible, and chaotic. It defies simplification or linear reasoning. We use our past encounters to recognize and codify what we find. Insoluble problems can arise at any time. No two encounters are the same. We cannot step in the same river twice. Preconceptions and rigid parameters can blind us and deprive us of the flexibility that we need to maintain an open system, capable of assimilating, accommodating, and progressively integrating an evolving narrative. The evidence is examined, not in abstraction, but in context. Our assessment of the evidence can be trusted only if we understand the context. This is more likely to be the case if we are able to influence and exert a degree of control over the context whenever possible or desirable. This elusive semblance of control and predictability can be approximated through implementation of our basic rules of technique, especially the principle of neutrality (Baker 2000, Franklin 1990). I will return to this point later to consider the task of the analyst in dealing with religious, cultural, and moral values of the patient in the course of psychoanalytic treatment.

FACT, FEELING, OR FAITH?

Based on its tradition of scientific orientation and reliance on objective evidence, psychoanalysis has maintained a skeptical and, at times, dismissive attitude toward assertions of religion and all matters of faith. Immutable certitude and unshakable belief, far from being admirable and devoutly desired, have been viewed as potential obstacles in the path of access to deeper levels or alternate states of understanding and development of enlightening insight that leads to broadening of horizons.

Throughout the history of scientific endeavor and on all

frontiers of research and scientific advancement, there has been a philosophical schismatic tension between the objectivity required of science and the subjective nature of faith. This tension peaked in the nineteenth century and moved toward a gradual resolution at the end of the twentieth century. In this respect, psychoanalysis as a body of knowledge, a research method, and a therapeutic tool has dealt with a similar kind of difficulty concerning the question of faith. Psychoanalysis has begun to establish a dialogue between the two sides of this continuum (Cavel 1999, Hanly 1999). The so-called intersubjective school of psychoanalysis (Greenberg 1986, Stolorow 1997), for example, emphasizes the role and inevitability of emotional resonance. It demonstrates how the psychoanalytic process is the product of the interaction between two poles of subjective reality. In this view, the possibility of establishing an objective stance, a blank screen, a reflecting mirror and the notion of neutrality of the analyst have been attacked. In this respect, the desirability and even the possibility of such an objectivity has been questioned. What has remained unquestioned as a principle is the primacy of the experience of the analysand. The analyst does not impose his own views, values, cultural standards, or religious orientation on the patient. As difficult a task as this is, examination and constant monitoring of the countertransference is the indispensable tool that makes this objective achievable. The goal is to systematically analyze rather than allow the force of countertransference to lead to enactment. To assure that this proceeds well and does so in an atmoshpere of honesty, neutrality, and respect is the responsibility of the analyst. He or she is the "conscience of the analysis" (Calef and Weinshel 1980).

CLOSE ENCOUNTERS OF NUMEROUS KINDS

In the course of the century in which psychoanalysis was born and became the dominant mode of explaining the workings of the mind and the underpinnings of psychological development, it gathered its material from the work of its practitioners with their patients in clinical encounters. As consumers and practitioners, many have participated in psychoanalytic treatment and investigation. Of these ventures, some have entailed intensive and exhaustive engagements using the couch. Others have been limited to brief encounters of clinical assessment, interdisciplinary consultation, counseling, or crisis intervention. Men or women on both sides of the therapeutic enterprise have come from homogeneous or divergent religious, national, cultural, and racial origins. Divergent or opposing frames of morality and cultural values have come face to face in the context of many therapeutic encounters numerous times.

This wide range of diversity in the history of therapeutic intervention has put the basic tenets of psychoanalysis to the test and has consolidated its basic doctrine resulting in the refinement of its technique. The psychoanalytic situation carefully enlarges and brings under microscopic scrutiny the unique attributes of the individual in their uncontaminated full expression. Interventions are technically gauged and targeted so as not to interfere with the unhampered unfolding of the process, exquisitely unique to each individual. Aiding the flow of free association, the analyst facilitates the unhindered unfolding of the dynamics governing emerging themes, structures, and conflicts. He tries to create and maintain an interpersonal context that feels safe as a holding environment that can contain impulses, tensions, and frustrations, while reflecting and clarifying the experiential and affective contents that have been buried from consciousness or have never been conscious. Using his familiarity with the process and the material presented, the analyst promotes the awareness of this internal universe. Discrimination of self from non-self, internal from external, fantasy from reality, past from present, and projection and denial from recognition leads to increase insight and self-awareness.

Focusing on the internal and clearly keeping the external where it belongs, the analytic process brings the patient more squarely face to face with himself and the disavowed aspects of him

which have been split off, repressed, or bypassed through denial.
The question becomes, What variety of impulses evoke what kind
of danger, experienced in what variety of anxiety, leading to what
forms of defensive behavior, symptoms, or adaptive compromise
formation? Where does the conscience stand in reaction to temptations pressing for transgression of limits and boundaries? What are
the individual's moral codes? Does their severity emanate from
identification with harsh and unyielding parental standards or is it
rooted in the intensity of sadomasochistic and infantile anal conflicts, perhaps remnants of an unresolved crisis of rapprochement?
In the case of sadistic parental introjects, what stands in the way of
liberating oneself from condemning influence of such an archaic
and self-punitive hindrance?

Through transference neurosis, the psychoanalytic situation
creates a vehicle that brings in to the present sense of the moment
the vivid reality of dormant needs and conflicts that are rooted
in the past long left behind. The principle of neutrality securely
guards the formation and eventual resolution of the transference.
Rather than educating, admonishing, counseling, moralizing, or
imposing his views, the analyst maintains an evenly hovering
attention in order to be able to appreciate and assess all the components of the conflictual material. Siding with the impulses or
with the prohibitions, advocating one value or another undermines
the analytic process and defeats its purpose, which is resolution of
the neurotic conflict, resumption of normal development, and
constructive integration of the past and present. The unhindered
emergence of unconscious affects, fantasies, and interpersonal
modes, in their original cast and color, will allow for discriminating
the past from present and ascertaining how the present is con-
taminated or dominated by the past. The analyst's consistency,
emotional availability, and empathic attunement in a position of
neutrality allows for the interpretation and reflection of the surface
of the material and provides a mirroring function that orients and
organizes the patient's new perception of himself. As the analyst
remains in this neutral position, the transference stands out more

vividly in sharp contrast to the real and new object that is the analyst and the reality of here and now that the psychoanalytic situation represents. Unresolved conflicts and their attendant archaic affects, along with infantile introjects and their interactional modes hereby reactivated, can be worked through and in time relinquished.

Psychoanalysis takes for granted that to various degrees the worldview of the analyst will differ from that of the analysand. A given individual with a particular national or cultural background can successfully analyze or be in analysis with someone from a different nationality, religion, race, or gender owing to the psychoanalytic principle of neutrality. The psychoanalytic experience can expand the horizons of both participants, which can lead, for the analysand, to an expansion of self-knowledge, and, for the analyst, to increased familiarity with a perspective different from his own. Moslem analysts or analysands, in my view, are no exception in this respect.

In my own work with my patients, the vast majority have been from a different background and religion. In a relatively small number, when our religious and national background have been the same, I have not found this sameness of any particular advantage. Sometimes these patients find the initial phase of our encounter more reassuring as they expect a greater degree of ease in communication and understanding. On the other hand, I can think of one such patient who decided after a while that seeing someone from another culture would allow her to express herself more freely, as if I might hold her to a higher standard in our common cultural value systems. On the other hand, on more than one occasion, patients have said that they chose to see me because of the difference in our background, as they thought I would be more objective and they would be treated with a fresh perspective and less judgmentally. More often, however, patients are likely to react to my name, accent, and appearance with a certain degree of reservation or hesitation. Would I know what it means to be in their shoes? Would I understand their slang? Would I be familiar with their religious orientation? And so on. For some women the question is whether as a man from the "Old World" I would have a demeaning attitude toward women. Would I be a rigid chauvinist? These reservations usually recede into the background and sometimes reemerge later as aspects of the transference, which we work on. I have never found a person's religious devotion or particular orientation in itself to be a hindrance to our work. When this is a problem, it usually turns out to be a by-product of psychopathology and not related to issues concerning religious considerations. Stated in one sentence, I would suggest that a person's religious orientation or devotion, as an analyst or analysand, may introduce an additional element, but by itself would be no hindrance to the analytic process or its successful outcome, if the standard psychoanalytic technique is sustained and adhered to.

HUMAN DRIVES AND SOCIAL REWARD

Concerning the illuminating paper by Ad-Dab'bagh, I wish only to comment on the important purpose it serves in familiarizing the Western reader with a significant world religion that is shrouded in an aura of mystery and frequently confusing misguided conceptions of exotic mysticism or else vague fears of violent intolerance. While the paper has delineated many of the basic principles and their distinct features unique to Islam, here I wish to add a few words to stress the similarities with the predominant religions of the Western world.

Many Westerners do not realize, for example, that Islamic principles and standards are derived from Judeo-Christian traditions that have descended from Abraham down through Moses and Jesus. This includes the entire content of the Torah as well as the Bible. Awareness of this fact may alleviate the confusion or disorientation a clinician might experience in first encountering a patient of Moslem faith. To be aware, for example, that a Moslem abides by the Ten Commandments, or that he believes in the teachings of Jesus, should similarly be beneficial. One might go so far as saying that almost all the essential rules and values governing social, interpersonal, familial, and moral precepts are similar in essence if not identical in all religions. For Moslems, as in Judaism or Christianity, selfish disregard for the well-being of others, cruelty, and trampling on the rights of others are condemned. Charity, self-sacrifice, and devotion to the welfare of one's fellow man and purity of intent in the service of God are central in the teachings of these, and perhaps all, religions.

I am somewhat skeptical about the assertion that for Moslems shame and guilt represent larger elements as determinants of moral or righteous behavior. I distinguish between the cultural-sociological facet of guilt and shame and their developmental-psychological aspects.

The developmental trajectory and the sequence of structure formation that lead to the establishment of conscience and moral ideals along with their affective regulators (shame and guilt) are universal and uniform across cultures and time in history. They are rooted in the biological drive toward self-fulfillment and socialization achieved in the context of a background of safety and secure attachment. There is an evolutionary trajectory from dependence toward autonomy and from helplessness toward self-sufficiency that leads to the acquisition of the capacity to function as a member of the society. The society as a pervasive milieu facilitates and nurtures the individual's growth and capacity for the pursuit of happiness.

Being capable of contributing to our community and to the well-being of others is the hallmark of successful adaptation and the ideal that all societies cherish and all individuals strive for. This is a major means of gaining approbation and affirmation, and feeling valued, useful, and respected. When this fails, the results are alienation, despair, self-loathing, or righteous indignation and rage directed at others or at oneself.

Psychoanalytic theory conceives of development in sequential stages throughout the life cycle, universal in their ontogenetic order of maturation and their age-specific tasks. These manifestations are variously influenced and even stimulated by environmental triggers that affect their nuances and texture, but their essential features, under more or less optimal or the "average expectable environment" (Hartmann 1950), are the same regardless of geography and cultural variation and have been so throughout human history. Infancy, childhood, latency, adolescence, and adulthood manifest essentially the same universal characteristics and present similar basic tasks and adaptive features regardless of the particulars of culture, tradition, or place of birth. It is as if the essential paradigm of human nature and evolutionary destiny provides one set of universal parameters regardless of the external influences, while environmental factors such as parenting, culture, geography, and other variables including religious beliefs, traditions, and practices provide and impose additional but extraneous influences. While separating these two factors may not always be easy, in psychoanalytic practice the predominance of one entity over the other is usually readily observable. In fact, frequently such a distinction and teasing apart of the intrapsychic from the environmental becomes an important objective in the course of treatment. For example, an intrapsychic conflict is frequently externalized and appears as if it is between the individual and his mate, parents, supervisor, rivals, the community, or perhaps all at once. The psychoanalytic focus on the intrapsychic can identify this hidden source of disturbance and subject it to examination and clarification instead of trying to devise means to extricate the unhappy patient from seemingly hostile external circumstances. Here the task of the analyst is to maintain the focus of attention on the internal dynamics, which are the primary determinants of motivation, behavior, compromise formation, emotional tone, and the underlying thought process that emerges in first view in matters of choice, opinion, and judgment.

Maintaining the focus on the internal dynamics does not imply that we ignore reality in order to attend to fantasy, or discount the external in order to cater to the internal. To the contrary, greater appreciation and demarcation of the external

internalized

reality is achieved when we keep in clear view the resistances and the wishes they conceal. This will soon allow us to account for the unconscious wishes that are the latent content and the main determinants of behavior, as distinct from the demands of reality and the influence of the internal object world (Jacobson 1964) with which they endlessly interact. This helps us establish a true grasp and more complete appreciation of the external and its influence on the state of the internal equilibrium. We can then more clearly delineate and demarcate the role of the environment and its agents, be it the breast, the caregiver, the objects of desire and/or aggression, social values and ideals, or religion and its institutions.

In a general sense, the more freedom from intrapsychic conflict and anxiety, the easier the adaptation to the vicissitudes of the external circumstances and the higher the resilience of the individual in confronting the challenges of a harsh and unwelcoming environment. When inner conflicts and anxiety deplete one's resources, resiliency is accordingly diminished. When inner conflicts are played out interpersonally, every encounter can turn into a feud. Each enterprise may become a source of defeat and any venture can begin a journey of anguish, guilt, and regrettable consequences. Events can be experienced as catastrophes and relationships as depleting ordeals of exploitation. Joy, peace of mind, affection, and trust have no chance. Fantasy and hopeless grandiose expectations serve as illusive islands of refuge from the pain of reality. Perceptions of reality contort to accommodate the reflections of inner distortions.

When early relationships are secure and optimally gratifying, a background of safety (Sandler 1960) is created and sustained. This allows for playful exploration, self-assertion, and a secure sense of mastery. A confident, stable, and secure sense of self can develop. The individual can supplement his secure sense of self by finding affirmation and supportive reassurance in his relations with others. In addition, he can utilize other available resources to contain and soothe himself and replenish his own mental reservoir of energy. Form the soft and familiar voice of a loving caregiver, to the calming murmur of a babbling brook, the scented aroma of a gentle breeze, a pleasant musical passage, a favorite prayer, a word of wisdom, a poem or a line of verse, strength can be gained and self-composure may be reestablished and dormant hope may be reawakened. For emotional stability, sustenance, and self-confirmation, we turn to our families, communities, cultural treasures, traditions, and religions.

Families provide for their members. Communities nurture the families that submit to its rules necessary for stability. The society protects and enriches the communities that contribute to its well-being. Responsibilities, duties, rules, and restrictions hold the individual securely in this hierarchical matrix. The highest order of this hierarchical structure consists of the relationship and the duties of the individual and the society to the higher authority of the Creator as represented in the mandates of religion. Man submits to the will of the Creator whose authority is believed to rule and regulate the entire universe. Unable to grasp the infinitely great dimensions of these attributes, man submits to God's word and will in faith. Faith suffices where knowledge cannot. As leading organizers of our societies, religions define and direct the means and manners in which man can place his faith and spiritual resources on the path of truth and servitude to this deity. In the context of the infinity that the individual needs to confront in this perspective, life does not begin at birth or end at the time of death. While the physical manifestations of life are limited to the span of time between birth and death, the spirit, which belongs to an eternal source of everlasting life, exists before birth and will not perish at the time of physical death. The soul is invested in the vessel of the physical self at birth and by death is emancipated into an eternal continuity that is not confined to the boundaries of time and space. In this sense, our life is a part of the eternity that exists before the creation of our physical self and extends beyond its demise. Our individual existence is thought to be experienced in two spheres. The material dimensions of this experience are based on perceptions, the senses, and immediate physical connsciousness. The spiritual dimension, on the other hand, is the other side of the coin. It is intuitive, concerned with meaning, and rises beyond perception or the senses and their physical limitations. Our physical existence and consciousness is a means to, but also an impediment to, the fulfillment of our spiritual potential. The spiritual reality and the eternal consciousness of which human existence is a small component is the source that can energize and govern values that should direct our lives. While our material needs and instinctual drives enslave us to needful temptations, blind self-indulgence, and sinful transgressions, spiritual strivings lift the soul and bring us closer to the eternal reality that contains the infinite intelligence that permeates, regulates, and maintains the universe. While material success might bring us passing worldly comfort and transient physical gratification, the spiritual journey takes us toward the eternal truth that can bring enlightenment and unbounded peace and inner harmony. True salvation is found in the spiritual domain as all material trappings are hindrances that come between us and the greater universal truth that reaches beyond the limitations of our senses and physical abilities.

All religions share this perspective. Religious practices are means to achievement of spiritual purity and grace through forgoing selfish material preoccupation and submitting oneself to the will of the Creator and to the ultimate truth that rules all that exists in a vast infinite unity, containing life and man's destiny in a predetermined order that transcends the confines of knowledge and the constraints of time and space.

Psychoanalytic theory is based on the understanding of innate drives and conflicts and can define developmental pathology and defenses (A. Freud 1936, Freud 1915). Normality, faith, and spirituality are not easily delineated in our theoretical frame. The soul and spirituality have no place in our concepts. This can create a nearly insurmountable impasse in dealing with those among our patients who place primary emphasis on this aspect. Many patients present with some concern around these issues, whether they be skeptics, seekers of answers, or devout practitioners of their religion. For the most part we have tended to sidestep questions of faith and spirituality. Our scientific tradition does not help much in this respect and does not give us a leg to stand on. At best we can be a witness to the unfolding of the patient's experiential state concerning faith, and help with resolution of its conflictual aspects, respectful and fully cognizant of the importance and centrality of faith in the life of the patient. We serve as an auxiliary ego to help our patients to use their own resources in reaching their own resolutions and arriving at their own personal answers. These answers have to pertain to their own circumstance and uniquely individual experiences. This unique experience is available only to the patient no matter how empathically close to its dimensions we may believe we are. Once the patient understands and resolves his own confusion or conflicted state, he can reach his own conclusion. He can then proceed on the basis of his own new and clearer understanding.

EXPECTING THE UNEXPECTED

In child psychoanalysis our objective is to work through the conflicts to the point that the child is back on his developmental track and can proceed free of the previous hindrances that had been impeding the normal course of his development. As we no longer confine the limits of development to the end of adolescence, we can maintain the same objective for our adult patients. Repairing developmental ruptures in adults, or resolving their infantile conflicts through psychoanalytic treatment, can pave the way for emotional and spiritual growth. As they become less self-absorbed and no longer developmentally arrested, they can become better adapted to their environment, more meaningfully engaged in their own cultural roots, and more capable of mutuality and intimacy with others. This provides for availability of motivation and energy that will be needed for pursuit of higher levels of meaning, faith, and spiritual strivings. In my view it should not matter if the level of devotion or paradigm of faith on the two sides of the couch are parallel or divergent. Whether or not the analyst and analysand are from the same gender, race, religion, culture, nationality, or value system, the analytic process does not have to suffer. Of course, problems will occur if countertransference blind spots and enactments go unrecognized or unchecked. This, however, is not a concern exclusive to matters of faith or religion.

If we leave aside the particular rituals, methods of worship, and observance in each religion, we are left with a number of common core principles that are based on higher, universally cherished ideals and moral standards. On the basis of this commonality, cultural divergence on the two sides of the couch should not create an insurmountable obstacle to the analytic work. Furthermore, there may be some advantages to lack of familiarity with the patient's cultural background. Running into a unique cultural feature for the first time in the course of analysis may be more meaningful than when we enter the analytic situation, prejudicially expecting that all members of a certain group present with certain characteristic features. After all, as analysts we believe that each individual has a unique perspective and his subjective experience is entirely unique to himself. We regard this uniqueness as a universal aspect of the human condition. We are therefore always braced for the unexpected and are ready to be surprised. Our preconceptions and prejudices have to be suspended and have no place in the analytic situation.

FAITH AS A STATE OF RELATEDNESS

I view faith as a state of relatedness to an object whose dimensions are beyond cognitive and emotional grasp. As the object in its complexity cannot be understood, conceptions and assumptions about it are essentially of a subjective nature and not possible to objectively or completely qualify. Faith in the benevolence of the object is rooted in early experience of the child when the mother's unconditional availability and the child's omnipotent illusion of symbiotic dual unity with the mother provide a constant background of safety. The quality of experience with the maternal object during the separation–individuation phase (Mahler et al. 1975) determines the state of relatedness to the mother and others after self and object constancy have begun. If this process is interrupted or incomplete, part objects and preambivalent states will be preserved. Self-reflection, self-constancy, modulated affective tones, and signal affects will not be available. Magical thinking and narcissistic defenses of a primitive nature will dominate. Self concepts and self-regulation will be vulnerable and the quality of relatedness to the object will remain based on states of need and deficit, which creates great instability and a sense of helplessness. This prevents the development of the capacity to empathize, reciprocate, and appreciate the other in its own right.

As a result of optimal development of object relationships, secure attachment and establishment of self and object constancy, appraisal of the qualities and emotional states of the other become possible. Understanding of one's own state of mind and the capacity to empathize with the other can grow. Mutuality becomes possible and used as an indispensable tool in relations and establishing gratifying object ties. Judgmental decisions based on the appraisal of the other individual's state of mind become realistic, objective, and more reliable. "Blind faith" or baseless optimism regarding others need not prevail, any more than paranoia and embittered disillusionment might sway. It has been said, "Knowing yourself is knowing your God." Someone who is incapable of knowing his own needs and inner states cannot know or appreciate the state of the mind of the other.

In this sense, faith as a state of relatedness entails stages of evolution and development. It can serve as an important provider of infinite potential of selfobject function and a source of stability and reliable orientation. An unambivalent relationship to the Creator can be a source of strength and selfobject function greater than any other relationship of a material nature. This is reflected in the

This is kept alive, thus it can be misused...

recent research (Gartner et al. 1991, Koenig et al. 1998) that shows faith is an important factor in recovery from malignancy, incurable conditions, and treatment of addictive and psychiatric diseases. Those who belong to a faith are healthier socially and physically and their children do better in many different respects. There are many anecdotal accounts of faith accomplishing improbable or impossible feats. As a state of relatedness to the Creator, that is, an object whose dimensions are beyond cognitive or emotional grasp, the quality and consistency of faith can vary. This parallels common variations we observe in the quality of ordinary relationships. For example, when emotional energies are depleted or depressed, or when a patient is depressed, there is a tendency toward withdrawal. The patient feels worthless, unwanted, and abandoned by God. His prayers are not heard. He feels forsaken and lost. When the quantity of unneutralized aggressive drives exceed that of libido, the self is experienced as beleaguered, assailed, fragmented, and in rageful anguish. Heaven and stars are malevolent and continue to parcel out nothing but torment and bad omens.

When arrest has occurred in the course of object relationships, we see interpersonal manifestations of this arrest manifested also in the individual's quality of faith and his relationship to God. This was striking in the following case.

A CLINICAL ILLUSTRATION

The patient began his current analysis at the age of 47, but he had been in psychotherapy on several previous occasions and had tried behavioral and group modalities of treatment as well. He was a professional but did not produce an income sufficient to meet his expenses. He was despised by his wife and his two teenage children. He was always depressed and felt "beset by demons." He was painfully anxious, and for relief he was using alcohol addictively. He spent endless hours in his office immersed in a stupor of masturbatory fantasy that depicted him as a suckling infant with irresistible physical features that endeared him to the "queen-mother-godhead" who had handpicked him to suck at her genital for her pleasure. The immense pleasure made him invaluable to her. Outside of his perpetual masturbatory preoccupation, he would pray in a submissive, masochistic manner that provided some relief and dissipated some of his guilt for his defiant and loathsome self-indulgence, which he was painfully ashamed of. Prayer also made him feel entitled to magical rescue and relief, which he unyieldingly expected. He railed against his fortune and the stars and thought of himself as "accursed." His alternate fantasy was of being a magnificent prince on a beautiful white horse who could deal with any situation with ease and grace, amazing and dazzling the ordinary onlookers with his prowess and facility. He in fact displayed these qualities with charm and chivalry in his profession. In a masterful dash of brilliant maneuvering he often "saved the day" as he dedicated himself to nearly lost causes, defending the underdog. Brilliant and dazzling in crisis and in brief spurts, he had no energy or motivation for the day-to-day grind of actual work, which he found to be too tedious. He was always tired, feeling beleaguered and "at sea." This severe narcissistic pathology and developmental arrest was based on the unfortunate events of his early upbringing.

He was born to a depressed woman who was married to a self-absorbed alcoholic and abusive man whom she despised. The birth of her son made her depression more unbearable. She could not attend to her infant whom she resented and rejected as he seemed to her to be "just like his father," that is, angry and hard to please. Thirteen months later she gave birth to her second child, a daughter. Her own mother was now available and helped her with the newborn. To her relief and delight, the care of the daughter was easier and with her mother's help went joyfully. At the same time, the young toddler became more uncontrollable and oppositional. Both mother and now also the grandmother reacted to him with disdain and contempt. The father's sister, who was a prominent clergywoman and childless, became the only source of emotional warmth and acceptance for the boy. By the time he was 4 years of age, he had completely disowned his parents and gained solace in interaction with his aunt who taught him about religion and means of worship. He became masterful in extracting adulation and praise from the women in the neighborhood who were the mothers of his playmates and who marveled at his mature charms and ability to attract and appease women. His native intelligence and talents, which he never fully developed, helped him survive school and later his professional school. As a professional he could not support his family and they had to rely on his wife's income, which was a meager salary.

His analysis lasted over seven years. The initial honeymoon period produced significant improvement and ease of his suffering. As the magical solutions that he expected failed to materialize, things bogged down. In a symbiotic cocoon of the transference, he verbalized and elaborated on many of his fantasies. Disillusionment, shame, narcissistic mortification, and rage followed and presented many problems of technique. His regressive and polymorphous fantasies needed containment and mirroring in the mother transference. In time he was able to work through his rage and mourn the passing of the "queen-mother-godhead" who no longer provided relief. Next came a consuming and moving working through of the negative oedipal conflict and his bisexual conflict. Once he had moved beyond preoedipal ambivalence and object constancy had begun, he was able to experience, express, and resolve his oedipal conflict through a series of evolving fantasies and dreams concerning the transference and fear of his father due to projection of his own aggression. Defensive constructs of idealized mother and father were now clearly noticeable in his thoughts and attitude concerning God. Gradual working through of these archaic introjects and expansion of his ego capacity was gradual and came as a result of careful working through. At the end of this very rewarding analysis he had moved from being a bedraggled, infantile, rageful, fragmented individual to becoming a mature and confident man able to function as a loving husband, a sensitive and caring father, a competent and productive professional, and a down-to-earth, modestly devoted church member who really enjoyed and appreciated the fellowship his church afforded him. His compassion and empathic capacity was liberating and a gratifying source of reciprocity and friendly connection with others. He could now see me in a realistic light, compassionately, and as a benevolent yet vulnerable individual that he respected and felt indebted to. He thought his analysis gave him a life which he had never known. He now knew his place in life, and was at peace and grateful for where he was. Now when he prayed he said it was like having an enjoyable visit with a magnanimous friend rather than desperately begging and never receiving relief.

THE HOLY ALLIANCE

In child analysis the idea of meeting the child at his own level is a frequently stressed aspect of the technique. This is based on the importance of the recognition of the ego state and emotional/cognitive specifics of the developmental stage in which we find our young patients. I believe this consideration holds no less true in working with adult patients. Here, too, the assessment of patients' ego states allows us to meet them at that level. This is how empathic attunement, "mirroring" (Kohut 1978), and containment, when needed, can be provided. Regarding the state of faith in a patient, the same approach usually applies. We do not have to share the same beliefs, worship in the same manner, or hold similar cultural values as our patients to be able to work with them successfully. We need only to be respectful, receptive, accepting, and open to their internal experience and cherished values. Without this receptive neutrality, the essential conditions for the formation of an alliance and working relationship cannot be mustered.

I was once called for consultation by a prominent colleague who had hospitalized a woman who was in a complicated state of health. Her poor health was additionally exacerbated by the fact that she was adamantly refusing all treatment, medication, food, and liquids, except in quantities and under conditions which she insisted upon. These demands made no rational sense and could not really be met. When I walked into her hospital room and announced myself, she demanded, with her back turned to me, that I leave, as she had no time or need for another one of my kind or my opinion. Her husband, standing near her, intervened to explain to me that their contact with several disciplines and many hospital personnel had been demeaning and infuriating. He felt they all had dismissed his wife's concerns as psychotic. Muttering and snickering, they had made sarcastic remarks in frustration faced with the patient's high-handed and unbending demands. The husband then made me aware of his background as one of the most distinguished figures of our national scientific community. He then patiently explained to me that although he had never taken anything of this sort in any way seriously, he had to tell me that recently his wife was "channeling God."

Before I could react, he added that his wife's impressive predictions recently had repeatedly amazed him. Some of her statements contained uncommon wisdom and depth and each of her many premonitory statements had actually materialized. He flatly admitted that he now believed that she did "channel God."

Duly impressed and somewhat intimidated by the husband's exalted stature, I was speechless. Channeling Pharaoh, Elvis, Mao Tse-tung or someone's late dear departed I had heard about, but never channeling God. Still I could not dismiss the solemn testimony of a scientist of such great stature. My state of bewilderment was then interrupted by the voice of the woman who now sounded grandly superior and unlike her previous tone. It was as if she were talking to a crowd, announcing herself as the creator of all beings. She was no longer asking me to leave. Her words and utterances were elegantly commanding and contained cosmic depth and breadth. I froze in my place. Her power, elegance, omniscient tone, and direct simplicity were mesmerizing. This could not be emanating from the mind of a mere human. What had seemed to be nothing short of preposterous now suddenly seemed genuine and palpably real. I had no reason to doubt my experience. The bizarre and preposterous claim of moments ago was now a compelling and incredible real event. Stunned and lost, I was now preparing to submit to the idea that I was participating in a rare moment, in the presence of an unusual human being capable of displaying unfathomable capacities. I thought I was a privileged recipient of the word of God "channeled" through a nearly terminal patient who by all accounts should have already died some time ago. Then trying to adjust to my state of awe and complete surrender, I felt as if I were being asked by God questions only he would know answers to. In a remotely perceptible way he was asking for the benefit of my opinion! Instantly I was relieved and regained my balance, feeling somewhat foolish but pleased. I reasoned that God would not need me to help him make decisions and would not turn to me for clarification!

Now I was back to being a clinician. In familiar territory as if playing out a story with one of my child patients, I could meet this patient on her ground, in her present ego state, and in terms of her own delusional inner experience. I could play with the same rules my patient was defining. I could follow her and let her lead me to where she needed to arrive. I interrupted to say I had nothing to offer regarding the matters of universe, but as a doctor I was trying to see if I might be able to understand the patient's fears and if I could assist in her treatment. The channeling came to a halt. In her own friendly and intimate tone, the patient now began to speak with me. Her husband was delighted and surprised that she was now engaged in such a trusting and open dialogue with me. She thanked me for listening, not dismissing and insulting her or treating her like a lunatic as others repeatedly had. For my caring and attention she expressed gratitude, deep respect, and affection. She then asked me about my diagnosis of her condition and my recommendations for her treatment. Together with her husband she secured my assistance in arranging for intensive inpatient medical-psychiatric care in a hospital closer to her own community.

This vignette dramatizes the point that if we are open, receptive, and empathically attuned to our patients' need for their defenses and symptoms, we will have a better chance of creating an alliance that may lead to a productive working relationship.

THE SOLE SAVIOR OF THE SOUL

Regarding our patients' religious convictions and the effects of these elements on the course of treatment, I cite the following example as another case in point.

I was evaluating a woman referred to me for chronic depression. She was an intelligent and talented woman who had taught and planned religious education for many years and was in the ranks of the clergy in her church. She was a minister's daughter. Her father had been a source of inspiration and a role model for her and many who had known him. In spite of her abilities and devotion, my patient had suffered many setbacks in her career. She had not received the recompense and status that she was due and had frequently been blocked and prevented from receiving institutional positions to which she aspired. She was uncertain about using treatment as a solution to her depression and chronic sense of failure and defeat. She thought her faith should be enough to solve her problems and resorting to any means other than divine intervention would prove her faith was fading. Her father in particular was adamantly opposed to her seeking treatment. Since she had no doubt in the strength of her faith she decided to try out the treatment in spite of furious protestation from her father, who wanted her to rely strictly on prayer for her problems.

Once we decided to embark upon her long and ultimately successful treatment, she devoted her heart and soul to our work together. This was a welcome development, but also of some concern to me because of her seeming total submission and what it might represent on a deeper level. She also confessed to me that her conjecture about my religion and national origin made it absolutely clear to her that I was exactly the wrong person for her to turn to. However, she reasoned that God had placed her in the hands of the ultimate enemy of her religion and of her people, and she was submitting to his will and what he was asking her to do. Her faith convinced her that the result would be miraculous and the treatment would succeed. She mused and laughed at the idea that in sending her to me, God was making an outrageous joke as she believed that God has a sense of humor!

The course of her treatment revealed a masochistic personality structure based on guilt and need for self-punishment. This was based on extended experiences of sexual abuse as a child, once during the oedipal period and another time in her preadolescence. Both these occasions coincided with times when her father was absent for a long time and she played out her oedipal fantasies with the father of her best friend who with no regard for her vulnerability and childhood innocence brutally exploited and callously abused her sexually.

It took a long time to recover fragments of memory and split-off affective states, which painfully and with great difficulty led to formation of recall and partial working through and recovery.

Her self view as a victim—used, soiled, humiliated,

mistreated, and discarded—had placed her in many past situations of defeat, humiliation, and painful disillusionment. As she was able to resolve her guilt and contain her self-directed destructive aggression, she became more accepting of her own strength and self-assertive urges. She was now more at home with her sense of envy, rivalry, aggression, sexuality, and oedipal longings. She could appropriately engage her anger at her abandoning father and his oedipal substitute, who had so brutally victimized her. Most importantly, without being flooded with self-loathing or denial, she was now able to identify with her very young vulnerable self and her active oedipal longings, which made her susceptible to the exploitations of her abuser. She no longer needed to deny her own wishes and sexual drives by assuming the posture of an innocently victimized subject who could only expect suffering and punishment for the transgression of her needs and ambitions. Rather than being at the receiving end of split-off sexual and sadistic attacks in a masochistic posture, she could now recognize, utilize, and assume responsibility for her own drives and id impulses. Now she was more productive, and felt happier and at ease with herself and in tune with others. She came to the realization that her assumptions about my religious and national identity were distorted and served to perpetuate her unconscious need to masochistically engage in relationships that expiated her guilt through pain, suffering, and humiliation.

At the end of her treatment, she was no less faithful to her religious traditions and practices. Her professional endeavor had grown in depth and clarity of purpose as had she. She felt that her perception of God had expanded and was greatly enhanced. She felt that as her understanding of herself and others had expanded, her appreciation of the greatness of God had increased. She said, with humor, "God is much greater than I ever realized." In a manner surprising to her, the quality of her relationships had changed as she felt closer to, safe with, and more equal to those she had clung on to ambivalently and in a helpless posture of victimhood. Her view of me as a real object had also changed as she saw me as a benevolent and reliable person whom she could call upon and rely on whenever she felt she needed to think through difficult situations. She said, "You understand me in a way that no one else can."

CONCLUSION

Although we can learn much from theology and would benefit from maintaining an open dialogue with experts and philosophers in this realm of human experience, in matters of faith and religious belief our psychoanalytic focus can only be on the intrapsychic dynamics, the psychic reality, and the emotional content of our patient's subjective state. We are in no position to establish values or construct levels of higher truth or reality for our patients. We cannot respond judgmentally. Our obligation to our patients is to help them remove obstacles from access to their own personal truth and ultimate judgment.

Divergence of value systems and opposing beliefs between the analyst and the analysand are taken for granted and pose no hindrance to the analytic process when the principles of technique are observed and adhered to.

The principles of neutrality, empathic attunement, and respect for our patients' perspectives and subjective experience guard against indoctrination or imposing values on our patients.

Spiritual faith and religious devotion as constituents of superego and ego ideal require robust and complicated developmental infrastructures. When these structures are deviant or deficient, faith and spirituality will bear the influence of defensive, regressive, or dysfunctional operations of these deviations.

In our analytic stance and functioning as an auxiliary ego, we pave the way for repair and conflict resolution via the vehicle of transference. This enhances the capacity for adaptation to the external reality and environmental challenges or resources including religion, cultural tradition, and social values.

Shame and guilt as affective signals that regulate behavior entail a universal developmental genesis that is common to all cultures and times of history. These signal affects cannot function optimally when their supporting structures are compromised. Neurotic or developmental pathology can interfere with their adaptive function regardless of the amplitude or pervasiveness of religious or cultural sanctions.

I have proposed that conceptualizing faith as a state of relatedness places the matter in the domain of object relations, ego psychology, attachment, self psychology, and developmental psychology, permitting clinical assessment and objective conceptualization. Since the dimensions of the object of this state of relatedness exceed the reach of cognitive and intellectual grasp, it can serve as a source of selfobject function of unlimited potential and endless resource.

REFERENCES

Baker, R. (2000). Finding the neutral position: patient and analyst perspectives. *Journal of the American Psychoanalytic Association* 48(1):129–153.

Calef, V., and Weinshel, E. (1980). The analyst as the conscience of the analysis. *International Review of Psycho-Analysis* 7:279–290.

Cavel, M. (1999). Knowledge, consensus and uncertainty. *International Journal of Psycho-Analysis* 80:1227–1236.

Franklin, G. (1990). The multiple meanings of neutrality. *Journal of the American Psychoanalytic Association* 38:195–220.

Freud, A. (1936). *The Ego and the Mechanisms of Defense.* London: Hogarth and the Institute of Psychoanalysis.

Freud, S. (1915). Instincts and their vicissitudes. *Standard Edition* 14:117–140.

Gartner, J., Larson, D. B., and Allen, G. D. (1991). Religious commitment and mental health: a review of the empirical literature. *Journal of Psychology and Theology* 19:6–25.

Greenberg, J. (1986). The problem of analytic neutrality. *Contemporary Psychoanalysis* 22:76–85.

Hanly, C. (1999). Subjectivity and objectivity in psychoanalysis. *Journal of the American Psychoanalytic Association* 47:427–444.

Hartmann, H. (1950). Comments on the psychoanalytic theory of the ego. In *Essays on Ego Psychology*, pp. 113–141. New York: International Universities Press, 1964.

Jacobson, E. (1964). *The Self and the Object World*. New York: International Universities Press.

Koenig, H. G., Larson, D. B., and Weaver, A. J. (1998). Research on religion and serious mental illness. *New Directions in Mental Health Services 1998* 80:81–95.

Kohut, H. (1978). The psychoanalytic treatment of narcissistic personality disorders: outline of a systematic approach. In *The Search for the Self*, ed. P. Ornstein, pp. 477–509. New York: International Universities Press.

Mahler, M., Pine, F., and Bergman, A. (1975). *The Psychological Birth of the Human Infant*. New York: Basic Books.

Sandler, J. (1960). The background of safety. *International Journal of Psycho-Analysis* 41:352–356.

Stolorow, R. (1997). Current conceptions of neutrality and abstinence: panel report. *Journal of the American Psychoanalytic Association* 45:1231–1239.

12

GOD AND THE UNCONSCIOUS: ETERNAL ANTONYMIES OR LONG LOST TWINS?:

Concluding Reflections

James S. Grotstein, M.D.

God created man in His own image, and man repaid Him in
kind.

Voltaire

In this book five distinguished classical psychoanalysts representing
five different religious faiths convened to share their respective
views about the interface between religion and psychoanalysis.
Ironically, whereas the contributors represent five different religious faiths, they compositely belong to the same psychoanalytic
"faith," classical ego psychology, which in turn represents a constrained perspective on the interface of religion and psychoanalysis.
Freud was, from one point of view, perhaps one of the foremost
atheists of all time, but, from another, was a devout worshiper at the
shrine of logical-positivistic (linear) "science," which itself has been
eclipsed by nonlinear theories of uncertainty, relativity, chaos,
complexity, and emergence theories. Ego psychology, of all the
schools of psychoanalysis, placed itself most closely to the older
theory of science in order to gain respectability, but "the moving
finger moves on" to newer paradigms such as the subjective-

intersubjective interface, and emotions have replaced drives as the putative organizer of unconscious mental life. In short, newer contributions from many analytic schools, freed from the shackles of a veritable Calvinistic scientific "straitjacket," now seem to be more supportive of and conducive to that area of the affective spectrum that can be allotted to spirituality as one of the undeniable instincts and passions of man.

I was originally "baptized" (or should I say "circumcised") in the "faith" of orthodox psychoanalysis (id analysis) in the earlier part of my formal training and then, later on, in modern American ego psychology, its legitimate successor in the United States. Afterward, I became analyzed and trained in the tradition of Fairbairn (British object relations), and finally in that of Klein and Bion. My psychoanalytic encounters with British psychoanalysis afforded me the opportunity to observe a more "religion-friendly" atmosphere in contrast to the more scientistically remote ego psychology, as I shall illustrate as I proceed. As an example, Meltzer (1978), a Kleinian, pointed out how religious and spiritual Klein's metapsychology was, particularly in terms of the transition (epigenesis) from the paranoid-schizoid to the depressive position, which traces the steps from veritable infantile paganism and idolatry to the spirituality, redemption, and salvation of the depressive position. Bion (1965, 1970, 1992) went even further by assigning the concept of "godhead" to his concept of "O" (which conflates God, fate, absolute truth, and/or ultimate reality) and by critiquing Freud for having overlooked man's religious passion in his instinct to worship.[1] He believed that psychoanalysis and religion were parallel universes experienced from different vertices. Fairbairn, who himself was religious and barely avoided becoming a clergyman in the Anglican Church of Scotland, viewed his endopsychic

---

[1]Bion was Anglo-Indian and was raised in India by an *ayah* (nanny). He frequently referred to Arjuna (from the *Bhagavad Gita*) in his works and has even more frequently been considered "Indian" in his mystical outlook. Comparisons between his ideas and those of Buddhism are remarkable.

structures as hell, which was the negative counterpart to the more blessed ideal object and its relation to the central ego. Here I can only allude to the deep spirituality that inheres in the works of Neville Symington, from the British independent school, whose work, *Emotion and Spirit: Questioning the Claims of Psychoanalysis and Religion* (1994), is an attempt to integrate them.

Let me state my opinion at the outset: Religion and psychoanalysis are parallel disciplines that have been examining the same truths and realities from differing vertices. They converge in philosophy. Religion, particularly in its spiritual dimension, is more psychoanalytic than it ever suspected, and conversely psychoanalysis is more spiritual than it (particularly ego psychology) has yet recognized.

MEISSNER'S CONTRIBUTION

Meissner's contribution is of interest, not only in its own right, but also because of the fact that the author is both a psychoanalyst and a Jesuit, a formidable combination. He wisely distinguishes between the theological and the psychoanalytic approaches to the problem and suggests that they are different approaches that can never be truly integrated. Each has its own methodology and ways of understanding. Meissner regrets Freud's dismissal of religious experience as pathological because of its being developmentally regressive ipso facto. While recognizing that psychic determinants infuse religious experiences, he believes that religious ideas can be pathologically misused by the neurotic.

The author divides the task as one that exists, on the one hand, in psychoanalytically understanding the determinants and motives behind one's religious beliefs, and, on the other, in realizing the profound truths religious thought offers us in regard to our existence. Bion (1992) would refer to these differing perspectives as matters of "vertices," or points of view, each of which had its own validity. Meissner then characterizes the manifold postulates of the religious vertex—the immortality of the soul, the reality and sustaining power of divine grace, the pervasive salvific will of God extended to all mankind—all having been accepted through revelation condoned by religious tradition through an act of faith, which means that they cannot be proved or empirically demonstrated. They are objects of true belief. "To those who believe, they are potentially sources of profound truth and existential guidance. To those who do not believe, they are illusions and deceptive fantasies and wish-fulfillments that fly in the face of reason and reality," he states.

Meissner's view about the origins of Freud's atheism is interesting. Freud apparently had been influenced by the view of Schleiermacher and Feuerbach, which in brief was a Promethean view in which man, having been created by God, took God back into himself as human nature. Meissner cites a passage from Feuerbach: "Religion arises when man 'projects his being into objectivity, and then again makes himself an object to this projected image of himself thus converted into a subject.'" This view, suffused as it is with projective identification, does actually conform to the view of God held by most of Freud's descendants. Yet it may tell only half the story. As I read this citation from Feuerbach, I could not help thinking that he was onto a profound truth. Might he not have been suggesting that God did indeed create man, but, because God is utterly *ineffable*[2]—as the subject-of-subjects ("Tell them I am that I am" [Exodus 3:13–14],[3] mankind can never know, see, face, or conceive of God, and, furthermore, cannot address God in the second person or discuss him in the third person. Any attempt to know God, I suggested, constituted "epistemic incest." As a result,

---

[2]Meissner cites Tillich's (1952) concept of a "transcending theism," a God beyond God who transforms all known forms of existence, which to me is similar to Keter Ayn Sof of the Lurianic Kabbala.

[3]In a recent contribution I suggest that God's ineffability lies in his being the subject who cannot be objectified (Grotstein 2000).

we are reduced to having to re-create our image of him, hoping that it will resonate with the unseen and unknowable one. Thus, another question must be posed: when individuals pray, do they pray to the God who is ineffable, one whom they must intuit, or do they pray to the God they feel impelled to re-create in order to have contact? Is this idea not confirmed in a way when we speak of "God, he or him?"

Meissner makes a significant point when he states that God belongs in the domain of psychical reality, not actual reality, but hastens to say that this does not mean that God does not exist in the latter. He affirms Rizzuto's notion of the "God representation,"[4] but then goes on to suggest that this God is "opaque to the analytic mind, but . . . is the object of convinced belief for the religious mind."

After discussing how many individuals project their psychopathology onto the God representation, Meissner then asks:

> In what sense and to what degree does the God representation reflect transference dynamics? To what extent does the God representation offer itself as a preferred target for therapeutic intervention or interpretation? Are there instances when the God representation can be worked on directly with therapeutic benefit, more advantageously . . . than less direct interpretive interventions dealing with the originative relationships? Does the God representation serve then as a convenient object of displacement or does it offer itself as a preferred and primary target for intervention? If so, when and how?

I believe these rhetorical questions ably reflect the therapeutic dilemma of the interface between religion and psychoanalysis.

---

[4] I have already suggested that God, being ineffable, cannot become a representation. That is objectifying God. Many religious Jews, when referring to the deity, spell it "G-d," knowing that his name is ineffable and inscrutable.

The Issue of Faith

Meissner distinguishes between faith and trust, stating that when psychoanalysts refer to faith they generally mean trust, whereas in religious issues faith transcends trust and involves divine grace. He suggests that religious faith has its own metapsychology, however, one that consists of the theological, the ontological, and the epistemological points of view. He believes that faith begins as a human response to revelation and is therefore grounded in psychology. Yet he also believes that the theological significance of the act of faith has little to do with psychological understanding and vice versa. Here one finally begins to grasp the presence of parallel tracks of inquiry that never meet but that are complete and valid within their own domain of inquiry—a dual track, as it were. He states:

> Faith involves and depends upon a particular relation to the divine that dispenses with every form of intermediary, whether community, state, church, or tradition. The individual thus enters into an immediate and absolute relation to the Absolute. . . . Faith reaches beyond the illumination of reason into the darkenss of paradox. . . . At this point we encounter the absurd. And the paradox is that man, by reaching through a veil of dread into the emptiness of the absurd, finds a relation to God stripped of all the trappings of the finite and in which man finds his own highest self-realization. And the further paradox is that beyond resignation man is enabled to live once again in the finite, but by virtue of a faithful relation to God that derives in no sense from understanding.

In these passages we experience Father Meissner, the Jesuit, who poignantly shows us what it is to be immersed in the wrappings of faith and be touched by godliness so as to be inoculated against the dread of cosmic aloneness and meaninglessness. Doctor Meissner, the psychoanalyst, then suggests: "Faith is not framed in terms of secondary process, and correspondingly reaches back to the most primitive levels of its originative experience and dynamic power. . . . Therefore, we can argue that faith has a regressive moment and that it can be at least partially accounted for in primary process terms."

Here we begin to get glimpses of Meissner's attempts at integration. Faith, he states, can be understood in part in psychological terms, for example, "primitive" and "primary process," and later, "regression," to which I would add, anticipating Ostow's contribution, "right cerebral hemisphere" functioning.

Meissner then addresses the issue of the "instinctual bases of faith" as a natural extension of his view that faith belongs to the domain of psychical reality and follows some of the same patterns as libido, but with many differences, the most important of which is that faith regresses to primitive states in order to become redefined in the face of infantile helplessness. With this regressive recertification of faith in divine providence in the face of one's infantile helplessness, religious belief restores to one the promise of life, beyond death and overcoming death, according to Meissner. Further, citing Erikson (1958), the author believes that "faith requires a developmental history that builds upon the infantile residues of trust." But he goes on to say, "The creative moment in faith is unique and beyond understanding, and beyond mere regression and mere recapitulation as well." In other words, faith is *ineffable*, yet constitutes a *pyschological* process at the same time.

Grace

Later in his contribution *Father* and *Dr.* Meissner informs us of the relationship between faith and grace:

> The Christian theological tradition teaches that faith requires the sustaining and confirming strength of God's grace. The action of divine grace remains mysterious but its effects can be more-or-less adequately considered on the psychological level in terms of the support and reinforcement of what we might regard as certain

ego-capacities and relational dispositions. We can conceive of grace, psychologically speaking, as operating to sustain the capacity of the self to mobilize its own inner resources and to carry out more effectively those ego-functions underlying regulation of instinctive motives, reinforcing the orientation and adaptation to reality, organizing and directing executive functions, and most significantly those that carry on the dynamic processes of synthesis and integration within the personality.

Why not the concept g...

I consider this particular passage to be an apogee of integration between theology and psychology. He goes on to say, "If faith requires basic trust and fidelity, it also creates them. . . . The psychological impact of the action of grace is profound and psychologically enriching, potentially changing, transforming, and in some sense reintegrating psychic capacities." The integration between theology and psychology reaches yet another apogee with Meissner's citation of St. Ignatius of Loyola: "Pray as though everything depended on God, but act as though everything depended on you." This citation is almost identical to passages I recall from the Hebrew *Mishnah*. The importance of this idea is that it affirms that a state of ambiguity or paradox must exist in which one must pray to God for help and yet count on oneself. Perhaps the resolution of this paradox might lie in the idea that, when one prays, that is, seeks God's grace, one is, at the same time and on another level, attempting to self-invoke one's own inner resources—that is, "hype-up," as athletes do when they go into noradrenergic reverie before they have to perform to the utmost of their capacities.

"Autochthony": The Infant as "God"

In his case presentation Meissner was confronted by a patient who suffered in part because of a posttraumatic stress disorder secondary to having been seduced by a priest. Meissner initially attempted, unsuccessfully, to deal with how the patient felt about being compromised. I have learned from Fairbairn (1952) that the analyst must never attempt initially to discredit an analysand's object of dependency without first working on the analysand's putative sense of omnipotent agency in believing that she, the analysand, was the cause of the sordid event. In later contributions I have called this putative sense of omnipotent agency the principle of *autochthony* (Grotstein 1997, 2000). What is relevant to the present theme in terms of that concept is the notion that the infant naturally feels it is a god, that everything that it opens its eyes to, it has created as it discovers it. It lives in a syncretic, narcissistic world where it is the center of all cosmogony and therefore feels inherently responsible for all that happens. When this feeling of responsibility is too overwhelming, it projectively reidentifies the source of causality in the object, thereupon creating persecutory anxiety in the paranoid-schizoid position (Klein 1946).

The concept of the infant-as-"God""was an ancient one in many different religions but reemerged with the advent of Jesus Christ and his legacy as the child who was both human and divine. Wordsworth (1807), the mystical poet, strongly alludes to this concept of the infant-as-"God" from another angle in his "Intimations of Immortality," in which his infants have intimations of the immortality in which they once dwelled before they became human upon birth. This theme is also explicit in the *Bhagavad Gita* in which Krishna shrank and left behind the universe, and in the Lurianic cabala in which Keter Ayn Sof shrank (the famous "zim-zum") and left the other nine sephirot (aspects of God) and the universe behind. Implicit in these themes is that the infant was once, in unconscious fantasy, the universe and shrank from grace and grandeur to become human. Moreover, this theme is implicit in Freud's (1914) paper "On Narcissism," in which he states that the ego and the ego ideal were once unitary. At birth the ego separates off and yields its narcissism in the form of grandiosity or omnipotence to the ego ideal, who continues to be a god, as it were, in the developing personality.

Conclusion

Meissner enriches our understanding of the interface between theology and psychoanalytic psychology by virtue of being able to straddle both disciplines. He introduces us to the concepts of faith, grace, and trust, and draws parallels between their operation and their quasi-counterparts in instinctual (motivational) and ego psychological terms. He helps us understand that the question "Does God help?" is an unanswerable one. I have reframed it as "Does *believing* in God help?" This question, which had not been asked of him, he answers in the positive. It was enlightening to read that he believes that the belief in God can better be understood from the standpoint of psychic reality, not actual reality, which is not to say that God is not real and actual.

RIZZUTO'S CONTRIBUTION

Rizzuto states from the outset: "The affirmation or negation of God's existence exceeds the level of our competence as experiential and empirical experts in understanding intrapsychic processes. We are, however, competent in comprehending the patient's subjective experience of God. . . . We can also understand the psychic 'use' of God as an object in everyday life and in pathological situations." This statement sets the tone for the author's subsequent discussion, that the existence of God is not a psychoanalytic issue. What is at issue is how patients use God as an object. She then refers to her extensive research on how the God concept arises developmentally in the form of God representations. Once again, as I have alluded to above with my critique of Meissner, the concept of a God representation is to objectify an ineffable subject whose very ineffable nature defies objectification:

> And Moses said unto God, Behold, *when* I come unto the children of Israel, and shall say unto them, the God of your fathers hath sent

me unto you; and they shall say unto me, What *is* his name? what
shall I say unto them?

And God said unto Moses, I AM THAT I AM: and he said, Thus
shalt thou say unto the children of Israel, I AM hath sent me unto
you. [Exodus 3:13–14]

In other words, "God" is the consummate subject-of-
subjects, ineffable, inscrutable, never the object of scrutiny, contemplation, or of language. A God representation is our antinomic
response, our idolatrously imaginative way of conjuring an object-
as-idol so that we can contemplate the uncontemplatable. Elsewhere I discussed this matter both from the concept of the
ineffability of the subject and from the concept of the transcendent
position, the bottom line of which is that the relationship to the
deity becomes most proximate when one transcends the paranoid-
schizoid position of unconscious fantasy and the depressive position
of reality and actuality, and ascends to the transcendent position
where one can "become"[5] the deity through resonance. Mystics,
according to Bion, can achieve a direct contact with the deity (and
thus with the unconscious) because of their unique ability to see
through the camouflage of facts and fantasy and view the thing-in-
itself.

After dealing at length with the issue of "help" in terms of the
idea of the interaction between God and man, Rizzuto concludes:
"God's help cannot bypass the psychodynamic laws that govern the
functioning of the psyche." In a very meaningful contemplation
about the similarities between the positions of the analysand's
relating to God and to the analyst, Rizzuto states:

As it happens, God too finds resistance to his capacity to see
everything and to hear everything the patient is thinking about

---

[5]Here I am using the linking verb "become" in the sense that Plato and Bion use
it, as always becoming but not achieving.

while trying to have the thought. As analysts we should not be surprised that what analysands want from us they also want from God. We both, analysts and God, as a believed supernatural being, find our emotional potential to help the patient in the fact that we both come to occupy as a natural process of the mind the *locus parentis* of earlier and later developments.

I believe these statements are profound. I find that, no matter how much analysts seek to resist such attribution, which commonly falls under the rubric of idealization, the analysand all too often relates to us as if we *were* God, prays to us for relief, and regards our comments as prophecies; moreover, they all too often hold us responsible for all that happens to them or even to the world at large. Perhaps someone should formulate the "God transference constellation." Rizzuto is quick to remind us, however, as do the other contributors, that this "God transference" constitutes a displacement from past object cathexes to parents.

Another very interesting feature in Rizzuto's work is her concept of the "private ad hoc God." She states:

There are the few who claim to have no God of any sort. Among them there are some who may be surprised by the discovery of a private and ad hoc God and an unconscious religion. To say it briefly, there are as many gods for an analyst to attend to as there are patients. I am talking here about God as a psychic conception of the patient, as a manifestation of the analysand's psychic reality that may or may not be integrated with participation in private or public religious practices. . . . For the patient God has a psychic reality that must be respected not so much because it is divine . . . but because it is personal creation of the patient as the result of his/her overall process of making sense of inner life, relational objects, and the world at large. . . . As Winnicott could say, the patient's God is a paradox that must be explored but not challenged.

I find that considerable wisdom inheres in this passage. The idea of an "ad hoc God" and an "unconscious religion" casts a new

light on personal and private theology. Perhaps we could safely say
that everyone, even an atheist, has one kind of faith or another, that
is, a system of beliefs about one's philosophy in regard to cosmic
uncertainty. Perhaps, on the other hand, even the most devout
religionists, after praying at their church of choice, go home and
unconsciously worship other gods.

The other point, that God is a psychic conception of the
patient's psychic reality, is also a profound observation, one that
the other contributors have also made. Perhaps God, heaven, the
angels, the devil, and hell constituted the prepsychoanalytic conception of what we today call psychic reality.

Rizzuto then seeks to describe how the infant constructs the
God representation: "Most God representations are collages of
significant aspects of primary object, significant adults (grandparents, aunts and uncles, and at times siblings and religious figures)
who have created meaningful, real or imagined libidinal ties with
the child. . . . We have also learned that God's psychic substance
has earlier and more complex antecedents than just the paternal
imago [postulated by Freud]."[6] Later she states that the God
representation undergoes changes as the primary objects change.
Here again I should like to interpose the organizing concept of God
preconception prior to experience as an archetype or inherent
preconception, in the platonic sense, or as a primary category
and/or noumenon in the Kantian sense, that awaits experience in
order to be realized as a conception—that it first begins as a
"background presence of primary identification" (Grotstein 1978,
p. 55) and misleadingly seems to emerge as a "representation" after
frustration. Again, God, being the subject, cannot really become a
representation (object) because of his ineffability and inscrutability,
but *can* be a background subject or presence. Rizzuto then goes on

---

[6]I feel compelled to reveal that when I was a very young child, I had a dream in
which my mother presented me to God. God sat on a throne and had a crown. In
retrospect he had the face of King George V, the reigning British monarch at the time,
whose visage I gleaned from British stamps.

to say that one of the most helping aspects of (the belief in) God is the "fact" that "he is always there." Conversely, there is no hiding from God because of his very ubiquity. Consequently, God can be considered to constitute a portion of the superego.

Some of Rizzuto's clinical recommendations in reference to God associations are of note:

> The analyst must not be concerned with the seemingly confusing, at times, unexpected emergence of . . . aspects of the God representation. . . . It is *indispensable that the analyst never make any pronouncement about God or religion.* Technically, such pronouncements disrupt the working through of the personal representation of God and of personal belief. It also conveys to the patient that the analyst knows God for sure, and has the right to demand that the analysand submits to the authority of the analyst.

And, when discussing praying:

> What is important . . . for these persons and other committed believers is the conviction of belonging to a deeply meaningful order of things governed by a loving and trusting God. . . . Prayer may be of great help to those who had found a God they trusted and feel related to. . . . God's help in relation to prayer varies along the lines of the type of God that is being prayed to, as well as the character structure and the psychic dynamic situation of the one who prays.

Here Rizzuto shows herself to be a respectful yet canny clinician. Clinically, belief in God is unassailable. *How* the analysand may choose to use—or misuse—prayer can become a clinical matter.

Conclusion

Rizzuto gives us the conception of the God representation and how it developmentally emerges in the shadow of primary object relationships. She also, like Meissner, believes that the God representation lies in psychic reality. Its putatively real existence is not a matter for psychoanalytic inquiry. Belief in God helps, according to Rizzuto, in part because it offers a concept of "the order of things," that is, a cosmic cosmology and/or container for what one would otherwise experience as chaos.

OSTOW'S CONTRIBUTION

Ostow postulates the existence of a "religious instinct" but hastens to state that his conception of it is metaphoric. Put another way, he believes that mankind behaves as if there were a religious instinct because of their need to pray and to worship. He defines the religious instinct as "the psychological readiness and need to engage with others in common submission to a divine entity recognized by the community of others." He believes that religious behavior seems to possess both primary or universal components and secondary individual components, the former being common to all individuals and the latter designating the cultural modifications or local manifestations of the universal tendency to be religious. He then divides his thesis into three parts—awe, mysticism, and apocalypse—depicting them as three universal and successive phases of religious history.

Awe

Ostow emphasizes awe in regard to the experience of preternatural vastness, such as the awareness of intensity, loudness, space, and so on. He cites the cathedral as an example of a structure that encompasses awe. The phenomenon of awe is then associated with the God-heaven concept. His next set of associations enter into the possible neuropsychological underpinnings of awe in the temporal lobe, particularly in the right hemisphere. Neurosurgical research on one patient is cited to show that stimulation of his right temporal lobe resulted in imaginary visualizations of "the House of the Lord"

and saints. Experiment with another patient resulted in the equivalent of an "oceanic feeling." Other clinical research findings demonstrated religious states and philosophic interests. Ostow then
states: "I associate awe with religious feeling in general and I take
these reports to suggest that awe might be associated with temporal
lobe function."

He then proffers yet another neuropsychological proposition
that uniquely interfaces with the theme of awe. After hyopthesizing
that memories are laid down categorically, that is, familiar facial
images are stored in the fusiform gyrus, while unfamiliar or inanimate images are stored in a region posterior to the fusiform gyrus,
he then states:

> I . . . suggest that when these categorical boundaries are crossed,
> the crossing is regularly accompanied by the appearance of a specific
> affect [of awe]. . . . Squire and Kandel report that memories are
> categorized by size. . . . Specifically they distinguish memories of
> objects that are inanimate and small from images of large objects and
> living creatures. Category-specific knowledge of the former is
> impaired by damage to the left frontal or temporal parietal region,
> and of the latter, by damage to the ventral and anterior temporal
> lobes. If size discriminates between categories, then the application
> to the experience of awe is immediate. Many awesome experiences
> depend on size, specifically large size. . . . If that is so, then we
> may imagine that when the individual who is aware of his human
> limitations confronts structures of an entirely different scale . . .
> he may experience a special affect, namely the sense of awe.

Ostow continues the theme of awe: "Since awe seems to be a
response to major discrepancies scale, it would seem reasonable to
attribute its origin to the earliest experiences of the infant who must
be impressed by, and respond to, large sizes, loud sounds, and
bright lights that he first encounters at the hands of his parents
and the world in which they live." Ostow then hypothesizes that
the infant's experiences with varieties of largeness of his parents

sets the stage for displacements for another category of largeness, presumably the awesome size of God himself.

Reverance, Awe, and the Imaginary

One is reminded here of Bion's paper, "Reverence and Awe" (in Bion 1992) and of the cabala and the *Bhagavad Gita*, the latter two of which I have already alluded to earlier in my discussion of Meissner's contribution. These myths presume an atavistic and therefore preexperiential template for the awesome largeness of the self prior to birth. Jaynes (1976) and Shlain (1998), the former from the standpoint of the notion of the archaic "bicameral mind" (right hemisphere/left hemisphere) and the latter from the perspective of the archaic primacy of the image prior to the advent of the word, describe a period in the infant's life, also alluded to by Subbotsky (1992), the Russian infant researcher, and by Lacan (1966), during which the image, as an aspect of the register of the imaginary, is predominant. If we add to that Klein's (1946, 1955) concept of projective identification, we can arrive at the probability that the infant's mental life is haunted by giants, by "Titans," as it were, prior to their shrinking into life-sized symbolic representations of objects when verbalization replaces the hegemony of the imaginary (with the attainment of the depressive position of separation-individuation).

Mysticism

Ostow defines mysticism,[7] the second of his holy triumvirate, as "the personal experience of contact with a deity or with a universal

---

[7]Could it be that Freud, who had been raised as a Jew, became atheistic, as have so many Jews, because of having been exposed almost exclusively to the compulsively ritualized observances that Jews often mistake for spirituality? Had he perhaps been more exposed to the more mystical side of Judaism, maybe his views on religion might have been otherwise.

secular entity." By contrast, Bion (1965, 1970, 1992, personal communication) defines the mystic as one who sees things clearly through the camouflage of knowledge, the one who "becomes" (transformed into) "O," his term for the ineffable. As I have already alluded to above, it is noteworthy that when some Orthodox Jews refer to the deity, they represent it as "G-d," eliminating the middle letter, in characteristically respectful Jewish fashion that proscribes the speaking or writing of the name of the deity outside the "tabernacle of the congregation" (temple or synagogue). The heart of the meaning of mysticism and its holy associations for Ostow is as follows:

> Classical mystical experiences reported to me have invariably been associated with longing for reunion with a lost object, usually an object of childhood, the mother, or the father. . . . Mystical dreams often present images of the maternal claustrum, a chair, a room, a garden, and an enclosure. I infer that the mystical experience represents a fantasy of reuniting with mother, undoing the experience of separation-individuation.

Ostow's hypothesis seems sound and constitutes a useful example of how psychoanalytic object–relations theory can interface with a theological concept. I myself would add the following hypotheses: Lacan (1966) theorizes that, when the infant is born, he experiences a loss, not of the object, but of the self, which the object had been a part of for him. He calls this "le petit a" ("a" for "autre" ["other"]). Recall that Freud (1914) hypothesized that the ego ideal assumed the grandiosity that the ego proper was compelled to surrender upon birth. What I am getting at here is that a preverbal stage of omnipotent (grandiose) imaginal mental life exists in nondeclarative memory and haunts the unconscious mental life of the infant and child, as has long been understood in Kleinian thinking.

Ostow goes on to suggest that mysticism owes its origin to a hypertrophied attachment drive and cites Panksepp, the neurodevelopmental biologist, for the location of the attachment drive in the anterior cingulate cortex. Other neural templates for the mystical experience lie in the occipito-parieto-temporal regions and in lateral aspect of the temporal lobe, where déjà-vu phenomena also arise.

Interestingly, Cath (1982) and Ramachandran and Blakeslee (1998) have found evidence that stimulation of the limbic system generally and the temporal lobe specifically, whether experimentally, by ictal seizure, or by a space-occupying lesion such as a tumor, will result in the release of varying forms of religious experience. This phenomenon can be artificially replicated, according to Cath, by varying forms of specific hallucinogens, ecstatic dancing, gospel-singing, and other measures. Cath goes so far as to suggest that God is living and well and resides in the amygdaloid nucleus. Could it have been that Saul of Tarsus, later to become St. Paul, suffered a temporal lobe seizure on the Road to Damascus, and the religious vision he experienced from that seizure changed the history of the Western world for all time to come? Further, if Cath, Ramachandran and Blakeslee, and now Ostow (and those whom he cites) are correct, may the Hebrew, Christian, and Islamic mystics, as well as the neoplatonists, the Gnostics, and the Zoroastrians, be right after all when they posited that "God" dwelled within us as well as residing beyond us as the Godhead?

From a more secular perspective Ostow concludes: "I am proposing that the attempt to restore unity with the parent gives rise to the mystical experience. . . . As I see it, the adult experience of awe recapitulates the earliest experience of the infant that is remembered, and the mystical experience attempts to revisit the archaic sense of union with the parent. The two experiences are often associated."

Apocalypse

The third member of Ostow's theological triumvirate is apocalypse or revelation. He states: "From the name given to the phenomenon, apocalypse, it is evident that theologians and scholars of scripture consider the phenomenon of revelation to be the essence. As a psychoanalyst, however, I find the succession of expectation of death and destruction, followed by the expectation of rebirth, the center of the issue." He then connects the religious phenomenon of apocalypse with the neuropsychological and neurophysiological aspects of mood regulation: "It becomes evident . . . that the anticipation of apocalyptic catastrophe is frequently no more than the anticipation of a depressive crash; and the anticipation of rebirth and salvation is an outward projection of our inner rebirth tendencies—the internal homeostatic correction."

Ostow then relates apocalyptic phenomena and mystical experiences as being integrally involved with alterations of mood. He proffers a sweeping yet seemingly credible hypothesis: "Mood oscillation and the apocalyptic complex, in which it is projected out onto the outside world, form one of the major archaic components of the religious instinct. . . . Perhaps the mystical experience represents the wish to undo the process of separation and individuation. And perhaps the apocalyptic phase reproduces the effort to acquire the capacity for mood regulation by the process of homeostatic correction." These hypotheses constitute a remarkable integration between theology, psychoanalysis, neurophysiology, and neuropsychology. It brings Ostow's talents into a remarkable synthesis. He is very well read in Scripture, is quite knowledgeable about neuropsychiatry, and is very well versed in the ego psychology school of psychoanalysis.

Conclusion

Ostow postulates the presence of a metaphoric "religious instinct," and under it he suggests there exists a triumvirate of universal experiences or phenomena—awe, mysticism, and apocalypse (revelation)—all of which ultimately relate to object relations phenomena and affect regulation. He states:

I have tried to show that the sense of awe derives from the new-born's nondeclarative memory of his impression of his adult, giant parents; that the tendency to mysticism derives from the infant's wish to undo the process of separation-individuation. . . . Together awe and mysticism create an affect that is generally described as religious. I adduce some evidence for this proposition that they are associated with temporal lobe function. . . . Persisting affects associated with nondeclarative memories leave a gap in the continuity of the conscious experience of the world. This gap is commonly filled by the image of the deity.

DISCUSSION

The first part of the title of this book is "Does God Help?" I immediately thought of another question that I believed was apposite: Does *believing* in God help? While reading the contributors' answers to the former question, I had the impression that they were also answering the latter one, and in so doing, shifted the scene of religious belief, in the psychoanalytic perspective, from actual reality to psychic reality.

I also thought of another question that goes to the very center of the mystical connection between God and man: If God is Almighty, why did he create man? What is the nature of the hidden covenant between them? This question never arose and therefore goes unanswered, yet I believe that it is of utmost importance. The little, dependent infant must feel (in psychic reality) that his love is of importance to the welfare of his objects for him to be regarded and self-regarded as a "member of the team." Likewise, God's parishioners must believe (in psychic reality) that their prayers and their worship revitalize God, who, paradoxically, is also omnipotent and therefore not in need of earthly succor.

Although this book has dealt with the theologies of different religions, the participants themselves all belong to the same psychoanalytic "religion"—ego psychology. (Other views that would have been relevant and interesting are those of Klein, Bion, Meltzer, Winnicott, Fairbairn, Jung, and Lacan.) This limitation is of some importance because, in my view, ego psychology is structured in a more deterministic and positivistic way than the others, and consequently is the least godly or spiritual of all the psychoanalytic schools or that of depth psychology (Jung). To me, it is much easier to reach God on the Klein, Bion, or Jung line than on the classical line; their complementary metapsychologies are in part religious, as Meltzer (1978) has commented. To cite but a few ideas, I would liked to have seen a discussion of Christian, Jewish, and Islamic mysticism, as Bion discusses, along with his notion of the religious instinct and his belief that man must create a god to justify his need to worship. I would also have liked to see a discussion of Bion's (1992) concept of wonder and awe, Meltzer's idea about the spiritual nature of Klein's psychology, and a development of Jung's ideas about God and religion (Stein 1985). Additionally, I thought of Coles's (1990) monumental study, *The Spiritual Life of Children*; Symington's (a member of the British Independent School) (1994) *Emotion and Spirit: Questioning the Claims of Psychoanalysis and Religion*; the Reverend Rodney Bomford's (1999) *The Symmetry of God*, in which he integrates theology with Matte-Blanco's (1975, 1988) concepts of symmetry, asymmetry, and bilogic; Spero's (1992) *Religious Objects as Psychological Structures: A Critical Integration of Object Relations Theory, Psychotherapy, and Judaism*; Spezzano and Gargiulo's (1997) *Soul on the Couch: Spirituality, Religion, and Morality in Contemporary Psychoanalysis*; Kirschner's (1996) *The Religious and Romantic Origins of Psychoanalysis*; and such works on the mystics as those by Sells (1994), McGinn (1994a,b), and Fox (1980).

My overall critique of the contributions I review here is that they are excellent, well thought out, and tightly reasoned disquisitions on the relationship between (one particular school of) psychoanalysis and religion or theology. They all hint, but do not explicate, that theology *is* psychology on a different level of comprehension. A common denominator in all of them is the theme that religion and psychoanalysis are akin but are different domains of study. Rizzuto's major thrust is to conceive of the God representation, a notion that I have critiqued earlier. She and Ostow have written excellent and moving contributions about the subject from the psychoanalytic vertex and from the psychoanalytic and neuroscience vertex respectively, whereas Meissner, being both a psychoanalyst and a Jesuit, tries to embrace the idea of psychoanalysis from the vertex of theology but still maintains a distinction between the two disciplines. I shall argue that they are all correct in doing so, but that they may have limited their researches by virtue of having been constrained to using a particular school of psychoanalysis that least lends itself to spiritual, mystical, and religious contemplation.

I believe that religion is more psychoanalytic than theologists realize, and that psychoanalysis is more spiritual than psychoanalysts realize. "The unconscious is as close to God as any mortal is likely to get and . . . it is occupied by the ineffable subject of the unconscious" (Grotstein 2000, p. xvii). The basis for my believing so follows leads from Bion (1965, 1970, 1992) and Matte-Blanco (1975, 1981, 1988). Bion perforated the bell jar of Freud's inner deterministic, drive-oriented cosmos by his conception of transformations in and evolutions of O. O is his way of designating the whole range of ineffable preexperiences awaiting a mind to experience them. He terms sensory-emotional stimuli that have not yet been processed "beta elements," which await "alpha function" (at first, mother's "reverie") to contain and then to transform into alpha elements that are suitable for further mental digestion as thoughts, feelings, memories, and so on. These beta elements are also associated with Kant's "things-in-themselves" and/or noumena, absolute truth, ultimate reality, and the godhead. In brief, O, which cannot be fantasied, imagined, symbolized, or thought about, "represents" the ineffable.

Thus, when we speak of the ego's defense mechanisms and ask what do they defend against, we would now proffer that they defend, not against the drives, which mediate O, but against the inexorable evolutions of O as it intersects our consciousness. See Kirschner (1996) for a similar view.

Matte-Blanco completed Bion's restructuring of the unconscious by proffering the notion that the unconscious consists of infinite sets of categories, that is, is infinite in itself and is governed by "bilogic," which is a binary-oppositional structure consisting of the propensity toward symmetry dialectically opposed to a propensity toward asymmetry. The religious implications are vast. In brief, the unconscious consists of many differing versions of God and, in a way, *is* God, something that psychoanalysts have secretly thought all along without realizing it.

Thus, if the unconscious can be associated with God and if God can be located within the amygdaloid nucleus or other aspects of the limbic system, then God is at hand via differing epistemological disciplines. Theologians and philosophers from the beginning of time have been involved with what we today would call psychic reality, albeit with seemingly different aims—absolution from the religious perspective and resolution from the psychoanalytic perspective. Religion, furthermore, evolved in part to help mediate the experience of chaos with the illusion of divine cosmological containment ("the order of things"), that is, a theory of meaning. Psychoanalysis can be regarded as a similar meaning-generating cosmology for the internal world, the one that theology failed to realize that it was studying.

REDDY'S CONTRIBUTION

Reddy intriguingly seeks to demonstrate parallels between psychoanalytic concepts and practice and the story of the *Bhagavad Gita*. He is meticulously careful in showing where the comparisons fail and is equally cautious in showing where they seem to apply. One of the major differences one notices from the outset is that the *Gita* is an heroic epic tale, not unlike *The Iliad*, *The Aeneid*, or *Morte D'Arthur*, whereas the psychoanalytic narrative is hardly an epic and is characterized by being improvisational (the "scripts" arrive unconsciously and only at the last moment for analysand as well as analyst).

The "Facilitating Object" and the *Gita* as Internal World

The author sees Krishna, the man-god, as a facilitating object for Arjuna and one who is trying to "treat" him for his acute loss of courage due to guilt for having murdered a relative who had become an enemy. The concept of the facilitating object has its ancestry in Winnicott's (1963a,b) concept of the "facilitating environment" and later became elaborated upon in a more active role by Bollas (1987) as the "transformational object," the one that facilitates changes in the subject. I myself have recognized the idea from another angle as the "existential coach," an archetypal role, in which the "coach" knows how far to stretch his/her client (Grotstein 2000). Reddy clearly recognizes that facilitation constitutes what psychoanalytic practice considers to be a parameter, but maybe we can get beyond that caveat if we were to consider that both the characters in the *Gita* are different aspects of the same person and that the whole tale can be thought of as a dream or fantasy (dream by day) in which Krishna occupies "a gradient in the ego" (ego ideal) within Arjuna's internal world. If this is credible, then perhaps we have an alternate possibility of linking the *Gita* with psychoanalysis, one in which Krishna is not the analyst but the ideal that exhorts the ego to courage. Put another way, what seems to emerge from this alternative speculation is something like self-analysis, perhaps as it might have been unconsciously conceived by the authors of the epic.

The Factor of Guilt

Reddy correctly raises the issue of the factor of guilt in Arjuna's assumption of cowardice or impotence. We learn that he feels guilt

for slaying a beloved kinsman, Bhishma, who, by the fortunes of
fate, had wound up on the enemy side. Here we are reminded in a
way of the tragedy of *Hamlet*, particularly as it has been interpreted
by Jones (1954), who assigned the factor of unconscious oedipal
guilt to explain Hamlet's reluctance to act. The unconscious sense
of guilt is assigned by Reddy (and by Jones) to oedipal impulses.
Perhaps we can borrow from Klein (1928) the idea of the first
(archaic) oedipal stage, which involves the infant's first series of
attacks against a "kinsman," the mother ("A special affection
develops between Arjuna . . . and Bhishma"). Having unconsciously pillaged her—or him—in fantasy, the subject now feels
primitive retaliatory guilt as persecutory anxiety and immobility.

In one portion of the text, Krishna instructs Arjuna to position
his chariot between the two armies, having friends and relatives on
both sides. Is this not a gripping picture of the ambivalence an
infant experiences when, upon becoming more separate and individuated, he enters the depressive position and anguishingly realizes
in retrospect the putative damage he believes he had committed on
his objects? If this is so, then perhaps we can detect a difference in
function between the ego ideal and the superego. The superego
would remind Arjuna of his guilt, whereas the ego ideal, more
responsive to shame in regard to weakness, would encourage him
to transcend his guilt in order to avoid shame—by doing his
allotted duty.

The Roles of Krishna

Reddy proposes that, despite the facilitating activity of Krishna on
Arjuna, the former can nevertheless be interpreted as occupying
the role of an analyst and participates in four differing roles with
Arjuna throughout the epic: (1) as close friends and companions,
(2) as warrior and charioteer, (3) as the ancient divine warrior/sage
pair, and (4) as devotee and god/divinity. From the beginning we
are confronted with the enigma of the phenomenon in which a god
becomes incarnate as a human, a whimsical practice with which we

are all too familiar in Greek legends and in many religions, particularly Christianity in the form of Jesus. One can possibly interpret the four phases from the standpoint of Kohut's (1971, 1977, 1978a,b, 1984) theory of selfobjects in the relationship as the normal epigenesis a child undergoes in relationship, first to a parent (as friend and companion, that is, a mirroring selfobject), then as facilitating selfobject (charioteer), then in an idealizing selfobject relationship with a parent (often father), and finally, after disillusionment with the parental selfobjects, the discovery of God.

We also learn that Arjuna was the same age as Krishna, a very important hint as to who Krishna really might be. Krishna is, if I can use—or misuse—a Hindu concept, an *avatar* of Arjuna, his lost erstwhile divine aspect. One recalls that Freud (1913) almost said this when he accounted for the separate fates of the ego and the ego ideal. The former, after being born and experiencing the hardships of life, is compelled to surrender its grandiosity (omnipotence), whereas the latter forfeits sensual life with the compensation of receiving the ego's abandoned grandiosity, and thereafter takes its place in a "gradient in the ego" (but, like Krishna, is "in service," that is, it has no life of its own).

The Transformation from the Paranoid-Schizoid to the Depressive Position

One of the most characteristic patterns of Krishna's behavior toward Arjuna was that of exhortation. We must remember that the zeitgeist of this epic, as in all epics, is one in which there is battle between the good forces and the bad forces and that it is necessary for the hero to align himself with the good forces to destroy the latter. What is needed is exhortation of the hero by a quasi-divine force to infuse courage into the hero. This pattern is suggestive not only of Klein's concept of the splitting processes that occur in the paranoid-schizoid position, but also of the political weltanschauung that is operant in that position—that of a hierarchy between a humble subject and an idealized object. The way for a weak subject to become strong is first to idealize an object (via projective attributions) and then complementarily identify with that object in order to obtain its strength.

From another standpoint the way for a beleaguered subject to feel better about himself is to find his blemishes and concretely blame them away. When an idealized object assumes this role, it is known as exhortation. In the depressive position, however, where equality replaces hierarchy, blemishes are aired as to the emotional meanings they convey. Exhortation is replaced by reparation of the sense of badness one had about oneself. Much, if not all, of the narrative of the *Gita* is exhortative in one way or another and thus characterizes the modus operandi of the paranoid-schizoid position. Arjuna did attempt to transcend this position and approach the threshold of the depressive position with feelings of guilt for having slain a friend and kinsman, but Krishna, who was still mired in the heroics of the paranoid-schizoid position, brought Arjuna back to the more archaic position and reinforced it with exhibitionistic revelations of his divine status and denial of death. In other words, Krishna's exhortations emphasize the use of omnipotence and the denial of reality and psychic reality. In order for Krishna successfully to exhort Arjuna to develop courage, he had to ensorcell him to deny his psychic reality, which is the opposite of psychoanalysis. In some ways Krishna resembles the "mythical trickster" of pagan religions, whose best-known descendants were Puck (Robin Goodfellow) and Peter Pan.

The Concept of the Bicameral Mind

Without knowing about Klein's concept of the positions, Jaynes (1976) postulated a revolutionary concept that beautifully accommodates Klein's theory, and that is apposite to the thesis of the *Gita*. Jaynes argues that the characters in *The Iliad*, like their contemporaries in real life, lacked the faculty of consciousness. When they had what we today call feelings, they would be relegated to a source that was extraterritorial to their awareness, that is, from exhortative gods. He then suggests this paradigm also applies to the preverbal infant, who is image-dominated, prereflective, and right-hemisphere dominated until the acquisition of verbal facility shifts hemisphere dominance to the left. In the more archaic state it is as if the infant's ego, which is located in the not yet fully functioning left hemisphere, is in a state of thralldom to voices emanating from the counterpart in the right hemisphere to the left hemisphere's future speech centers. These "voices" are "God voices" (the origin of the archaic superego?) which exhort, command, ensorcell, and educate the hapless, enthralled ego. Later, they are to become known as unconscious feelings and intentions (drives, impulses). Put another way, the "God voices" emanating from the right hemisphere, which Krishna incarnates in the *Gita*, are to become known as the unconscious itself. Jaynes made another comment, one which struck me as being profound. He suggested that Freud viewed the unconscious from the perspective of consciousness, rather than the other way around.

Conclusion

Reddy has made an interesting and apt study of the possible applications of psychoanalytic ideas to the drama of the *Gita*. While in agreeing with him on his major points, that is, that the role of Krishna in some ways resembles that of an analyst vis-à-vis Arjuna, I believe that another psychoanalytic application is suggested. It is my belief that the *Gita*, as an epic, constitutes the group equivalent of activity that is apposite to Klein's paranoid-schizoid position. Further, I believe that the entirety of the epic can be understood as transactions of Arjuna's internal world; that is, Krishna is an idealized and deified phantom.

AD-DAB'BAGH'S CONTRIBUTION

While perusing this treatise on the Islamic faith, I could not help reminiscing on my boyhood background in my own religion,

Judaism. I had been struck even as a child by what I felt was a great schism in my experience of Judaism, a religion dominated by a wrathful god who created human beings in order to sing his praise, constitutive of the Torah, and, markedly separated from this cant, a system of laws known as the Talmud, which dealt with the minutist aspects of human relationships, such as the respect that children must have for their parents and vice versa, respect owners must have for their slaves, and so on. In other words, the Torah emphasized command obedience to a temperamental deity, and the Talmud was an ordinance of ethics. Even then I missed the phenomenon of spirituality, which I was later to find in Jewish mysticism.

I had a veritable déjà-vu experience, consequently, when I read the author's treatise on Islamism. It was so much like the Judaism I had been raised in, the same god, and the same or similar rules of ethics. It was as if the Qur-ān (Koran) and the Torah and Talmud converged. Moreover, when I read about the principle of the median, I could not help recalling Ecclesiastes from the Old Testament, which emphasizes the median in all things more than any other portion of the Bible. Thus, I felt very much at home here, as I did with Mortimer Ostow's contribution.

The Concept of the Median

The Ariadne's thread running through the author's thesis is the notion of the median between any and all extremes. In the first instance this suggests that the Islamic parishioner is entitled to have extreme thoughts but, if he controls his impulses and follows the middle path of emotional temperance, he is on the right path and is following Allah. Islamism consequently devolves into a series of dialectical ideas and practices and seeks mediation as the reconciling synthesis. On the other hand, Allah is absolute but mediates his commandments to his followers between faith and reason.

Islamism and Cosmology

Islamism, like all religions, tries to deal with first causes, that is, how was the world and the creatures who inhabit it created? The author states: "Divine omnipotence and predetermined destiny are always the source of the entirety of causation. They cause humans to cause events. However, each individual perceives his or her actions to be autocratic. . . . Does what I intend to do fit in with God's plan? If so, why was I chosen to do it? What is it about me that brought this choice upon me?"

The concepts of creation, cosmology (cosmogony, world-view), and the origins of intentionality have preoccupied theologians from virtually every religion since the dawn of time. It seems as if it is the task of religion to offer the group a doctrine of accountability for creation, circumstance, and man's will. Virtually every religion, and even psychoanalysis itself, seems to have settled for ambiguous answers to these unanswerable questions. The ambiguous "solution" is that God's will (or the unconscious, in terms of psychoanalysis) is the numinous and mysterious prime cause, but man (consciousness) must claim responsibility. The Hebrew Mishnah states that God is the source of all action but man must act if he is the source. This reasoning amounts to a theological catch-22. Christians, following the Jews, ordained the concept of original sin to account for man's propensity toward sin and evil.

From a newer psychoanalytic perspective one might hypothesize that the deity, as pure essence, is unknowable and without desire. The deity we "know" is one we create through projective identification (projective attribution, idealization, deification) in order to mediate our religious instinct to worship. In other words, we need to create a god to justify our need to pray and to worship a preternatural essence. The deity that is (or may be) is utterly independent and extraterritorial to our "creation" of "him" ("her," "it").

Cosmogony is the principle that helps the infant organize all

the events that happen to him and in his surrounds into a pattern
that has meaning (one that makes unifying sense). At first this
cosmogony will be organized around the infant's narcissistic (syn-
cretistic, solipsistic, autochthonous) way of thinking: "I am the
cause of everything that happens. Causation radiates from me."
This mode of thinking is prereflective and characterizes the
paranoid-schizoid position. Once the infant achieves the depressive
position, where he is separate from the object and is individuated,
he becomes self-reflective and allows for the other to have a
separate mind and thereby encounter schemes of causation that are
independent of self. One recalls Schreber's cry for justice and his
invoking the order of things as the highest form of justice, a
haunting concept that harkens back to Plato's idea of the "memory
of Justice" (Freud 1911).

What seems to characterize religions such as the Islamic,
Hebrew, and Catholic is the practice of observances, which act as a
socially unifying instrument to encourage tribal bonding and unity.
This set of practices characterizes the paranoid-schizoid position
insofar as these observances, like obsessive-compulsive rituals, borrow from superstitious magic. In the depressive position one begins
to shorn imitative magical observances and superstitions and to
contemplate one's own interiority (introspection) in search of one's
inner soul. The author frequently used the term *spirituality*, but I
did not know how he was using it. Spirituality, as distinguished
from religion, seems to be more individualistically private and
soulful.

I was surprised to learn that there was no original sin in the
Islamic religion. The author states: "The *Qur-ān*'s stress on the
purity of the original state of humans cannot be underestimated." I
find this concept to be unique. It seems to substantiate the primacy
of human innocence, a state that has been denied the human being
in virtually all other religions and even in the older schools of
psychoanalysis until Fairbairn, Winnicott, and Kohut and the
subjective-intersubjective revolution. Later the author states:

An internal observing agency, whether preexisting or introduced, is at the forefront of Islamic theology. *Taqwa*, or piety in Arabic, literally means protection from peril. . . . *Taqwa* is a quality in the Muslim that is only developed through constant self-examination to the extent of truthful appraisal of one's thoughts, impulses, emotions, moral values, and beliefs. It utilizes a disciplined and informed observing ego that attempts to see beyond self-deception arising from personal desires, family interest, or group demands.

How remarkably close these ideas are to the traditional psychoanalytic concept of the superego! In a subsequent passage the author remarks that Muslims are unusually vulnerable to feelings of shame.

On a more practical level the Muslim is more family-bound than most Westerners. The author states:

Separation from parents in Islam is neither encouraged nor seen as essential for the development of autonomy. A total relinquishment of the real maternal figure in favor of the internal mother arguably never takes place in the mind of a Muslim reared in an Islamic society. Although presently considered unusual in a Western society, such a situation creates in the mind a continuous balance between the demands of the internalized and the real mother.

From my own experience with Muslim patients I can attest to the truth of Ad-Dab'bagh's statement. This may be another way of stating that Muslims may still be more tribal in their social organization than Westerners have become.

Returning to the issue of the soul, the author states: "Although faith in the presence of the soul is part of Islam, no elaboration, definition or description of the soul is provided. This is in contradistinction to the word *self*, which is used to mean personhood. One's mind is a component of one's person, which is contained in the outer body. Although distinction between the self and the body exists, the radical doctrine of mind–body dualism does not."

I found these observations interesting. It would seem that the
Islamic religion in many ways paralleled the history of the Hebrew
faith in becoming less soulful and more pragmatic in terms of
psychological issues that interfaced with the faith.

The author's description of the fate of applying various forms
of psychotherapy was interesting and speaks for itself. Moderation
(achieving the mean) seems to be the organizing principle behind
their notions of therapeusis.

Conclusion

The author skillfully puts us into the immediacy of Muslim religious life. It was intriguing to learn the nature of the issues that
confront the Muslim in his daily life and how he strives utmostly to
be ethical by worshiping Allah and the median. As a Jew I felt a
kinship with these ideals and recall them from my own religious
training. Nevertheless, one gets the impression that the spirit of
psychoanalysis, that is, self-reflection in line with psychological
mindedness with regard to the presence of an unconscious mental
life, is missing from their social consciousness.

FINAL COMMENTS

It was a privilege to have had this exposure to such rich and varied
examples of religious life from the observational perspectives of
individuals trained in psychoanalysis. I have already shared my
specific comments as I proceeded through the various texts. But
more generally, enriched as I was by the care for details the authors
showed in their contributions, my insatiable epistemophilia on the
interface of religion and psychoanalysis would like to have had the
following themes addressed as well: (1) the relationship between
ritual and stoicism in religion and psychoanalysis; (2) the mediation
of sensuality in each; (3) the role of the change from matriarchal to
patriarchal emphases in religion and psychoanalysis; (4) a clearer

delineation between the holy and the secular aspects of religion
(and psychoanalysis); (5) an admission that, in the primeval past, the
arbitrariness of circumstance became God's will; (6) an emphasis on
the religious experience itself, with emphasis on what Bion (1992)
terms "reverence and awe." I would also like to see studies that
compare religious experiences with altered states of consciousness.
Here I have in mind studies on temporal lobe epilepsy, which I
have cited earlier, and the ictal release of the "God experience"
(Cath 1982, Ramachandran and Blakeslee 1998). Could it have
been that Saul of Tarsus suffered a temporal lobe seizure on the
Road to Damascus which gave him divine visitations, then became
St. Paul, and altered Western civilization forever? Finally, what is
meant by "sacred" and "holy"? Don't religious and psychoanalytic
experiences converge, from different vertices, in the domain of the
transcendent?

Finally, I wish to repeat an opinion I stated at the beginning:
religion (spirituality) is more psychoanalytic than it has realized, and
psychoanalysis is more religious and spiritual than it realizes.

REFERENCES

Bion, W. R. (1965). *Transformations*. London: Heinemann.
———— (1970). *Attention and Interpretation*. London: Tavistock.
———— (1992). *Cogitations*. London: Karnac.
Bollas, C. (1987). *The Shadow of the Object: Psychoanalysis of the Unthought Known*. New
    York: International Universities Press.
Bomford, R. (1999). *The Symmetry of God*. New York: Free Association Books.
Cath, S. H. (1982). Adolescence and addiction to alternative belief systems: psychoana-
    lytic and psychophysiological considerations. *Psychoanalytic Inquiry* 2(4):619–676.
Coles, R. (1990). *The Spiritual Life of Children*. Boston: Houghton Mifflin.
Erikson, E. H. (1958). *Young Man Luther*. New York: Norton.
Fairbairn, W. R. D. (1952). *Psychoanalytic Studies of the Personality*. London: Tavistock.
Fox, M. (1980). *Breakthrough: Meister Eckhart's Creation Spirituality in New Translation*.
    New York: Doubleday.
Freud, S. (1911). Psycho-analytic notes on an autobiographical account of a case of
    paranoia (dementia paranoides). *Standard Edition* 12:3–84.
———— (1913[1912-1913]). Totem and taboo. *Standard Edition* 13:1–64.

————— (1914). On narcissism: an introduction. *Standard Edition* 14:67–104.

Grotstein, J. (1978). Inner space: Its dimensions and its coordinates. *International Journal of Psycho-Analysis* 59:55–61.

————— (1997). Integrating one-person and two-person psychologies: autochthony and alterity in counterpoint. *Psychoanalytic Quarterly* 66:403–430.

————— (2000). *Who Is the Dreamer Who Dreams the Dream? A Study of Psychic Presences.* Hillsdale, NJ: Analytic Press.

Jaynes, J. (1976). *The Origins of Consciousness in the Breakdown of the Bicameral Mind.* Boston: Houghton Mifflin.

Jones, E. (1954). *Hamlet and Oedipus.* New York: Garden City Publications.

Kirschner, S. R. (1996). *The Religious and Romantic Origins of Psychoanalysis: Individuation and Integration in Post-Freudian Theory.* Cambridge, UK: Cambridge University Press.

Klein, M. (1946). Notes on some schizoid mechanisms. In *Developments of Psycho-Analysis,* ed. J. Riviere, pp.292–320. London: Hogarth, 1952.

————— (1955). On identification. In *New Directions in Psycho-Analysis,* ed. J. Riviere, pp. 309–345. London: Hogarth.

Kohut, H. (1971). *The Analysis of the Self: A Systematic Approach to the Psychoanalytic Treatment of Narcissistic Personality Disorders.* New York: International Universities Press.

————— (1977). *The Restoration of the Self.* New York: International Universities Press.

————— (1978a). *The Search for the Self: Volume 1,* ed. Ornstein. New York: International Universities Press.

————— (1978b). *The Search for the Self: Volume 2,* ed. P. Ornstein. New York: International Universities Press.

————— (1984). *How Does Analysis Cure?,* ed. A. Goldberg and P. E. Stepansky. Chicago: University of Chicago Press.

Lacan, J. (1966). *Écrits: 1949–1960,* trans. A. Sheridan. New York: Norton, 1977.

Matte-Blanco, I. (1975). *The Unconscious as Infinite Sets.* London: Duckworth.

————— (1981). Reflecting with Bion. In *Do I Dare Disturb the Universe? A Memorial to Wilfred R. Bion,* ed. J. S. Grotstein, pp. 489–528. Beverly Hills, CA: Caesura.

————— (1988). *Thinking, Feeling, and Being: Clinical Reflections on the Fundamental Antinomy of Human Beings.* London/New York: Tavistock and Routledge.

McGinn, B. (1994a). *The Foundations of Mysticism: Origins to the Fifth Century.* New York: Crossroad.

————— (1994b). *The Growth of Mysticism: Gregory the Great through the 12th Century.* New York: Crossroad.

Meltzer, D. W. (1978). *The Kleinian Development.* Perthshire, Scotland: Clunie.

Ramachandran, V. S., and Blakeslee, S. (1998). *Phantoms in the Brain: Probing the Mysteries of the Human Mind.* New York: William Morrow.

Sells, M. A. (1994). *The Mystical Languages of Unsaying.* Chicago: University of Chicago Press.

Shlain, L. (1998). *The Alphabet and the Goddess: The Conflict between Word and Image.* New York: Penguin/Arcana.

Spero, M. H. (1992). *Religious Objects as Psychological Structures: A Critical Integration of Object Relations Theory, Psychotherapy, and Judaism.* Chicago: University of Chicago Press.

Spezzano, C., and Gargiulo, G. J., eds. (1997). *Soul on the Couch: Spirituality, Religion, and Morality in Contemporary Psychoanalysis.* Hillsdale, NJ: Analytic Press.

Stein, M. (1985). *Jung's Treatment of Christianity: The Psychotherapy of a Religious Tradition.* Wilmette, IL: Chiron.

Subbotsky, E. V. (1992). *Foundations of the Mind: Children's Understanding of Reality.* Cambridge, MA: Harvard University Press.

Symington, N. (1994). *Emotion and Spirit: Questioning the Claims of Psychoanalysis and Religion.* London: Cassell.

Tillich, P. (1952). *The Courage to Be.* New Haven, CT: Yale University Press.

Winnicott, D. W. (1963a). The mentally ill in your caseload. In *The Maturational Processes and the Facilitating Environment*, pp. 217–229. New York: International Universities Press, 1965.

———— (1963b). Psychiatric disorder in terms of infantile maturational processes. In *The Maturational Processes and the Facilitating Environment*, pp. 230–241. New York: International Universities Press, 1965.

Wordsworth, W. (1807). Ode: Intimations of Immortality from Recollections of Early Childhood. In *William Wordsworth: The Poems: Volume One*, pp. 523–529. London: Penguin, 1977.

Index